Education in the Asia-Pacific Region: Issues, Concerns and Prospects

Volume 47

More information about this series at http://www.springer.com/series/5888

Yuto Kitamura • Toshiyuki Omomo
Masaaki Katsuno

Editors

Education in Japan

A Comprehensive Analysis of Education
Reforms and Practices

 Springer

Editors
Yuto Kitamura
Graduate School of Education
The University of Tokyo
Tokyo, Japan

Toshiyuki Omomo
Gakushuin Women's College
Tokyo, Japan

Masaaki Katsuno
Graduate School of Education
The University of Tokyo
Tokyo, Japan

ISSN 1573-5397   ISSN 2214-9791   (electronic)
Education in the Asia-Pacific Region: Issues, Concerns and Prospects
ISBN 978-981-13-2630-1   ISBN 978-981-13-2632-5   (eBook)
https://doi.org/10.1007/978-981-13-2632-5

Library of Congress Control Number: 2018961384

This Springer imprint is published by the registered company Springer Nature Singapore Pte Ltd.
The registered company address is: 152 Beach Road, #21-01/04 Gateway East, Singapore 189721, Singapore

Foreword

I am now writing this foreword while looking at the results of the American 2018 midterm election, which affected not only America but also the world in a global age. In such a global age, public education that has been institutionalized as part of the nation-state is now about to be largely reconsidered along the following three points.

First, the image of citizens cultivated through public education is greatly swaying between people who make up the nation-state and more multicultural and multilayered ones based on the increasing prevalence of immigrants and refugees.

Second, as symbolized by the OECD's PISA, economic globalization promotes the globalization of school education evaluation standards, creating a problem of widening inequality and an aporia of social inclusion and social exclusion.

Third, the transformation of the environment pushes forward the sustainability of society as a global issue. We are now forced to reconsider the old concept of education that has assumed economic growth.

It is in this situation that this book was planned. All the chapters of this book were written by faculty members (as well as a former faculty member) of the Faculty of Education and Graduate School of Education of the University of Tokyo. The Faculty of Education of the University of Tokyo was founded in 1949 after World War II. Among faculties of the University of Tokyo that have histories of nearly 140 years, our faculty is relatively new and was created as a symbolic existence of a new university responsible for the construction of postwar democracy. It has contributed to the democratization of education in Japan and has left a brilliant footprint as the base of postwar democracy.

However, 70 years after the war, Japan and the world are about to change greatly. In 2016, Britain decided to withdraw from the EU (European Union) by a referendum, and Donald Trump was elected president of the United States. In Japan, education and society systems that have existed for 70 years since the end of World War II are now undergoing major changes. For example, the connection between primary and secondary education and higher education and the relationship between society as a whole and school education are about to be revised toward the abolition of the National Center Test for University Admissions in 2020. The realization of the 18-year-old voting rights that began in 2016 can be said to symbolize such a change.

Under such a postwar system, our Faculty and Graduate School of Education are now trying to enter the new stage of fulfilling a mission that matched these new times while taking into consideration the past achievement as the base of postwar democratic education.

This book is exactly the result of such a new stage. I am convinced that this book will deepen the understanding of Japanese education and will provide prescription of educational reforms in such a globalized world.

Dean and Professor, Faculty of Education   Shigeo Kodama
and Graduate School of Education
The University of Tokyo
Tokyo, Japan
November 7, 2018

Series Editors' Introduction

This volume by Yuto Kitamura, Toshiyuki Omomo and Masaaki Katsuno on *Education in Japan: A Comprehensive Analysis of Education Reforms and Practices* is the latest book to be published in the long-standing Springer book series *Education in the Asia-Pacific Region: Issues, Concerns and Prospects*. The first volume in this Springer series was published in 2002, with this book by Kitamura, Omomo and Katsuno being the 47th volume to be published to date.

Education in Japan: A Comprehensive Analysis of Education Reforms and Practices is, to date, the most comprehensive resource for education in Japan, tackling the different education levels and issues inherent in the sector. Chapters written by local experts give readers the needed insight into Japanese education and provide a critical assessment of matters that shape and influence the sector given the global trends in educational reform.

Divided into two main parts, theoretical, empirical and historical approaches are used to give readers an overview of the country's education system and understanding of the challenges and reforms in line with the goal of ensuring quality education towards greater sustainable development. Matters such as teacher education, disparities in education, multiculturalism, internationalisation, and community and school engagement are just some of the pressing concerns reviewed in this book that capture the realities and challenges of education in Japan.

This book will be an invaluable resource to those interested in understanding Japanese education and the actualities inherent within it. It is a solid contribution to Japanese education literature while at the same time bridging the often limited voices of local educational researcher in mainstream literature.

In terms of the Springer book series in which this volume is published, the various topics dealt with in the series are wide ranging and varied in coverage, with an emphasis on cutting-edge developments, best practices and education innovations for development. Topics examined in the series include the environmental education and education for sustainable development; interaction between technology and education; reform of primary, secondary and teacher education; innovative approaches to education assessment; alternative education; most effective ways to achieve quality and highly relevant education for all; active ageing through active

Series Editors' Introduction

learning; case studies of education and schooling systems in various countries in the region; cross-country and cross-cultural studies of education and schooling; and sociology of teachers as an occupational group, to mention just a few. More information about this book series is available at http://www.springer.com/series/5888.

All volumes in this series aim to meet the interests and priorities of a diverse education audience including researchers, policy-makers and practitioners; tertiary students; teachers at all levels within education systems; and members of the public who are interested in better understanding cutting-edge developments in education and schooling in Asia Pacific.

The reason why this book series has been devoted exclusively to examining various aspects of education and schooling in the Asia-Pacific region is that this is a particularly challenging region which is renowned for its size, diversity and complexity, whether it be geographical, socio-economic, cultural, political or developmental. Education and schooling in countries throughout the region impact on every aspect of people's lives, including employment, labour force considerations, education and training, cultural orientation, and attitudes and values. Asia and the Pacific is home to some 63% of the world's population of 7 billion. Countries with the largest populations (China, 1.4 billion; India, 1.3 billion) and the most rapidly growing megacities are to be found in the region, as are countries with relatively small populations (Bhutan, 755,000; the island of Niue, 1600).

Levels of economic and socio-political development vary widely, with some of the richest countries (such as Japan) and some of the poorest countries on earth (such as Bangladesh). Asia contains the largest number of poor of any region in the world, the incidence of those living below the poverty line remaining as high as 40% in some countries in Asia. At the same time, many countries in Asia are experiencing a period of great economic growth and social development. However, inclusive growth remains elusive, as does growth that is sustainable and does not destroy the quality of the environment. The growing prominence of Asian economies and corporations, together with globalisation and technological innovation, is leading to long-term changes in trade, business and labour markets, to the sociology of populations within (and between) countries. There is a rebalancing of power, centred on Asia and the Pacific region, with the Asian Development Bank in Manila declaring that the twenty-first century will be 'the Century of Asia Pacific'.

We believe this book series makes a useful contribution to knowledge sharing about education and schooling in Asia Pacific. Any readers of this or other volumes in the series who have an idea for writing their own book (or editing a book) on any aspect of education and/or schooling, which is relevant to the region, are enthusiastically encouraged to approach the series editors either direct or through Springer to publish their own volume in the series, since we are always willing to assist perspective authors shape their manuscripts in ways that make them suitable for publication in this series.

Office of Applied Research and Innovation   Rupert Maclean
College of the North Atlantic – Qatar
Doha, Qatar

Zhejiang University   Lorraine Symaco
Hangzhou, China
25 June 2018

Contents

Chapter 1
Background and Context of Education System in Japan

Yuto Kitamura

1.1 Introduction

Japan has been known for its success in building an efficient and effective educational system, particularly for school education. International academic achievement tests such as PISA and TIMSS have shown significant performance for Japanese students at the primary and secondary levels. At the tertiary level, Japan's higher education system has been academically productive compared to its foreign counterparts, especially those in Asia. However, today Japanese education is considered one of the major reform areas, because of its rigidity and inflexibility despite rapidly changing environments inside as well as outside Japan. Many people in Japan are raising questions over whether Japanese education can still produce good-quality human resources who will be able to respond to the needs and demands of a knowledge-based society in the twenty-first century.

To answer this question, we need to understand the nature of Japan's education system and identify its strengths and weaknesses, as well as the socioeconomic environment surrounding education in contemporary Japanese society. The main objective of this book is to help readers grasp these issues. As Japan deals with advancing globalization, the transition to a knowledge-based society and other events, this book intends to show how various attempts have been made to improve the method of providing education and the system for quality assurance, through governance reform of the education system in Japan. Although the term "governance reform" has been defined in various ways, in this book it refers to the reform of relational structures and methods of providing/managing public services. It should be noted that a growing awareness of the issue of equity in education is also part of the background behind these attempts.

Y. Kitamura (✉)
Graduate School of Education, The University of Tokyo, Tokyo, Japan
e-mail: yuto@p.u-tokyo.ac.jp

© Springer Nature Singapore Pte Ltd. 2019
Y. Kitamura et al. (eds.), *Education in Japan*, Education in the Asia-Pacific Region: Issues, Concerns and Prospects 47,
https://doi.org/10.1007/978-981-13-2632-5_1

1

In Japan, issues relating to quality assurance for education in results-oriented governance reform have been a central concern in educational reforms, particularly in the 2000s and later. This book describes the basic institutional structure of each educational stage, in an overview of today's school education in Japan, presenting analyses of the status of implementation of important policies and the progress of reform at each stage. This educational stage-based analysis focuses on primary and secondary education, higher education, and lifelong education/social education. This book also describes the current situation of the educational administration systems that support education at each stage while analyzing various relevant issues, including the evaluation system.

In addition to an educational stage-based analysis, this book also analyzes the status of and problems with various issues that are considered important for education in Japan today, utilizing knowledge from diverse academic disciplines. Educational subjects addressed in this book include teachers, lesson studies, schools and the community, educational disparities, education and jobs, multiculturalism, university reforms, internationalization of education and English language education, education for sustainable development, and others, covering diverse fields. Through an analysis of these subjects, this book aims to provide a comprehensive picture of education in contemporary Japan.

The objective of this book is to illustrate the status and problems of governance reform and quality assurance in the field of education in Japan, employing the expertise of diverse academic disciplines. Although similar books have been written, this one is unique in its attempt to comprehensively understand and analyze the educational field in Japan by applying a multidisciplinary approach.

Of course, various important attempts have already been done that adopted comprehensive and holistic approaches to understanding the education sector in Japan. To name a few, previous studies include Stephens (1991), Okano (1999), Gordon et al. (2009), and Decoker and Bjork (2013). There have also been more focused studies on particular topics and aspects of Japanese education, including Hood (2001), Hebert (2011), Tsuneyoshi et al. (2011), Kariya (2012), and Jones (2010). Each of these studies has presented interesting phenomena relating to Japanese education and has generated insightful and thought-provoking discussions; however, in this book we try to present more updated works and collective efforts by experts from a wider range of academic disciplines. This volume is the most current and complete treatment of contemporary educational issues in Japan, including the most up-to-date reforms at different educational levels and specific topics relevant to current trends in Japanese education. As editors of this volume, we hope that readers will refer to our book and to some of these previous studies to deepen their understanding of contemporary Japanese education.

All the contributors here are influential and have a wealth of experience in the field of education in Japan. Contributors to this book are specialists across a range of academic fields related to education, including public administration, sociology, history, linguistics, and anthropology. It should be emphasized that all are also leading researchers in their respective academic fields in Japan. Incidentally, contributors are faculty members of the Graduate School of Education at The University of

Tokyo (UTokyo), except for Toshiyuki Omomo, who previously was Dean of this graduate school and retired from it in 2017. The Graduate School of Education at UTokyo has led educational studies in Japan over the years, and this book was accomplished through the all-out efforts of this school. The project for the book was developed out of feelings of regret that only a small number of Japanese educational researchers have been active in promoting attempts at reorganizing and conveying to the world the results of research in diverse academic disciplines relating to education in Japan from a comprehensive viewpoint.

We would like to emphasize that this book is particularly timely in that it also addresses issues that presently affect many other countries around the world. The discussion and findings presented in this volume relate to and inform responses to global trends in educational reforms in the context of our knowledge-based societies of the twenty-first century.

1.2   The Development of Education in Postwar Japan

In this introductory chapter, we would like to first review the historical development of Japanese education over the last half-century or so. Following the end of World War II, Japan, a defeated nation, was placed under the occupation of the Supreme Commander for the Allied Powers (SCAP; usually referred to in Japan as the General Headquarters or GHQ) charged with democratizing the militarist imperialist nation. In democratizing Japan, an extremely important role was played by education, especially school education. At the GHQ's request, the American government sent the United States Education Mission to Japan in 1946. This group, comprising 27 American experts in education, put together a set of proposals to democratize Japan's education. They emphasized the importance of introducing an American-style, democratic educational system, in which individual freedom and dignity would be respected. To realize such a democratic educational system, the Mission recommended transforming the country's highly centralized and uniformist education administration in order to limit the power of the Ministry of Education, as well as establishing prefectural and municipal boards of education comprising publicly elected members. The Mission's proposals led to a number of specific changes: government-designated school textbooks were abolished; the academic subjects of National History and Moral Education were replaced by the American-style Social Studies; 6 years of primary education and 3 years of lower secondary education were made compulsory; public schools that had been gender-segregated until then were made coeducational; and 3 years of upper secondary education were designated, thereby establishing a 6-3-3 school year system.

The establishment of boards of education, in particular, was based on the reflection that the prewar system had concentrated administrative authority in the Ministry of Education, allowing excessive control and centralization in the field of education. After the war, decentralization was thus pursued, prompting the introduction of American-style boards of education at prefectural and municipal levels. Each of

Japan's first boards of education comprised several members publicly elected from among local residents and a director who executed decisions made by the members. This new institution, however, caused much confusion in various forms during its initial years. To adapt it to the Japanese social context, the Act on the Organization and Operation of Local Educational Administration was promulgated in 1956. Accordingly, the public election of board members was abolished and replaced by appointment by the head of each prefectural or municipal government. At the same time, the Act reinforced the hierarchy between the Ministry of Education, prefectural boards of education, and municipal boards of education.

In 1952, the Treaty of Peace with Japan came into force, thereby officially ending the "state of war" in Japan and returning sovereignty to the country. At that time, during the first half of the 1950s, the Japanese economy began improving remarkably through the sale of large quantities of military supplies mainly to the US forces engaged in the Korean War. This was soon followed by Japan's rapid economic development in the 1960s and 1970s. Such sudden economic recovery and growth greatly impacted the country's education, among other areas. Against the backdrop of stabilization of the household economy, expansion of the urban middle class, increase in employment due to the shrinking primary-industry population, and spread of credentialism, people's demand for higher levels of education increased. This first manifested itself in the growing percentage of lower secondary school pupils continuing on to upper secondary schools. The trend gradually expanded to the next level, raising the percentage of upper secondary school students going on to higher education (see Fig. 1.1).

Japan's school education began showing positive effects in international academic achievement surveys. In the First International Mathematics Study (FIMS) conducted by the International Association for the Evaluation of Educational Achievement (IEA) from 1964 through 1967, Japan was ranked first, alongside Israel, in terms of academic performance by 13-year-old pupils in Mathematics, among the 12 countries studied, including European countries, the United States, and Israel. In the IEA's subsequent Science Study (1970–1973), Japan's fifth-year primary school pupils and third-year lower secondary school pupils were ranked first in Science among the 19 countries surveyed. As attested by the high academic standards of Japanese pupils in these studies, it can be said that Japanese education has succeeded in producing human resources who contribute to the country's economic, social, and cultural development. Japanese education has indeed produced many individuals equipped with basic knowledge and skills responsive to industrial structural change, as well as discipline, diligence, patience, and the ability to work in group in a harmonious manner.

At the same time, Japanese education has had to face a variety of challenges. Many experts and opinion leaders have criticized Japan's school education in which strict management places excessive emphasis on standardization and student behavioral control. The intense competition among students vying for admission to prestigious senior high schools and universities has caused tremendous psychological pressure for these students and their parents. The situation surrounding the frenzied

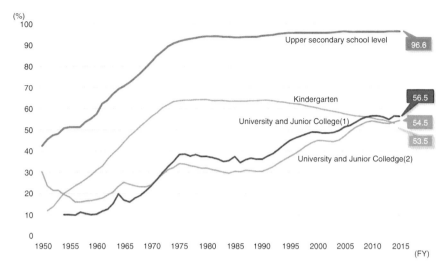

Fig. 1.1 Enrollment and advancement rate 1950–2015. (Source: Database of the Statistics Bureau, Ministry of Internal Affairs and Communications, Japan (in Japanese: http://www.e-stat.go.jp/SG1/estat/List.do?bid=000001066158&cycode=0 [Retrieved July 24, 2017]))
• Kindergarten graduates as a percentage of enrollments in the 1st year of elementary school
• Upper secondary school data exclude those advancing to correspondence courses of upper secondary schools. Figures include completion numbers of lower division of secondary school
• University and junior college (1) indicate new entrants to university and junior college, as a percentage of the 18-year-old age cohort
• University and junior college (2) indicate new graduates from upper secondary school who advanced to university and junior college upon graduation, as a percentage of the total upper secondary school graduates for each year, excluding those advancing to correspondence courses of universities and junior colleges

competition in entrance examinations was even described as "examination hell" from the 1970s to 1980s. Criticism has also been made about the widespread practices of rote memorization and "cramming" of knowledge, accused of depriving pupils of opportunities to develop their intellectual curiosity and creativity. The percentage of pupils who fail to keep up with their peers in school work has increased, while many parents send their children to *juku*, commercially operated after-school study centers, to complement school work. Since the 1970s, the aggravation of other problems has also been underscored, including increasing numbers of cases of truancy, school violence, bullying, juvenile delinquency, and youth suicide.

At the outset of the 1980s, the Ad Hoc Council on Education was established to explore new ways of education in the face of these challenges. The Council promoted an educational reform orientation, which is discussed in Chap. 1. In the 1990s, Japan pursued educational reform that shifted the focus from education centering on rote memorization and cramming to what was called *yutori*, or pressure-free, education. Nevertheless, in the 2000s, yet another educational reform policy was adopted that focused on improving pupils' scholastic ability as a somewhat reactionary response to the *yutori* approach. Chapter 1 also provides a look into the changes in educational reforms in Japan during this period. Since the 2000s, children's poverty and differences in academic ability between social classes have come to be generally recognized as major social problems relating to education. These in fact are also some of the negative effects of the long-term economic downturn since the 1990s.

Another problem that has come to the fore in more recent years is education for minority children in Japanese society. These children, especially those of "newcomers," that is, of Brazilian or Peruvian immigrants (often of Japanese descent) who began arriving in large numbers in the 1990s, are said to lack opportunities for qualitatively adequate education. While problems of education had already been pointed out with regard to minority children, especially children of ethnic Chinese and Korean residents and Japan's indigenous Ainu, such problems had not been given due consideration until recently, largely due to the relatively homogeneous ethnic and cultural makeup of Japanese society.

As stated above, Japan's education system is confronted with various challenges. Contemplating how we should tackle and overcome these challenges was the starting point of this book. The following chapters are intended not to simply enumerate problem areas in Japan's education, but to discuss and analyze various thoughts on education and educational institutions and practices, in the hope that these discussions will offer clues that may also be useful for examining many other issues in education. Some chapters take up themes that may appear, at first glance, not directly related to education in Japan today. This is because these chapters discuss topics that are highly relevant when one attempts to understand the characteristics (both positive and negative) of Japan's education in a broader context.

In around 2020, education in Japan is expected to reach a major turning point. From 2018 to 2019, a new Course of Study (Japan's National Curriculum) will be introduced. This is expected to mark a significant departure from the conventional rote memorization-oriented education, highlighting the importance of allowing pupils to engage in proactive learning. It is also expected to emphasize the possibilities of new approaches to education, such as Education for Sustainable Development (ESD), Active Learning, and other new teaching/learning methods. In 2020, Japan's university admission system will also be reformed, with entrance examinations redesigned so that candidates are evaluated on the basis of, not the amount of knowledge they have acquired but, the depth of their reflection and how they mobilize and apply the knowledge they have gained to solve problems. We believe that, in examining such a new orientation of educational reform, the discussions in the chapters that follow serve as a useful reference for readers.

We invite readers to also refer to "A Chronological Table of Education Reforms in Postwar Japan," which follows this chapter, for a detailed overview of education in postwar Japan.

1.3   Emerging Awareness About the Importance of Early Childhood Education

In this book, we have focused mainly on the formal education system (i.e., primary, secondary, and tertiary education) and lifelong learning, but could not cover the earlier stage of education. However, as globalization advances and society undergoes major transformation, it is important to note that the environment surrounding young children and ways of learning in early childhood are changing. Globalization is also steadily progressing in Japanese society, thus rendering the issue of diversity increasingly conspicuous in the field of practice of early childhood education (ECE). Concretely, the number of children of foreign origin attending kindergartens and day nurseries in Japan has been increasing in recent years (Shibuya 2010). Another significant factor relating to growing diversity among young children is widening socioeconomic inequality, which affects children's daily lives and manifests itself in greater differences in dietary habits, learning experiences, and the like. Therefore, in this introductory chapter, we would like to address one of the most important issues of early childhood education in Japan today, which is autonomous learning for children in a multicultural environment. We consider this issue of autonomous learning in the early stage of education is essential to examine the whole education system in Japan because it would affect teaching and learning in the later stages of education, particularly in such an increasingly diversifying society as Japan.

Regarding how learning should take place in early childhood, the Kindergarten Educational Guideline of the Ministry of Education, Culture, Sports, Science and Technology of Japan (MEXT), for example, designates objectives in five domains of childhood development so that children may cultivate the emotions, motivation, and attitude that they are expected to develop by the end of kindergarten and that constitute the foundation of "zest for living."[1] The five domains are as follows (MEXT 2008, p. 3):

1. Health: the domain concerning children's mental and physical health
2. Interpersonal relationships: the domain concerning children's interactions with others
3. Environment: the domain concerning children's interactions with the local environment
4. Language: the domain concerning children's language acquisition
5. Expression: the domain concerning children's sensibility and expression

---

[1] "Zest for living" has been one of the most important key phrases in Japanese educational reforms since the 1990s. The 15th Central Council for Education submitted a report called "The Model for Japanese Education in the Perspective of the Twenty-first Century" in July 1996 and it explains that "fostering zest for living is a vitally important task in our so-called lifelong-learning society, in which there is an increase in the needs for the learning required for self-realization along with demands for appropriate adaptation to social change" (excerpted from MEXT website [http://www.mext.go.jp/b_menu/hakusho/html/hpae199601/hpae199601_2_042.html] accessed on January 13, 2018).

These five domains will be kept and re-emphasized in a new Kindergarten Educational Guideline that should be revised in 2018. This Guideline has been revised at the same time as the revision of the Course of Study (Japan's National Curriculum), approximately once every 10 years. A new guideline is scheduled to be introduced in 2018, and a new Course of Study is planned to be introduced successively for primary education in 2020, lower-secondary education in 2021, and upper-secondary education in 2022.

The importance of children's autonomous learning is also highlighted under all the objectives of the Kindergarten Educational Guideline. As an approach to education that promotes children's autonomous learning, Active Learning has been attracting attention in recent years in Japan. Active Learning is a "generic term for teaching and learning methods that largely consist of the learner's active participation in the learning process." Its ultimate goal is "the development of general-purpose abilities through learning actively pursued by the learner, including cognitive, ethical and social abilities, general culture, knowledge, and experience." Accordingly, Active Learning "encompasses such approaches as learning through discovery, problem-solving learning, learning through experience, and learning through investigation, and group discussions, debates, and group work in the classroom are also effective methods of Active Learning" (MEXT 2014).

Today, the importance of Active Learning in primary, secondary, and higher education is being discussed in Japan, as education is repositioned toward the goal of developing students' knowledge, skills, and attitudes compatible with the new visions of learning for a knowledge-based society in the twenty-first century. It is important to recognize that the starting point of such autonomous (and thus active) learning is learning in early childhood. It is generally understood that it is through active and autonomous learning that children develop in the five domains of the Kindergarten Educational Guideline, which represent the foundation for learning in primary school and onward. While Active Learning is championed as an approach that will better prepare children and students to acquire the abilities that enable them to continue learning throughout their lives and think autonomously, this is indeed the learning goal of today's ECE.

With the growth of diversity in children's backgrounds in contemporary Japanese society, some children of foreign origin or from single-parent families find themselves in a socioeconomically challenging situation. While kindergartens and day nurseries can serve as a "breakwater" providing them with protection, such institutions are also required to ensure equitable learning for them (Akita and Sagawa 2011).

At the same time, it should be noted that greater emphasis on autonomous learning could also lead to even wider socioeconomic inequalities. Autonomous learning involves and requires various daily experiences conducive to forming close interpersonal relationships and engaging in rich communication with others. It is important not to overlook the fact that some children with minority backgrounds cannot easily access such experiences or encounters, due to restrictive family environments or economic difficulties. Requiring such children to pursue autonomous learning without any consideration could thus end up expanding the disparity between them and their peers living in more privileged environments. It is therefore essential for educational practitioners to understand the diverse backgrounds of children and interact with them with ample consideration.

To sum up our discussion on ECE, we would like to emphasize specifically the importance of continuing reflection on how ECE should be operated to promote cross-cultural understanding through autonomous learning, toward the eventual realization of an equitable society, through collaborative consultation by educational practitioners, parents, administrators, researchers, and all others involved in early childhood education and development.

1.4 Organization of the Book

Following to this introductory chapter (Chap. 1), this book is composed of two parts: **Part I: The Education System in Japan** presents an overview of the Japanese education system by describing each educational stage, primary and secondary education, the most fundamental education stages, in Chap. 2, higher education in Chap. 3, and lifelong education and social education—targeting adults—in Chap. 4. In each chapter, the basic institutional structure is outlined, and the status of implementation of important policies and progress of reform in recent years are analyzed. On the basis of this analysis, major reform achievements and problems are then discussed. After these educational stage-based outlines have been presented, Chap. 5 outlines the changes that have taken place in Japan relating to the educational administrative systems at both the national and municipal levels, primarily since the 2000s. This chapter deals with the circumstances of change in national educational administration. Moreover, the chapter covers circumstances concerning municipalities and presents the characteristics of recent municipal educational policies, describing both the circumstances and an outline of the 2014 reforms relating to the now-implemented system of the Board of Education. By going over these matters, Chap. 5 should help readers better understand the trends in Japan's national and local educational administrations.

Since the 1980s, basic structures of relationships—not only between national and local governments but also between the government and the market or society—have been reviewed in many countries around the world, making governance reform an urgent task. In other words, many countries have been promoting structural reforms of their administrative systems, reforms represented by decentralization, deregulation, and introduction of the principle of competition and merit-based systems. The field of education is no exception to these trends.

Part I of this book should help readers grasp the basic structures of the education system in Japan while deepening their understanding of the achievements and problems addressed by important policies and reform in recent years.

Part II: Educational Issues in Japan focuses on various issues relating to education in Japan today, analyzing them using expertise from a range of academic disciplines. These subjects do not directly relate to the issues of governance and quality assurance; however, in their respective contexts, all chapters deal with essentially important educational issues that have directly or indirectly influenced current educational reforms in Japan. We believe the chapters in Part II should help readers better understand why and how today's structural reforms in Japan's education system, which are outlined in the chapters of Part I, are promoted. Below is an outline of each of the chapters in Part II.

Chapter 6 gives an overview of various issues surrounding teachers in Japan today. The subjects addressed in this chapter include teaching qualifications/ licenses, teacher evaluations, and teachers' professional autonomy. In recent years, circumstances surrounding teaching as a profession have been changing dramatically: a system has been introduced requiring periodic renewal of teaching licenses, there have been moves to link teacher treatment to performance evaluations, and graduate schools of teacher education have been established. Discussions concerning these issues are critically analyzed in this chapter.

Chapter 7 introduces lesson study, which has been practiced in Japanese schools over the years, and currently increasing numbers of teachers in different countries are practicing it. Lesson study is an approach in which teachers collaborate with one another and mutually criticize/review their lessons, to autonomously achieve progressive improvement of their teaching. This is an activity that has been developed through educational practices in Japan since the Meiji period, functioning as a forum for teachers' self-enlightenment/development. Regarding lesson study, which has been attracting much attention worldwide in recent years, this chapter outlines how it has been developed and how it is being practiced today and discusses what lesson study will be like in the future.

Chapter 8 looks closely at teachers from a historical perspective. Traditionally in Japan, many teacher discourses have been recorded in various forms, including lesson records, classroom journals, classroom newsletters, personal diaries, and letters. Through analysis of these discourses and stories told by teachers themselves, this chapter illustrates how and on what basis teachers of educational philosophy have engaged in education practice in Japan during each historical period.

Chapter 9 is also a historical analysis of educational issues in Japanese schools. Recently, the importance of community participation in school management has been widely recognized around the world. In Japan, communities have actively supported schools since the mid-nineteenth century, when the modern school system was introduced. This chapter reviews the history of this community participation in school management and clarifies how and under what conditions such support has been provided. We hope that the analysis will serve as a basis for understanding the relationship between schools and communities in Japan today.

Chapter 10 highlights one of the biggest social problems in Japanese society today—the issue of "disparity." In the field of education, the issue of disparity is also widely recognized as a critical problem. Various educational disparities, as represented by disparities in academic performance, obviously exist among students, among schools, and among communities. It should be noted that these educational disparities are closely linked with employment opportunities for the young generation. This chapter gives an overview of the status of these educational disparities and discusses how they are influencing the youth labor market, with particular focus on the impact of the bursting of the economic bubble since the 1990s and the major earthquake that occurred on March 11, 2011.

Chapter 11 examines how education in Japan has been increasing its multicultural aspects and analyzes how schools are responding to this trend in terms of providing minority children with opportunities and preparing them for their future lives. The chapter reveals the ways in which minority children (i.e., long-existing minority groups as well as newcomers) interact with "mainstream Japanese" children through their school lives.

Chapter 12 focuses on approaches for assuring education quality, from among the various approaches to reforming Japan's higher education system in recent years. Following an explanation of the systems that have been established for quality assurance and accreditation in universities, the approaches taken by individual universities are presented. These analyses enable critical discussion of the ability of universities to meet social expectations for higher education in Japan.

Chapter 13 focuses on the international aspects of Japanese education with linguistic interests. As society becomes increasingly knowledge-based, the internationalization of education is widely recognized as a crucially important social task for Japan. Given these circumstances, particularly the development of human resources who can exercise their abilities in the international community, there are high expectations for reforming English language education. Reflecting such expectations, however, populist discussions and policies are often perceived in relation to English language education. This chapter therefore aims to critically examine the role English language education should play in promoting the internationalization of Japanese education.

Chapter 14 explains how the Great East Japan Earthquake of 2011 has heightened public interest in safety education in Japan. It is important to promote comprehensive safety education covering not only disaster prevention but also crime prevention and traffic safety. However, since safety education is a relatively new field, practices and academic verifications have been insufficient. Under these circumstances, employing the viewpoint of Education for Sustainable Development (ESD), an international discussion of education, enables development of a comprehensive concept for safety education. Thus, this chapter examines theoretically the form of ESD-based safety education while presenting the results of research on how parents and teachers actually perceive safety education.

We would like to draw readers' attention to there being some differences in terms of the length of chapters and the way each chapter conducts its discussion. Since this book is composed of two parts, Part I for more general overviews of each educational level and Part II for selected topics and issues analyzed theoretically, historically, and/or empirically, we try to keep some flexibility and space for each chapter's author to conduct his/her own discussion in a more appropriate manner for his/her chapter. This approach has resulted in having some chapters relatively shorter (or longer) and/or more descriptive (or analytical) than others. We believe that such variety of chapters should be considered as an asset for responding to diverse interests and expectations readers may have.

By applying theoretical, historical, and empirical approaches toward the current structural reforms of the education sector while dealing with widening socioeconomic disparities in Japan, the ultimate goal of this book is to show the wider audience beyond Japan's borders how contemporary Japanese society has been trying to improve the quality of its education. Both the editors and authors of the individual chapters hope that readers will be able to grasp how dynamically the education sector has been developing over the years and how the various obstacles and challenges in education that we are facing in Japan today are being dealt with.

Acknowledgment The chapters of this book are outcomes of the research project called "Theoretical and Empirical Studies on Governance Reform and Quality Assurance in Education" led by Toshiyuki Omomo, which has been funded by the Japan Society for the Promotion of Science (KAKENHI Research No.: 26245075). Also, for the creation of the Chronological Table of Education Reforms in Postwar Japan, we are grateful for extensive support from Mr. Naofumi Sueoka, a Master's student in Graduate School of Education, The University of Tokyo.

Chronological Table of Education Reforms in Postwar Japan

【1945–1954】 Beginning of postwar education reforms: democratization of education		
1945	September 15	The Ministry of Education, Science, Sports and Culture (MOE) publishes the Educational Policy for the Construction of a New Japan (eradicating militarism from education)
	October 22–December 31	The General Headquarters of the Allied Forces (GHQ) issues four major directives relating to education, including the Directive concerning the Administration Policies of the Educational System of Japan (inspecting educational content, purging militant teachers, removing Shinto education from schools, and suspending courses on morals, Japanese history, and geography)
1946	April 7	The GHQ publishes the US Education Mission Report (recommending a 6-3-3 school system)
	May 15	The MOE issues the Guideline for New Education
	August 10	Education Reform Committee established (as an advisory body to the prime minister that led to subsequent educational reforms)
1947	March 20	The national course of study (a tentative plan) published (placing emphasis on experience-based learning, introducing new subject areas, Social Studies, etc.)
	March 31	The Basic Act on Education and the School Education Act promulgated
	April 1	Primary schools and lower secondary schools established under the new school system
	June 8	Japan Teachers' Union established

(continued)

1948	April 1	A new upper secondary school system opened (under the three principles of small school districts, coeducation, and comprehensive curriculum)
	July 15	The Board of Education Act promulgated (a public election system for BOE members). The first elections held in October
1949	January 12	The Special Act for Education Public Service Personal promulgated
	May 31	The National School Establishment Act, the Act for Establishment of the Ministry of Education, and the Education Personnel Certification Act promulgated (introducing an open system)
1951	May 6	The Ordinance Revision Commission established (an unofficial advisory body to Prime Minister Yoshida to re-examine the education reforms that had been enacted during the occupation)
1952	June 6	The Central Council for Education (CCE) created as a successor to the Education Reform Committee (which had been renamed the Education Reform Council in 1949)
	July 31	Sweeping revisions to the Act for Establishment of the Ministry of Education implemented (authorizing the MOE to give guidance, advice, and recommendations to local public bodies, etc.)
1954	June 3	The Act for Partial Amendments to the Special Act for Educational Public Service Personnel, the Act on Temporary Measures for Securing Political Neutrality of Education in Compulsory Education Schools (known as the "Two Major Educational Acts"), and the School Lunch Program Act promulgated

【1955–1964】 Economic growth and the massification of upper secondary schools: Widening of educational opportunities

1956	June 30	The Board of Education Act abolished. The Act on the Organization and Operation of Local Educational Administration (hereinafter "Local Educational Administration Act") promulgated
	October 1	An appointment system for the members of the boards of education introduced in accordance with the Local Educational Administration Act
1957	November 9	The Curriculum Council decides to reintroduce moral education into the school curriculum as an informal subject
	November 28	The Association of Prefectural Board of Education Chairpersons develops the standards for performance evaluation in accordance with the Local Educational Administration Act
1958	April 25	The Act on National Treasury's Sharing of Expenses for Facilities of Compulsory Education Schools, etc. promulgated
	May 1	The Act on the Standards for the Class Formation and Fixed Number of School Personnel of Public Compulsory Education Schools (hereinafter "Compulsory Education Standards Act") promulgated (class sizes of up to 50 students)
	October 1	The revised national courses of study for primary schools and lower secondary schools announced (making the curricula binding, emphasizing on systematic learning, introducing moral education as an independent area of teaching)

(continued)

1960	March 31	The Curriculum Council issues a report on the improvement of upper secondary education curricula (introducing a general education course, etc.)
	June 21	The MOE requests advice on the establishment of a system for supervising and disciplining students at upper secondary schools (as a precaution against the student movement)
	October 15	The revised national course of study for upper secondary schools announced (separating the general education program from vocational education programs)
1961	June 17	The School Education Act revised (to create a technical college system)
	November 6	The Act on the Establishment of Public Upper Secondary Schools, Their Proper Distribution, the Standards for the Fixed Number of School Personnel, etc. promulgated
1963	January 14	The Economic Council issues a report on the problems and measures for developing human capabilities in the high economic growth period
	December 21	The Act on the Free Distribution of Textbooks to Compulsory Education Schools promulgated. (Free distribution started for first graders and expanded in stages year by year to higher graders (until full-scale implementation in all compulsory education schools in the 1969 academic year). The Compulsory Education Standards Act revised (a class size of up to 45 students)
1964	June 19	The School Education Act revised (to establish a permanent system for junior colleges, which started on an ad hoc basis in 1949)

【1965–1974】 The government's strong intervention in education: Improvement of educational conditions and the spread of the ability-first principle

1966	October 31	The CCE issues a report on the expansion and development of upper secondary education (appending "The Image of the Ideal Japanese," proposing the diversification of upper secondary education and placing an emphasis on a sense of patriotism)
1967	August 11/ October 3	The Council on Scientific and Industrial Education (established within the MOE) issues a report on the diversification of vocational education in upper secondary schools (in August) and another report on the establishment of courses relating to science and mathematics in upper secondary education (in October). These reports led to the establishment of 18 new courses in upper secondary school education
1968	July 11	A revision to the national course of study for primary schools announced (modernizing the curriculum and placing emphasis on Japanese traditions and a sense of patriotism)
	December 6	A committee for discussing university problems established within the MOE (to deal with widespread campus disturbances)
1969	April 14	A revision to the national course of study for lower secondary schools announced (modernizing the curriculum, as in the case of primary schools)
	May 15	The Compulsory Education Standards Act revised (to improve the allocation of teachers and eliminate multiage classes)
	August 3	The Act on Temporary Measures concerning University Management formulated (giving the government the power to directly intervene in university administration)

(continued)

1971	June 11	The CCE issues a report proposing basic policies for comprehensive reforms of school education. (An ambitious report known as "*yon-roku toshin* (46 report)," since it was compiled in the 46th year of the Showa era. It recommended the reorganization of the education system as Japan's third major education reform and advocated lifelong learning)
1972	January 1	The Act on Special Measures concerning Salaries and Other Conditions for Education Personnel of Public Compulsory Education Schools, etc. enacted
	July 3	The Council on Educational Personnel Training proposes measures to improve teacher training
1973	February 20	The Act on Special Measures for Securing Capable Education Personnel in Public Compulsory Education Schools for the Maintenance and Enhancement of School Education Standards decided by the Cabinet (and enacted in February 1974, providing teachers with a salary increase)
1974	September 1	The School Education Act revised to include a provision for the post of assistant principal
【1975–1984】 Fiercely competitive entrance exams and the spread of disruptive behavior in schools: Tighter classroom management		
1975	July 3	The Bill on Subsidies for Private Schools and the Bill on Specialized Training Colleges (*senshu gakko*) passed by the Upper House in the plenary session and enacted
	December 8	The primary and secondary education team of the Liberal Democratic Party's education division issues a proposal for reforming the system and educational content of upper secondary schools (suggesting a policy course for the diversification of upper secondary schools)
1976	March 1	A revision to the Enforcement Regulations for the School Education Act enforced (introducing a head/senior teacher system in primary and secondary schools)
	September 8	The MOE issues an official notice on the use of tests developed by commercial educational companies, etc. (as a precaution against the spread of deviation-value-oriented education)
	October 6	The Curriculum Council issues a report on improvements to curriculum guidelines (placing emphasis on *yutori* (latitude or being free from pressure) and fulfillment)
1977	April 22	The National School Establishment Act revised. The National Center for University Entrance Examinations established (the first unified first-stage exam started in 1979)
	July 23	The revision to the national courses of study for primary and lower secondary schools announced (the careful selection of curriculum content with emphasis on *yutori* and fulfillment)
1978	June 16	The CCE submits a report on improving teachers' quality and competence (proposing systematic training for teachers)
	August 30	The revision to the national course of study for upper secondary schools announced (more flexible curricula)
1979	April 1	A compulsory system for special education schools implemented.
1980	April 25	The Compulsory Education Standards Act revised (class sizes of up to 40 students)

(continued)

1981	February 12	Tokyo's Nakano Ward implements the first local quasi-public election for education board members in Japan in accordance with an ordinance passed by the Ward's council (the election system was abolished later)
	April 29	The MOE compiles a collection of cases of violent and disruptive school behavior (to ensure tighter oversight of students' behavior)
	June 11	The CCE issues a report on lifelong learning
1982	November 24	The MOE announces the revision to the authorization criteria for school textbooks (by adding the so-called Neighboring Country Clause)
1983	March 10	The MOE issues a notice urging educational officials to ensure tighter management of disruptive, violent, and other problem behaviors of students in schools
1984	February 26	The National Teachers Federation of Japan holds its inaugural meeting
	August 21	The Ad Hoc Council on Education created (an advisory body to Prime Minister Nakasone)
【1985–1994】 Rise in bullying and nonattendance cases and a new view of academic ability		
1985	October 25	The MOE issues a notice to prefectural boards of education, etc. regarding the thorough implementation of tighter school management as countermeasures to bullying
1987	August 7	The Ad Hoc Council on Education issues its final report (presenting the three principles of educational reform: emphasis on the individuality of students, lifelong learning, and the responses to internationalization and advancements in information technology)
1988	May 31	The revised Special Act for Educational Public Service Personnel promulgated (introducing an induction training system for newly appointed teachers based on the recommendations issued by the Ad Hoc Council on Education)
	July 1	The Lifelong Learning Bureau established within the MOE
1989	March 15	The revision to the national courses of study for primary and secondary schools announced (presenting a new view of academic abilities, placing emphasis on students' motivation to learn, adding a new subject, Living Environment Studies, to the primary school curriculum, and recommending the introduction of competency-based education in lower secondary schools)
	December 22	The Education Personnel Certification Act revised (creating new certificate categories for the specialized teacher's license and special teaching certificate and increasing the requirements for teacher certification)
1990	June 29	The Lifelong Learning Promotion Act promulgated

(continued)

1991	April 19	The CCE submits a proposal for reforming various systems relating to education to cope with a new era (developing more diverse and flexible admission criteria for upper secondary schools and universities and laying the foundations for lifelong learning)
	June 3	The Ministerial Ordinance for partial amendments to the Standards for Establishment of Universities promulgated (to relax the standards)
	December 19	The MOE proposes the phased introduction of a five-day school week (every second Saturday became a holiday from September 1992)
1993	February 22	The MOE issues a notice regarding entrance screening for upper secondary schools (introducing more diverse screening methods of applicants)
1994	December 9	An urgent anti-bullying meeting convened, issuing an emergency appeal. (The MOE urged local educational officials around the country to conduct full-scale investigations of suspected bullying in schools)
【1985–2004】 *Yutori* (pressure-free) education and society in the twenty-first century		
1995	March 13	The MOE issues a report on the urgent anti-bullying meeting as a notice concerning measures that should be taken immediately to stop and prevent bullying
1996	July 19	The CCE submits the first report on "The Model for Japanese Education in the Perspective of the Twenty-first Century" (proposing the cultivation of *ikiru chikara* (competencies for positive living or zest for living), the creation of schools that have their own distinctive characteristics and can help children to develop their own individuality, and the establishment of periods of integrated studies)
1997	January 24	The MOE formulates an Educational Reform Program (full-scale introduction of a five-day school week in the academic year 2003, etc.)
	June 26	The CCE submits the second report on "The Model for Japanese Education in the Perspective of the Twenty-first Century" (proposing a more flexible school education system, such as early entrance to university and the selective introduction of combined lower and upper middle school education)
1998	June 30	The CCE issues a report, "How we can help children cultivate competences to carve out a new era?—The traditional model for nurturing the next generation is being shaken" (emphasizing the *ikiru chikara* (zest for living) and reaffirming the roles of home, community, and school)
1999	April 1	Six-year secondary schools open as a result of the revision to the School Education Act (introduction of combined lower and upper middle education system)
	July 16	The Act on Revisions of Related Acts for Promoting Decentralization ("Omnibus Decentralization Act") enacted. (The abolishment of the system in which the heads of prefectural governments and ordinance-designated cities appoint and approve the superintendent of the local board of education)
	August 13	The Act on National Flag and Anthem promulgated
	September 17	The MOE issues a notification regarding the use of the national flag and anthem in schools

(continued)

2000	January 21	A revision to the Enforcement Regulations for the School Education Act enforced (introducing the School Councilor System)
	March 27	The National Commission on Educational Reform established (prime minister's advisory body)
	December 22	The National Commission on Educational Reform submits its final report (listing 17 proposals for making changes to education: emphasis on moral education, the development of a basic plan for the promotion of education, a review of the Basic Act on Education, etc.)
2001	January 6	Central Government Reform. The Ministry of Education, Culture, Sports, Science and Technology (MEXT) created through the merger of the MOE and the Science and Technology Agency
	January 25	MEXT formulates an educational reform plan for the twenty-first century, the Rainbow Plan (developing "solid academic abilities," promoting small class size and competency-based education, etc.)
	February 1	The CCE and six other councils integrated into a new Central Council for Education
	June 11	Policies for structural reform of national universities (Tohyama Plan) announced (reorganization and consolidation of national universities, transformation into a national university corporation, allocation of funds based on third-party evaluation, etc.)
2002	January 17	MEXT releases a document titled "*Manabi no susume* (Encouraging self-motivated learning)," describing policies for developing solid academic abilities
	April 1	A five-day school week schedule and new courses of study for primary and lower secondary schools implemented (development of a "zest for living," pressure-free education, 30% reduction in curriculum content, and the introduction of periods for integrated studies)
2003	July 16	The National University Corporation Act and five other related Acts promulgated. The incorporation of national universities started from the following academic year
2004	June 9	The Local Education Administration Act revised to introduce the School Management Council system (community schools)
【2005–2017】 Creation of a new school system and a new education system		
2005	October 26	The CCE issues a report titled "Redesigning Compulsory Education for a New Era" (proposing national strategies for compulsory education reform)
	December 8	The CCE issues a report on a new system for promoting special education
2006	October 1	Centers for Early Childhood Education and Care opened
	October 10	The Education Rebuilding Council (an advisory panel to the prime minister) established
	December 22	The Basic Act on Education revised (adding the provisions on the duties and powers of the national government in education)

(continued)

2007	January 24	The Education Rebuilding Council submits its first report titled "Education Rebuilding by Society as a Whole—The First Step toward Rebuilding Public Education" (recommending the review of *yutori* education and the system of the boards of education, etc.)
	March 10	The CCE issues a report on the changes that should be made immediately to the school education system in response to the revision to the Basic Act on Education (reviewing the school administration system and the roles of the boards of educations and the national and local governments, introducing a teacher license renewal system, etc.)
2008	March 28	The revision to the national courses of study for primary and lower secondary schools announced (increasing the number of hours devoted to major subjects and introducing foreign language activities in the primary school curriculum)
	April 1	The School Education Act revised (allowing schools to add more managerial posts, such as vice principal and managing teacher)
	July 1	The Basic Plan for the Promotion of Education formulated (a comprehensive 5-year plan designed to promote education and realize the visions stipulated in the Basic Act on Education)
2009	April 1	The teacher license renewal system introduced. (Some universities and other institutions implemented the system in the previous academic year on a trial basis)
2010	April 1	The Act on Free Tuition Fees at Public High Schools and the High School Enrollment Support Fund System enacted (making tuition for public upper secondary schools free and providing a certain amount of financial assistance for tuition to private school students)
2011	January 31	The CCE issues a report on a future vision of career education and vocational education at school
	April 1	The revised national course of study for primary schools implemented fully (standard class sizes of up to 35 pupils for first graders in public primary schools)
2012	July 23	The CCE releases a report on the promotion of special needs education to develop an inclusive education system toward creating a cohesive society
	September 5	MEXT develops comprehensive policies for anti-bullying, school safety, etc. in response to the October 2011 suicide of a junior high school boy in Otsu, Shiga Prefecture, who had been severely bullied
2013	January 15	The Education Rebuilding Implementation Council (ERIC) established and submits its first proposal, "Measures to solve bullying and other problems" (upgrading moral education to a formal subject, etc.) in February, and its second proposal, "The role of the boards of education system, etc.," in April
	March 13	MEXT issues a notice regarding the prohibition of physical punishment and the improvement of instruction of students based on a thorough understanding of the actual situation, in response to the December 2012 suicide case of a high school boy in Osaka City, who had been subjected to harsh physical punishment

(continued)

2014	July 3	ERIC submits its fifth proposal, "School system for the future," recommending the extension of the periods of free-tuition education and compulsory education, the introduction of combined primary and lower secondary school education, etc.
2015	January 16	Plan for Implementing the High School/University Articulation Reforms formulated (discussions on the establishment of a Council for High School/University Articulation System Reform, a new examination that will replace the National Center Test for University Admissions, Active Learning, etc.)
	March 4	ERIC submits its sixth proposal, "New education for creating a society that features lifelong learning and participation by all and realizing regional revitalization," proposing to consider the establishment of free schools, night classes at lower secondary schools, etc.
	March 27	The national courses of study for primary and lower secondary schools partially revised (to introduce moral education as a special subject into the curriculum for primary schools in the academic year 2018 and for lower secondary schools in the academic year 2019, using government-approved textbooks)
	April 1	The revised Local Educational Administration Act implemented, partially making changes to the board of education system (such as the consolidation of the superintendent and chairman posts)
	June 24	The revised School Education Act promulgated, allowing the establishment of new nine-year "compulsory education schools," which integrate primary and lower secondary schools
	December 21	The CCE submits a report on the idea of a school as a team and future improvement measures, etc.
2016	January 25	MEXT develops a Plan for Creating Next Generation Schools and Communities
	March 31	The Council for High School/University Articulation System Reform (established in February 2015) submits its final report, proposing the introduction of a "High School Basic Academic Skills Test (tentative name)" and "Scholastic Assessment Test for University Applicants (tentative name)," etc.
	May 20	ERIC issues its ninth proposal "Creating an education system that helps all children develop to their full potential" (preparation of individual education records of children with special needs, etc.)
	May 30	The CCE submits a report regarding how we can diversify education and secure the quality of education to help students develop to their full potential to realize a society that features participatory problem-solving, recommending the promotion of vocational education, etc.
	December 21	The CCE submits a report on improvements to the courses of study for kindergartens, primary, secondary, and special needs education schools and necessary measures (making proposals to strengthen foreign language education; make "comprehensive geography," "comprehensive history," and "citizenship" compulsory in upper middle schools; and introduce new selective subjects, including "advanced Japanese history," "advanced world history," and "advanced geography," to the upper middle curriculum)

(continued)

| 2017 | March 31 | The revised national courses of study for primary and lower secondary schools announced, advocating "self-directed, interactive, and deep learning" and placing emphasis on the enhancement of education related to tradition and culture, science and mathematics education, foreign language education, etc. (to be implemented fully at primary schools in the 2020 academic year and at lower secondary schools in the 2021 academic year) |

Note: In order to develop this table, the editors referred to Nihon Jidou Shinkou Zaidan [The Foundation for the Advancement of Juvenile Education in Japan] (eds.) (2016). *Gakko-Kyouiku no Sengo 70 Nen Shi* (*70 Years of the Post-War History of Japanese Education*). Tokyo: Shogakkan

References

Akita, K., & Sagawa, S. (2011). Hoiku no shitsu ni kansuru judan kenkyu no tenbo [A vision for transversal research into the quality of childcare]. *Bulletin of the Graduate School of Education, The University of Tokyo, 51*, 217–234.

Decoker, G., & Bjork, C. (Eds.). (2013). *Japanese education in an era of globalization: Culture, politics, and equity*. New York: Teachers College Press.

Gordon, J. A., Fujita, H., Kariya, T., & Letendre, G. (Eds.). (2009). *Challenges to Japanese education: Economics, reform, and human rights*. New York: Teachers College Press.

Hebert, D. G. (2011). *Wind bands and cultural identity in Japanese schools*. Springer.

Hood, C. P. (2001). *Japanese education reform: Nakasone's legacy*. London/New York: Routledge.

Jones, M. (2010). *Children as treasures: Childhood and the middle class in early twentieth century Japan*. Cambridge: Harvard University Asian Center.

Kariya, T. (2012). *Education reform and social class in Japan: The emerging incentive divide*. London/New York: Routledge.

MEXT. (2014). "*Yogoshu*" [Glossary] in *Chuo Kyoiku Shingikai "Aratana mirai o kizukutame no daigaku kyoiku no shitsuteki tankan ni mukete: shogai manabi tsuzuke shutaiteki ni kangaeru chikara o ikuseisuru daigaku e (toshin)*" [The Central Council for Education report "For a qualitative turn in university education for building a new future: for universities that enable lifelong learning and develop proactive thinking]. http://www.mext.go.jp/b_menu/shingi/chu-kyo/chukyo0/toshin/1325047.htm. Accessed on 13 June 2015.

MEXT (Monbukagakusho: Ministry of Education, Culture, Sports, Science and Technology). (2008). *Yochien kyoiku yoryo* [Kindergarten educational guideline]. Tokyo: MEXT.

Okano, K. (1999). *Education in contemporary Japan: Inequality and diversity*. Cambridge: Cambridge University Press.

Shibuya, M. (2010). *Nyuyoji o torimaku tabunkateki jokyo no shinten: 2006 iko no jokyo o chushin ni* [Development of multicultural situations surrounding infants and young children: Mainly situations since 2006]. In *Tabunka ni ikiru kodomotachi: nyuyojiki kara no ibunkakan kyoiku* [Children living in multiple cultures: Cross-cultural education since infancy and early childhood], C. Yamada (Ed.). Tokyo: Akashi Shoten.

Stephens, M. D. (1991). *Japan and education*. New York: Palgrave Macmillan.

Tsuneyoshi, R., Okano, K. H., & Boocock, S. S. (2011). *Minorities and education in multicultural Japan: An interactive perspective*. London/New York: Routledge.

Part I
The Education System in Japan

Chapter 2
Primary and Secondary Education

Toshiyuki Omomo

2.1   Introduction

Primary and secondary education in Japan has undergone drastic changes in the past few decades. The starting point was the establishment of an Ad Hoc Council on Education (*Rinkyoshin*) in 1984. Yasuhiro Nakasone became Prime Minister in 1982 and undertook radical reforms of the post-World War II regime. Education reform was one of his major concerns, and the Rinkyoshin was created as his advisory panel.

In Japan, the national education system was organized after the Meiji Restoration in the late nineteenth century and reorganized after World War II. The Rinkyoshin report referred to the reform after the Meiji Restoration as "the first education reform" and the reform after World War II as "the second education reform." Although there were rather big differences between the two reforms, the Rinkyoshin argued that the second reform complemented the education system created after the first reform and that it was a system by which Japan could catch up with modernized Western countries. According to the Rinkyoshin report, although this system contributed to the development of the country, it became uniform and inflexible and caused serious problems. In addition, the second reform had aspects to deny the distinctive and positive features of traditional Japanese culture, to downplay moral education, and to cause an imbalance between the sense of right and that of responsibility. Therefore, the Rinkyoshin argued that the education system should enter a stage of drastic reexamination and reform (Rinkyoshin 1985, pp. 7–10).

This chapter begins with a brief overview of the post-World War II education system and points out several factors which led to the establishment of the Rinkyoshin. Then, it analyzes the debates at the Rinkyoshin and the later development

T. Omomo (✉)
Faculty of Intercultural Studies, Gakushuin Women's College, Tokyo, Japan
e-mail: toshiyuki.omomo@gakushuin.ac.jp

© Springer Nature Singapore Pte Ltd. 2019   25
Y. Kitamura et al. (eds.), *Education in Japan*, Education in the Asia-Pacific
Region: Issues, Concerns and Prospects 47,
https://doi.org/10.1007/978-981-13-2632-5_2

of the reforms which the Rinkyoshin proposed. Finally, it examines the present situation and specifics of primary and secondary education reforms in Japan. In these analyses and examinations, the chapter pays specific attention to the influence of governance reform. As in many other countries, education reform in the past few decades in Japan has proceeded in close relation to governance reform.

2.2   Centralized System of Education

After World War II, the new constitution and new education laws were enacted, and education reforms were implemented. The constitution prescribed "the right to receive an equal education" as one of the fundamental rights of the people (Article 26), and the Basic Act on Education prescribed the principle of equal educational opportunity (Article 3). Instead of the complicated, multi-track system that existed before the war, a so-called single track school system was adopted to guarantee equal educational opportunities. The system was composed of kindergarten (1–3 years in duration), elementary school (6 years), lower secondary school (3 years), upper secondary school (3 years), university (4–6 years), and schools for special education (kindergarten, primary, lower secondary and upper secondary divisions). Although there were many types of educational institutions in Japan, these schools prescribed in Article 1 of the School Education Act had a specific status, and only the national government, local governments, and school corporations prescribed by the Private Schools Act were permitted to establish these schools. The 6-year primary education and 3-year lower secondary education were compulsory. This basic school system structure has not changed until the present, although, as stated later, some important modifications have been made.

The national government set up a Course of Study for each academic subject, and school textbooks were compiled according to the Course of Study. Private companies compiled most textbooks, but the Ministry of Education retained the right to approve them through strict examinations. Some textbooks for subjects with a limited number of students were compiled by the Ministry of Education itself. Every school at the elementary and secondary education level was required to use textbooks that the Ministry of Education approved or compiled. The national government also set up precise national standards for school organization and facilities and prescribed teacher certification requirements in detail through laws and regulations. With this centralized system, the national government aimed to provide universal and common education throughout the country. No matter where children lived, they could receive education on the same subjects, based on almost the same textbooks, and by teachers with the same qualifications (Omomo 2012, pp. 129–130).

Under this centralized system, the enrollment ratio at the compulsory education level has been stable at almost 100%. The ratio of students who went on to upper secondary schools exceeded 50% in 1954 and 90% in 1974. The ratio of students who went on to university increased from about 17% in 1960 to 24% in 1970 and again to 32% in 1980 (MOE 1998, pp. 28–29). Along with the rise in the ratio of advancement to upper secondary and higher education, entrance examinations became extremely competitive and were accused of placing excessive pressure on students. The severe competition was often referred to as "examination war" or "examination hell." Although the cause and effect relationship was not clear, during the period from the end of the 1970s to the mid-1980s, juvenile delinquency became a serious problem.

2.3   Background to the Establishment of the Rinkyoshin

Among many factors involved in the establishment of the Rinkyoshin, the direct one was the increase in juvenile delinquencies or students' problematic behaviors. According to national government data, the number of violent incidents in schools increased by about 1.7 times in 2 years from 1979 to 1981. In particular, violence toward teachers at the lower secondary school level greatly increased, by about 3.5 times, in the same period. In 1981, the ratio of young people (age of 14 years and upward) who committed criminal offences became the worst after World War II (MOE 1982, pp. 13–14, Council on Juvenile Problems 1982, p. 65). In addition, in the early 1980s, serious juvenile crimes took place, including murder.

This situation raised awareness of the need for educational reforms. Although it is not correct to identify juvenile delinquencies as educational problems, school education was accused of being a cause for these youth problems. "The deterioration of education (*Kyoiku Kohai*)" became an often-used phrase. To cope with these problems, the Ministry of Education and its advisory panel proposed various measures such as taking resolute postures regarding students' problematic behaviors, organizing more collaborative systems among teachers, and establishing cooperation with related organizations (MOE 1983; Panel on Recent Problematic Behaviors at Schools 1983). However, there arose strong demands for more fundamental reforms of the post-World War II educational resume.

We can point out the influence of so-called neoliberal ideology as another factor for the establishment of the Rinkyoshin, in relation to these demands for more radical reforms. During the 1980s, the welfare state regime was radically reexamined through neoliberal policies, not only in Japan but also in other countries such as the United Kingdom and the United States. There were various definitions of neoliberalism, and its policy developments were diverse among countries. However, if we define the neoliberal policy as emphasizing the reduction of governmental functions in both regulation and finance, use of private sector initiative, introduction of market mechanisms along with resulting competition, and expansion of consumer choice, we can trace the demands for such policies in education reform arguments.

One example was the Final Report of the Ad Hoc Commission on Administrative Reform in 1983. In the 1980s, the national government advanced radical administrative and financial reforms under the slogan of "financial reconstruction without tax increases." Yasuhiro Nakasone was in charge of administrative and financial reforms as the head of the Administrative Management Agency and then as the

Prime Minister. Under the Nakasone administration, Nippon Telegraph and Telephone Public Corporation, Japan Tobacco and Salt Public Corporation, and Japan National Railway were privatized. The Final Report of the Ad Hoc Commission included demands for the reduction of budgets as well as for more active use of private sectors in the area of education (Ad Hoc Commission on Administrative Reform 1983, pp. 134–137).

Another example was the Seven Proposals for Revitalizing School Education by the Kyoto Group for Thinking about the World (*Sekai wo Kangaeru Kyoto Zakai*), a group of influential people not only in academia but also in the business community. This report criticized the present education system as being uniform and inflexible and proposed the elimination or relaxation of regulations to the extent possible. The proposals included the diversification of school providers and types of schools, the expansion of school choice, and the recruiting of diverse people as teachers by relaxing regulations (Kyoto Group 1984). This report was issued in March 1984, just before the establishment of the Rinkyoshin, and some of the Kyoto Group became the members of the Rinkyoshin and played important roles in its debates.

Along with the neoliberal trend for reform, we can add the conservative demand for education reform as another factor for the establishment of the Rinkyoshin. As already mentioned, Prime Minister Nakasone aimed at radical reform of the post-World War II regime, and he wanted to revise the Basic Act on Education which was the basis of the post-World War II education regime. Later, Nakasone mentioned that the Basic Act on Education had few cardinal elements such as our own country's tradition and culture, community, state and nation, responsibilities, and duties and that education could not come into effect without Japanese elements (Nakasone 2004, pp. 197–198).

According to Kenzo Uchida, a member of the Rinkyoshin, most opposition parties resisted the establishment of the Rinkyoshin for fear that educational reform led by Nakasone would become a milestone on the road to constitutional revision. The national government made two compromises. First, the Rinkyoshin would advance education reform according to the spirit of the Basic Act on Education. Second, the appointment of its members would be approved by the Diet, and its recommendations would be reported to the Diet (Uchida 1987, pp. 9–11). These points were incorporated in the Establishment Act of the Rinkyoshin. However, the reports of the Rinkyoshin were to include the conservative demands.

2.4   Liberalization of Education and Emphasis on Tradition

One major issue in the debates at the Rinkyoshin was the "liberalization of education (*kyoiku no jiyuka*)." At the early stage of the Rinkyoshin debates, a core member of the Kyoto Group as well as the Ad Hoc Commission on Administrative Reform, Hiroshi Kato emphasized the importance of deregulation and privatization at a hearing, and this was referred to as the beginning of the "liberalization of education" arguments at the Rinkyoshin (Otake 1993, p. 17). Kato was a professor of Keio

University and was known as the translation supervisor of Milton and Rose Friedman's work, *Tyranny of the Status Quo*. He was a strong advocate of "freedom, competition, and diversification" in education (Kato 1984). Among the Rinkyoshin members, the most prominent proponent of the "liberalization of education" was Kenichi Koyama, who was "a central figure in the Nakasone education reform debate" and had "ideas very close to his (Nakasone's) own" (Hood 2001, pp. 16, 104). Koyama defined the "liberalization of education" as "the relaxation of national uniform control, approval and regulation, etc., on education" (Koyama 1985, p. 239).

In Japan, as stated previously, "Article 1 schools" providers were limited to the national government, local governments, and school corporations. Schools established by the national government, local governments, and school corporations were called national, public, and private schools, respectively. At the compulsory education level, the municipal boards of education designated the public school that each child should attend. Parents could choose national or private schools for their children, but the number of such schools was few, except for in large cities. "Liberalization of education" proponents argued for relaxing regulations to create diversity among school providers and provide freedom regarding school choice. According to them, diversifying providers would create competition, thereby making school education more responsive to consumers, or parents and children, in the case of education. Such arguments as diversifying providers, introducing market mechanisms, and responding to consumer needs were in accordance with those of administrative reform.

To the criticism that Japanese education was uniform and too rigid, the Ministry of Education admitted the necessity of diversifying school education or introducing more flexibility in education. However, the Ministry strongly opposed the idea of the "liberalization of education," especially relaxing regulations on school education providers and freedom of public school choice at the compulsory education level. The Ministry criticized the former as threatening the stability or public nature of school education and the latter as making competition more intense at the early stage of school education (MOE 1985, pp. 55–56). Among the Rinkyoshin members, the most prominent opponent of the "liberalization of education" was Kazuhisa Arita, who had an educational career as a high school principal and a member of a prefectural board of education as well as a member of the Central Council for Education (*Chukyoshin*), a major advisory panel to the Minister of Education. Like the Ministry of Education, Arita strongly criticized the liberalization of school providers and public school choice at the compulsory education level (Arita 1985).

After fierce debates, instead of the "liberalization of education," the Rinkyoshin used the phrase "the principle of respecting individuality" in its reports. The reports made such recommendations as diversifying secondary education and increasing elective subjects in order to respond to the different needs of individual students. The reports also recommended a shift from a system that heavily emphasized school education in the early stage of life to a lifelong learning system, thereby relieving the excessive stress of the competitive school system. Addressing diversification of school education providers and public school choice, the reports pointed out the necessity of "relaxing regulations on the establishment, maintenance and management of schools" and of "devising various measures for the gradual expansion of school choice opportunities" (Rinkyoshin 1987a, pp. 207, 262). Both the diversification of school providers and public school choice at the compulsory education level were to be implemented in the later reforms, as well as the diversification of school education.

As previously stated, we can also find conservative aspects in the Rinkyoshin reports: the demands for a love for the country and respect for the national flag and anthem. These were required in relation to responding to internationalization. For example, the final report mentioned that "it is necessary not only to have a love for the nation as a Japanese but also to aim for character formation from the broader international and humane perspective, without judging issues only from narrow national self-interests," and that "in this relation, it is important to foster minds and attitudes to understand and respect the meaning of the national flag and anthem, and they should be treated adequately in school education" (Rinkyoshin 1987b, p. 277).

In present-day Japan, the *Nisshoki* (or *Hinomaru*) is prescribed by law as the national flag and *Kimigayo* as the national anthem. However, there was strong opposition to their use as the national flag and anthem, as both were regarded as "reminders of Japan's past and the results of 'unhealthy nationalism' that led to war" and "symbols of the right wing's desire for greater nationalism" (Hood 2001, p. 70). Further, at the time of the Rinkyoshin debates, there was no clear legal recognition for either. Hideo Otake, a political scholar, pointed out that the Rinkyoshin eliminated the national elements as much as possible by incorporating the national anthem and flag issues into internationalization (Otake 1993, p. 21).

2.5   Diversification and Downsizing of School Education

Through the end of the 1980s to the early 1990s, new types of upper secondary school courses were adopted. One was the "credit system," which was introduced to part-time and correspondence courses in 1988 and to full-time courses in 1993. In credit-based courses, students could learn without a grade framework and graduate when they completed the necessary credit requirements. Another new course type was the "integrated course," which was introduced in 1994 and allowed students to select both general and vocational subjects according to their purposes. These new courses aimed to more flexibly meet the diversified purposes and learning paces of individuals. Eventually, in 1998, a new type of school, the secondary education school, was institutionalized to provide consistent 6-year education to the graduates of elementary schools. Along with the introduction of the technical college in 1961, this reform added modifications to the simple 6-3-3-4 single track school system. The technical colleges provide 5-year education in specific areas to the graduates of lower secondary schools. The 6-year compulsory education school was institutionalized in 2015.

New cross curricular studies were also introduced. In 1992, sciences and social studies in the first and second grades of elementary school were combined to form a new subject: Living Environment Studies. Its aim was to use practical activities and experiences to help pupils become interested in the relationships among themselves, the people around them, society, and nature (MEXT 2015a, p. 1). A more radical reform was the Period for Integrated Study, created by revisions to the Course of Study in 1998 and 1999. Introduced in every grade from the third grade of elementary school to the final grade of upper secondary school, it emphasized cross synthetic studies, problem-solving, and inquiry activities (MEXT 2015b, p. 1). However, the Ministry of Education did not prescribe its contents but left them to each municipality or school. Along with relaxing regulations, promoting decentralization was the major purpose of administrative reforms. Under these revisions, each upper secondary school was also permitted to set up its own subjects. In addition, around the turn of the century, national regulations on class sizes were relaxed.

In terms of downsizing school education, the 5-day school week system was implemented in a phased manner: once a month since 1992, twice a month since 1995, and completely since 2002. Implementing the 5-day school week system and introducing the Period for Integrated Study greatly shortened lesson hours for academic subjects. For example, the 1998 and 1999 Course of Study revisions shortened the requisite hours for Japanese language study at elementary schools from 1601 to 1377 and the hours for arithmetic from 1011 to 869. At lower secondary schools, Japanese language study hours were shortened from 455 to 350 and the hours for mathematics from 385 to 315. Accordingly, the content of the subjects was radically reduced. Also, the number of credits required for graduation from upper secondary school was reduced.

The Chukyoshin, an advisory panel to the Minister of Education, pointed out the importance of fostering comprehensive abilities necessary to live in difficult times of rapid change (*ikiru chikara*), including abilities to find problems by oneself and solve them properly and to control oneself and cooperate with others. According to its report in 1996, it was important that children, schools, and society at large have more relaxed or stress-free conditions (*yutori*) in order to foster *ikiru chikara* in children (Chukyoshin 1996). This report was the basis for the 1998 and 1999 Course of Study revisions, and *ikiru chikara* and *yutori* became keywords for the later educational reforms. However, the *yutori* education regime would soon be severely criticized.

2.6 Freedom of School Choice and Diversification of School Providers

Before discussing the criticisms of *yutori* education, I would like to review another issue regarding the relaxation of regulations: freedom of school choice and the diversification of school providers. As stated previously, at the compulsory education level, the public school which each student attends is designated by the municipal boards of education. Generally, the boards set up school attendance zones and required parents to send their children to the school located in their zone. Public school choice started with relaxing the regulation for the school attendance zone system.

In 1996, about 10 years after the fierce debates at the Rinkyoshin, the Administrative Reform Committee voiced their opinion for advancing freedom of public school choice. The Committee critically examined the anti-school choice arguments and insisted that the national government instruct municipal boards of education to take various measures allowing more flexibility in school choice. Next year, the Ministry of Education issued a notification to require boards of education to make efforts for more flexibility in the school attendance zone system (MOE 1997). After this notification, municipal boards of education, especially in urban areas, began to introduce public school choice at the compulsory education level.

In the 2000s, national committees on administrative reform continued to insist on the expansion of school choice. Their arguments included the introduction of voucher systems as well as the expansion of public school choice. For example, in 2004, the Council for the Promotion of Regulatory Reform pointed out the need to examine the validity of introducing voucher systems by referring to those in foreign countries (Council for the Promotion of Regulatory Reform 2004, pp. 86–87, 89, Omomo and Kira 2018). However, until now, no voucher system has been introduced in Japan. Also, even public school choice has not spread widely. Instead, as will be examined later, participatory reform has been promoted.

The diversification of school education providers was introduced under the more direct influence of governance reform. In 2002, the national government enacted the Act on Special Districts for Structural Reform, which aimed to advance deregulation or the relaxation of regulations by setting up areas where regulatory exceptions would be adopted for specific purposes. In the districts, business corporations and nonprofit organizations were permitted to establish and maintain "Article 1 schools." However, as with freedom of school choice, school education providers have not been widely diversified.

2.7 Reinforcement of Schooling and Implementation of National Assessment of Academic Abilities

Around the turn of the century, declining student academic abilities became a controversial issue. One of the factors was a drop in the rankings and average scores in the Programme for International Student Assessment (PISA) tests, conducted by the Organisation for Economic Co-operation and Development (OECD). The ranking and the average score of Japanese students in mathematics literacy have changed from 1st (557) in 2000, to 6th (534) in 2003, and 10th (523) in 2006; science literacy from 2nd (550) in 2000, to 2nd (548) in 2003, and 6th (531) in 2006; and reading literacy from 8th (522) in 2000, to 14th (498) in 2003, and 15th (498) in 2006. It is difficult to define students' academic abilities and to judge their decline, but, under the advancement of globalization, the drop in rankings and scores in such comparative international tests was used as a persuasive indicator.

If there are real declines in the academic abilities of Japanese students, there are many possible causes. University entrance examinations are not as competitive as before, due to the decline in the number of students. The number of 18-year-old children in 2008 was roughly 60% of what it was in 1992. Now, many universities cannot meet their student quotas. Also, changing lifestyles and social conditions might influence students' motivation to study hard. However, educational policies, especially *yutori* education, were accused as the cause for declining academic abilities.

Under the 2008 and 2009 Course of Study revisions, the Ministry of Education again increased lesson hours and contents of academic subjects by reducing hours for the Period for Integrated Study and elective subjects. The number of municipalities which began supplementary Saturday classes has increased. Even the Ministry of Education started measures to support such activities on Saturdays. Also, there are strong opinions promoting the reintroduction of the 6-day school week system.

While modifications to the *yutori* education regime have proceeded, the Ministry of Education has continued to position *ikiru chikara* as a key concept in Japanese education. The 2008 Central Council for Education report, a basis for the 2008 and 2009 Course of Study revisions, referred to the "key competency" proposed by the OECD and its PISA. According to the report, the awareness of the international validity of school education is strong, but *ikiru chikara* takes the idea of key competency in advance (Chukyoshin 2008, pp. 9–10). Both key competency and *ikiru chikara* include non-cognitive abilities as well as cognitive skills.

Another measure aimed at improving academic abilities or performance was the implementation of the National Assessment of Academic Abilities. This national test was launched by the Ministry of Education in 2007 for students in the sixth year of elementary school (for Japanese language and arithmetic) and the third year of lower secondary school (for Japanese language and mathematics). It consists of two types of questions. Type A questions assess accumulated knowledge, while Type B questions assess students' abilities to utilize knowledge and skills and to solve problems. The Type B test is designed along the lines of PISA (Fujita 2010, p. 26). In 2012, science was added. The Ministry of Education points out the importance of using the results of this national assessment test for improving educational policies and classroom teaching (MEXT 2015c). We may point out here the influence of the results-oriented governance reform.

2.8 Introduction of Evaluation Systems and Promotion of Participation

One important government document on governance reform in the 2000s was the Basic Policies for Economic and Fiscal Policy Management and Structural Reform, which was issued every year from 2001 to 2007. The first Basic Policies document asserted that New Public Management (NPM) was a new global trend among administrative reform methods. It aimed to provide more effective, higher- quality administrative services by introducing business management methods. According to the first Basic Policies document, NPM theory is based on three ideas: the introduction of a thorough competition principle, performance-/results-based evaluation, and division of policy planning and implementation (Cabinet Office 2001, p. 29).

We can find an emphasis on evaluation in many other government documents. For example, the report of the Council for Regulatory Reform issued the next year insisted that it was "necessary to urgently establish a system to support ex-post-facto monitoring, such as information disclosure and third-party evaluation, in order to ensure the quality of education and proper competition." The report proposed to change "the conventional nationally uniform education system" by relaxing "advanced regulations" but also insisted on the importance of the ex post facto check system (Council for Regulatory Reform 2002). This report typically shows that regulation reform in Japan was not mere deregulation or the relaxation of regulations but the shift of regulations from the input stage to the output or outcome stage, and evaluation became an important measure.

Evaluation systems have been introduced or reinforced at various levels of educational administration and management. In 2007, under revisions to the School Education Act and its implementation order, school self-evaluation and the publication of its results became mandatory, and each school was expected to make efforts to implement school evaluations by parents and local community members. In addition, each school was required to submit its evaluation results to its founder, or the board of education in the case of public schools. The Ministry of Education issued the Guideline for School Evaluation at Compulsory Education Schools in 2006 and a revision including upper secondary schools in 2008. The Guideline described one of the purposes of school evaluations as ensuring a certain degree of educational quality and raising it through measures based on the results of school evaluations (MEXT 2006, p. 1, MEXT 2008, p. 1). The Guideline was revised again to include a third-party evaluation guide in 2010 and to correspond to the institutionalization of the 6-year compulsory education school in 2016 (MEXT 2010, MEXT 2016).

The boards of education were also required to self-evaluate their measures and publish the results under the 2007 Local Educational Administration Act revision. In addition, a teacher evaluation system was introduced at almost all schools. In Japan, teacher evaluation is not directly tied to students' scores on standardized tests such as the National Assessment of Academic Abilities. However, they will be exposed to more pressure to raise test scores if each school's result on this national assessment is published.

School participation has been promoted, along with school education reinforcement and the introduction of various evaluations and assessments. The most significant example is the 2004 establishment of the School Management Council system. This is the first system in Japan which permits parents and local community members to participate in school management with substantive powers. The Council consists of parents, local community members, and others and is endowed with powers to approve school management plans formulated by the principal and to submit opinions on school management and personnel to the principal and the board of education. The law does not require that every school should have a council.

Rather, under the decentralization policy, each board of education retains the authority to decide which schools should have a council. The Ministry of Education calls the schools with a School Management Council "community schools."

As stated previously, public school choice at the compulsory education level has not spread widely in Japan. Recently, some municipalities have begun to abolish it. In order to respond to the demands of committees for administrative reform, the Ministry of Education issued notifications calling for more flexible school attendance zone systems and issued some booklets showing examples of school choice. However, the Ministry does not seem particularly enthusiastic about promoting school choice. As we have already observed, at the time of Rinkyoshin debates, the Ministry strongly opposed public school choice at the compulsory education level. On the other hand, the Ministry has actively promoted community schools by various measures such as opening forums and setting up the community school adviser system (Omomo and Kira 2018).

The Basic Act on Education, revised in 2006, requires the national government to formulate the Basic Plan for the Promotion of Education. The Second Basic Plan for the 2013–2017 school year prescribes "building bonds and establishing vibrant communities" as one of the four basic policy directions and proposes further expansion of community schools. It stresses the importance of establishing "various networks and a cooperative system positioned as the core of the community that contributes to the promotion and recreation of schools and social education facilities for communities" (MEXT 2013). A similar, yet stronger demand is expressed by the Education Rebuilding Implementation Council, an advisory panel to the Prime Minister, which proposed to change all schools to community schools in its Sixth Report in 2015. Like the Second Basic Plan for the Promotion of Education, it argued for the importance of forming cooperation systems between schools and communities and building communities where schools should become the core of the community (Education Rebuilding Implementation Council 2015, p. 11).

In the 2000s and the 2010s, awareness increased regarding problems such as the isolation of individuals, the reproduction of socioeconomic and educational disparity, and even the decline of local communities. The above two documents reflect such awareness. The national government is trying to respond to these problems by forming stronger ties between schools and communities while introducing various result- or outcome-based evaluation and assessment systems to ensure the quality of school education.

2.9 Development of Conservative Policies and Moral Education

Finally, I would like to review the development of conservative aspects in education policies since the Rinkyoshin debates. Despite the general trend toward relaxing regulations, the regulation on the use of the national flag and anthem, and the position of fostering respect for the country and its traditions in school education, have been strengthened. In terms of the former, the Course of Study before the Rinkyoshin prescribed that it was "desirable" to raise the national flag and sing the national anthem at school ceremonies. However, under the 1989 revision, the national flag and anthem became mandatory at school ceremonies. In 1999, the Act on National Flag and Anthem was enacted, with *Nisshoki* legally prescribed as the national flag and *Kimigayo* as the national anthem.

As previously stated, *Nisshoki* and *Kimigayo* were sometimes understood in relation to the wartime experiences or nationalism. By 1999, most schools used *Nisshoki* and *Kimigayo* at school ceremonies, but there were still strong oppositions. Under the severe controversies between those who required the use of them at school ceremonies and those who opposed it, the principal of an upper secondary school in Hiroshima prefecture committed suicide, which led to the enactment of the above-mentioned law (Hood 2001, pp. 70–77, Ichikawa 2011, 322–332). Soon after this legislation, the Ministry of Education issued a notification to require more proper implementation of the instruction about the national flag and anthem at school ceremonies. (MOE 1999). Harsh punishments were imposed on teachers who resisted the raising of *Nisshoki* or refused to sing or play the piano for *Kimigayo*.

In terms of the latter, such phrases as "love the country" or "respect Japanese culture and traditions" were used in the Course of Study, even before the Rinkyoshin. The major change was that such phrases were inserted in the prescription of the Basic Act on Education under the 2006 revision. The Act prescribes one of the purposes of education as follows:

> To foster an attitude to respect our traditions and culture, love the country and region that nurtured them, together with respect for other counties and a desire to contribute to world peace and the development of the international community. (Article 2)

As with the final Rinkyoshin report, fostering an attitude toward the country and its traditions and culture is mentioned in reference to international relations.

As previously stated, the increase in problematic behavior of students was a direct factor for the establishment of the Rinkyoshin. Currently, there are still many serious problems related to student behavior, such as bulling among students and violence against teachers. The strengthening of moral education is demanded to prevent these problems. When moral education was introduced to compulsory education schools in 1958, it was not as a formal school subject. The Education Rebuilding Implementation Council, the above-mentioned advisory panel to the Prime Minister, pointed out that the existing moral education did not necessarily work well and proposed to upgrade moral education to a school subject in its first report in February 2013 (Education Rebuilding Implementation Council 2013, pp. 1–2). This was just after a student's suicide caused by bulling. Next year, the Chukyoshin, an advisory panel to the Minister of Education, submitted a report supporting the upgrade of moral education, and the Ministry of Education decided to make moral education a special subject.

At the classes of moral education as a formal subject, teachers are to be required to use textbooks compiled according to the national Course of Study and approved by the Minister of Education or textbooks which the Ministry of Education itself compiles, as is the case with other subjects such as Japanese, mathematics, and social studies. The School Education Act prescribes the mandatory use of such textbooks for school subjects and punishments for noncompliance with this requirement. At the introduction of moral education in 1958, there were strong objections from those who feared that it would become a way to indoctrinate specific values as in the period during and before World War II. The same kind of fears about instilling into students the values which the national government prefers are being expressed regarding the present upgrade of moral education into a formal subject.

Upgraded to a formal subject, evaluations are also required for moral education. Unlike other formal subjects, descriptive evaluation is to be used for moral education as a "special subject." Evaluating students' activities by grades such as the five-grade evaluation system and comparing them with those of other students are considered unsuitable for moral education. However, it is quite difficult to evaluate and describe students' activities related to their mental and moral development. With these disputes and difficulties, new moral education as a special subject starts in 2018 at elementary schools and in 2019 at lower secondary schools.

2.10 Conclusion

The diversification and downsizing of school education proceeded after the Rinkyoshin reports. Also, public school choice at the compulsory education level was promoted by relaxing regulations on the school attendance zone system, and business corporations and nonprofit organizations were permitted to establish and maintain schools due to the relaxing of regulations on school providers in the Special Districts for Structural Reform. These reforms were in accordance with the general trends of governance reform, such as relaxing regulations, reducing governmental functions, responding to the various needs of consumers, and introducing market mechanisms.

However, if the market and autonomous actors cannot be unconditionally trusted to ensure the quality of the public services provided, there would still be a need for governmental regulations. Instead of conventional ex ante regulations, governance reform demanded the establishment of ex post facto check systems, and, in the area of education, various evaluation systems and a national assessment test were introduced. Further, amidst disputes over declining student academic abilities, the national government again increased the lesson hours and contents of academic subjects and began to promote Saturday supplementary class activities. In addition, public school choice and diversification of school providers have not spread widely, and instead, community schools based on the participation of parents and local community members have been strongly promoted. Thus, the present trends of primary and secondary education reforms are toward the reinforcement of school education by forming participatory systems as well as by strengthening educational standards and ex post facto regulations.

Despite these swings in reforms, regulations on the use of the national flag and anthem, or the legal position of fostering respect for the country and its culture in school education, have been consistently strengthened. Also, it has been decided to upgrade moral education to a school subject. In addition, the importance of nurturing not only cognitive but also non-cognitive skills has been progressively more emphasized. To what extent, and how will school education be involved in the psychological development of individuals? This basic question of public education has again become an important issue in Japan.

References

Ad Hoc Commission on Administrative Reform (1983). *Gyosei kaikaku ni kansuru daigoji toshin (saishu toshin)* [The fifth (final) report on administrative reform] (March 14, 1983). In *Rincho Saishu Teigen* [The final proposal of Ad Hoc commission on administrative reform]. Tokyo: Institute of Administrative Management.

Ad Hoc Council on Education (Rinkyoshin) (1985). *Kyoiku kaikaku ni kansuru daiichiji toshin* [The first report on education reform] (June 26, 1985). In *Kyoiku kaikaku ni kansuru toshin* [The reports on education reform] (in Japanese), Tokyo: Printing Bureau, Ministry of Finance.

Ad Hoc Council on Education (Rinkyoshin) (1987a). *Kyoiku kaikaku ni kansuru daisanji toshin* [The third report on education reform] (April 1, 1987). In *Kyoiku kaikaku ni kansuru toshin* [The reports on education reform] (in Japanese), Tokyo: Printing Bureau, Ministry of Finance.

Ad Hoc Council on Education (Rinkyoshin) (1987b). *Kyoiku kaikaku ni kansuru daiyoji toshin (saishu toshin)* [The fourth (final) report on education reform] (August 7, 1987). In *Kyoiku kaikaku ni kansuru toshin* [The reports on education reform] (in Japanese), Tokyo: Printing Bureau, Ministry of Finance.

Arita, K. (1985) *'Gakko Kyoiku no jiyuka' ni tsuite* [Concerning "Liberalization of school education"] (in Japanese) (April 26, 1985). In *Rinkyoshin to kyoiku kaikaku* [Ad Hoc council on education and education reform] (Vol. 1), Tokyo: Gyosei.

Cabinet Office (2001). *Kongo no keizai zaisei un'ei oyobi kozo kaikaku ni kansuru kihonhoshin* [Basic Policies for Economic and Fiscal Policy Management and Structural Reform] (in Japanese) (June 26, 2001).

Central Council for Education (Chukyoshin). (1996). *21 seiki wo tenbosita wagakuni no kyoiku no arikata ni tsuite (daiichiji toshin)* [Concerning the ways of education in our country for the 21th century (the first report)] (in Japanese) (July 19, 1996). http://www.mext.go.jp/b_menu/shingi/old_chukyo/old_chukyo_index/toushin/1309579.htm

Central Council for Education (Chukyoshin). (2008). *Yochien, shogakko, chugakko, kotogakko oyobi tokubetsushiengakko no gakushushidoyoryo no kaizen ni tsuite* [Concerning Improvements of the Course of Study at Kindergarten, Elementary School, Lower Secondary School, Upper Secondary School and Special Support School] (in Japanese) (January 17, 2008). http://www.mext.go.jp/b_menu/shingi/chukyo/chukyo0/toushin/__icsFiles/afieldfile/2009/05/12/1216828_1.pdf

Council for Regulatory Reform. (2002). *Second report regarding promotion of regulation reform: Priority regulatory reform measures to promote economic vitalization* (Tentative translation) (December 12, 2002). http://www8.cao.go.jp/kisei/en/021212report/index.html

Council for the Promotion of Regulatory Reform. (2004). *First report on the promotion of regulatory reform and the opening up of government-driven markets for entry into the private sector* (December 24, 2004). http://www8.cao.go.jp/kisei-kaikaku/old/publication/2004/1224/item041224_02e.pdf

Council on Juvenile Problems (1982). *Seishonen no hikoto mondaikodo eno taio* [Coping with juvenile delinquency and problematic behaviors] (June 24, 1982). In *Kyoikuiinkai geppo* (in Japanese) Vol 34 (7).

DeCoker, G., & Bjork, C. (Eds.). (2013). *Japanese education in an era of globalization: Culture, politics, and equity.* New York: Teachers College Press.

Education Rebuilding Implementation Council. (2013). *Daiichiji teigen* [The first proposal] (in Japanese) (February 26, 2013). https://www.kantei.go.jp/jp/singi/kyouikusaisei/pdf/dai1_1.pdf

Education Rebuilding Implementation Council. (2015). *Dairokuji teigen* [The sixth proposal] (in Japanese) (March 4, 2015). https://www.kantei.go.jp/jp/singi/kyouikusaisei/pdf/dai6_1.pdf

Fujita, H. (2010). Whither Japanese schooling? Educational reforms and their impact on ability formation and educational opportunity. In J. A. Gordon, H. Fujita, T. Kariya, & G. LeTendre (Eds.), *Challenges to Japanese education: Economics, reform, and human rights.* New York: Teachers College Press.

Hood, C. P. (2001). *Japanese education reform: Nakasone's legacy.* New York: Routledge.

Ichikawa, S. (2011). *Aikokushin—kokka · kokumin · kyoiku wo megutte* [Patriotism: Concerning state, nation and education] (in Japanese) Tokyo: Gakujutsushuppankai.

Kato, H. (1984). *Gakkokan no kyoso de kyoiku ni miryoku wo* [Making education attractive by introducing competitions among schools] (in Japanese) In *Kikan Kyoikuho* (vol 52), Tokyo: Eideru-Kenkyujo.

Koyama, K. (1985). *'Kyoiku no jiyuka' ronso no rekishiteki igi* [Historical meaning of "Liberalization of education" disputes] (in Japanese) (May 8, 1985). In *Rinkyoshin to kyoiku kaikaku* [Ad Hoc council on education and education reform] (vol. 2), Tokyo: Gyosei.

Ministry of Education, Culture, Sports, Science, and Technology (MEXT). (2006). *Gimukyoiku shogakko ni okeru gakko hyoka gaidorain* [Guideline for school evaluation at compulsory education schools] (in Japanese) (March 27, 2006). http://warp.da.ndl.go.jp/info:ndljp/pid/286184/www.mext.go.jp/b_menu/houdou/18/03/06032817/003.pdf

Ministry of Education, Culture, Sports, Science, and Technology (MEXT). (2008). *Gakko hyoka gaidorain* [Guideline for school evaluation] (in Japanese) (January 31, 2008). http://warp.da.ndl.go.jp/info:ndljp/pid/286184/www.mext.go.jp/b_menu/houdou/20/01/08012913/001.pdf; http://warp.da.ndl.go.jp/info:ndljp/pid/286184/www.mext.go.jp/b_menu/houdou/20/01/08012913/002.pdf

Ministry of Education, Culture, Sports, Science, and Technology (MEXT). (2010). *Gakko hyoka gaidorain* [Guideline for school evaluation] (in Japanese) (July 20, 2010). http://www.mext.go.jp/component/a_menu/education/detail/__icsFiles/afieldfile/2012/07/12/1323515_2.pdf

Ministry of Education, Culture, Sports, Science, and Technology (MEXT). (2013). *The second basic plan for the promotion of education* (Provisional translation) (June 14, 2013). http://www.mext.go.jp/english/lawandplan/1355330.htm

Ministry of Education, Culture, Sports, Science, and Technology (MEXT) (2015a). *Section 5 living environment studies* (p. 1). http://www.mext.go.jp/component/english/__icsFiles/afieldfile/2011/03/17/1303755_006.pdf

Ministry of Education, Culture, Sports, Science, and Technology (MEXT) (2015b). *Chapter 5 The period for integrated studies* (p. 1). http://www.mext.go.jp/component/english/__icsFiles/afieldfile/2011/03/17/1303755_012.pdf

Ministry of Education, Culture, Sports, Science, and Technology (MEXT) (2015c). *Improvement of academic abilities* (Courses of study). http://www.mext.go.jp/english/elsec/1303755.htm

Ministry of Education, Culture, Sports, Science, and Technology (MEXT). (2016). *Gakko hyoka gaidorain* [Guideline for school evaluation] (in Japanese) (March 22, 2016). http://www.mext.go.jp/component/a_menu/education/detail/__icsFiles/afieldfile/2016/06/13/1323515_02.pdf

Ministry of Education, Science, Sports and Culture (MOE). (1982). *Seitoshido shiryo* [Documents of student guidance] (Vol. 17) (in Japanese). Tokyo: Printing Bureau, Ministry of Finance.

Ministry of Education, Science, Sports and Culture (MOE) (1983). *Konaiboryokuto jidoseito no mondaikodo ni taisuru shido no tettei ni tsuite* [Concerning complete implementation of guidance on students' problematic behaviors as school violence and others] (in Japanese) (March

10, 1983) In MOE (1987). *Jidoseito no mondaikodo no jittai to monbusyo no shisaku ni tsuite* [Concerning the real situation of students' problematic behaviors and the measures by the Ministry of Education].

Ministry of Education, Science, Sports and Culture (MOE). (1985). Wagakuni no shoto chuto kyoiku [Elementary and secondary education in our country] (in Japanese) (January 23, 1985). In K. Nagai & S. Miwa (Eds.). *Shiryoshu: rinkyoshin: kyoiku kaikaku no doko* [Collection of documents: The Ad Hoc council on education and the status of education reform] (in Japanese). Tokyo: Eideru-Kenkyujo.

Ministry of Education, Science, Sports and Culture (MOE) (1997). *Tsugaku kuiki seido no danryokuteki unyo ni tsuite* [Concerning the flexible operation of school attendance zone system] (in Japanese) (January 27, 1997).

Ministry of Education, Science, Sports and Culture (MOE). (1998). *Statistical abstract of education, science, sports and culture (1998 edition).* Tokyo: Printing Bureau, Ministry of Finance.

Ministry of Education, Science, Sports and Culture (MOE) (1999). *Gakko ni okeru kokki oyobi kokka ni kansuru shido ni tsuite* [Concerning the instruction about national flag and anthem at schools] (in Japanese) (September 17, 1999).

Nakasone, Y. (2004). *Jiseiroku: rekisihotei no hikoku to shite* [Meditations: As a defendant at Historical Court]. Tokyo: Shinchosya.

Omomo, T. (2012). Japan. In C. L. Glenn, J. De Groof, & C. S. Candal (Eds.), *Balancing freedom, autonomy and accountability in education* (Vol. 4). Nijmegen: Wolf Legal Publishers.

Omomo, T., & Kira, N. (2018). Policy formation and implementation of school choice reform in Japan: An example of local adaptation of educational borrowing. *Bulletin of Gakushuin Women's College,* vol. 20. Tokyo: Gakushuin Women's College.

Otake, H. (1993). *Rinkyoshin ni yoru kyoiku no jiyuka no kokoromi* [Attempts at the liberalization of education by the Ad Hoc council on education] (in Japanese) *Leviathan,* vol. 12. Tokyo: Bokutakusha.

Panel on Recent Problematic Behaviors at Schools (1983). Teigen [Proposals] (in Japanese) (March 8, 1983) In MOE (1987). *Jidoseito no mondaikodo no jittai to monbusyo no shisaku ni tsuite* [Concerning the real situation of students' problematic behaviors and the measures by the Ministry of Education].

Uchida, K. (1987). *Rinkyoshin no kiseki: kyoiku kaikaku no 1100 nichi* [Trajectory of the Rinkyoshin: 1100 days of education reform]. Tokyo: Daiichihoki.

Chapter 3
Higher Education in Japan: Its Uniqueness and Historical Development

Hideto Fukudome

3.1 Introduction

Japan has one of the largest higher education systems in the world. Today, about 80% of Japanese 18-year-olds proceed to various types of higher education institutions after they graduate from high school. About 60% of them enter four-year and two-year colleges and universities, and about 20% enroll in the nonuniversity sector, that is, technical and vocational training colleges and technology colleges without degree-granting status. Some countries have larger percentages of students who enroll in higher education than Japan; however, given Japan's relatively larger population, its higher education system matriculates a larger number of students. The percentage of high-school graduates advancing to higher education has rapidly increased over the past 20 years, and most young people have had access to some kind of higher education in recent years (MEXT 2017). Japan has built one of the most well-structured higher education systems in the world, indicating a "massified" democratized higher education system, of which we should be proud. However, this massive system is not usually seen as a major indicator of the success of the Japanese higher education system. Despite the attainment of this large-scale democratic educational system, higher education has experienced some major issues in terms of quality.

In this chapter, I will discuss the uniqueness and development of Japanese higher education mainly from a historical perspective. The development can be discussed in four main stages: beginning and early development in the prewar era, drastic change in the postwar era, the period of expansion and disorder during the economic growth of society between the 1960s and 1980s, and the post-1990s period of reforms.

H. Fukudome (✉)
Graduate School of Education, The University of Tokyo, Tokyo, Japan
e-mail: fukudome@p.u-tokyo.ac.jp

© Springer Nature Singapore Pte Ltd. 2019   41
Y. Kitamura et al. (eds.), *Education in Japan*, Education in the Asia-Pacific
Region: Issues, Concerns and Prospects 47,
https://doi.org/10.1007/978-981-13-2632-5_3

3.2   Uniqueness of the Japanese Higher Education System

Before discussing the historical development of Japanese higher education, elaborating on some of its basic characteristics would be insightful. One of the unique features of the Japanese higher education system in terms of the number of institutions and undergraduate students is its huge private sector. This is a common distinction among higher education systems in major Asian countries compared with those in Europe and the United States (Altbach and Umakoshi 2004). The Japanese higher education system's public sector is divided into two types: national universities supported by the national government and local public universities funded by local governments such as prefectures or cities. According to 2017 statistics, the college and university sector accounts for 780 institutions in total, 604 (77%) of which are private. In terms of the number of four-year undergraduate students, 2,007,207 (78%) are enrolled in private colleges and universities (MEXT 2017).

In the public sector, there are 86 national universities and 90 local public universities in 2017. The latter slightly outnumber the former but are smaller in size. National universities have approximately 600,000 students including four-year undergraduate students, graduate students, and auditing students—four times the number in local public universities, which have around 150,000 students.

At the graduate level, national universities dominate because they include major research-intensive universities that emphasize academic research and research training at graduate schools. Nearly 60% of graduate students enroll in national universities, with the percentage increasing to 66% when considering only doctoral students (i.e., excluding masters and professional degree students).

The Japanese higher education system was established in the late nineteenth century with the national (at that time, imperial) university sector. After the Second World War, the expansion of higher education was focused on the private sector, which played the major role in the "massification" of higher education. Most large and comprehensive national universities assumed the principal role in providing cutting-edge research and graduate research training, particularly at the doctoral level. And, the local public sector sustained the regional demand for higher education opportunities. This was the basic structure of the Japanese higher education system after the Second World War, which mainly depended on the private sector for undergraduate education opportunities and was financially supported by the private initiatives market, including education providers and students/parents. At the same time, the market was controlled and regulated by the national government. Regulatory control by the national government was another traditional underpinning of the Japanese higher education system.

Burton R. Clark, an eminent higher education researcher in the United States, discussed the higher education system from an international comparative perspective (Clark 1983). In his well-known triangle of decision-making authorities, Clark argued that Japanese higher education was positioned in a strongly market-oriented system. This is partly true because in Japan, both providers and consumers of higher education are composed mainly of private initiatives. However, although almost 80% of higher education opportunities are provided by the private sector, in reality, the Japanese higher education system depends just as much upon the national government's regulatory initiatives.

In recent decades, particularly after the 1990s, national government's higher education policies have attempted to loosen regulatory control, emphasizing instead market competition among higher education institutions on the one hand and granting considerable autonomy to individual institutions on the other. However, this aim has not exactly translated into reality. On the contrary, in some senses, the higher education system depends more on the national government. Yet, this does not mean that universities are still directly controlled by national government policies as they were until the 1990s. Rather, they are often forced to follow national policy directives to secure financial support from the national government. This means that, for higher education governance, the national government has oversight. Besides, in Japan, the proportion of the gross domestic product (GDP) assigned to public subsidy for higher education is the lowest among members of the Organization for Economic Co-operation and Development (OECD) (MEXT 2013). This implies that financially, Japanese higher education depends on private initiatives for providers and consumers of education.

Even though both policy makers and officials in higher education institutions have gradually come to understand the value of autonomous governance in institutions, it has been rather difficult to change the traditionally fostered mentalities of government officials and academicians. The Japanese higher education system has maintained its quality at a minimal level mainly through regulation by the national government.

3.3 Formation of Japanese Higher Education in the Prewar Era: The National Government's Initiative

3.3.1 Founding of National Universities

In Japan, few educational institutions existed during the Edo era and earlier ages, some of which provided education substantially equivalent to higher education level (Okubo 1997). However, the foundation of the University of Tokyo in 1877 was an epoch-making event that laid the foundation for Japanese higher education, because the full-fledged university was created by the newly established Meiji government—the national institution overseeing the emerging public education system. The most remarkable attribute of the University of Tokyo at that time was that its principal purpose was the training of personnel who would become essential for building the new nation (Amano 1986).

The University of Tokyo was founded by merging several existing professional training institutions. It was the first higher education institution established by the Ministry of Education. In 1886, the university was renamed the Imperial University according to the Order of Imperial Universities. It was the first comprehensive university with five "branch universities": law, medicine, engineering, letters, and sciences (Nakayama 1978). It also held the postgraduate tier (though not exactly a graduate program) and awarded a Ph.D. degree in 1888 for the first time in Japan. In 1897, a second Imperial University was established in Kyoto, and the original Imperial University renamed itself the Imperial University of Tokyo (Ushiogi 1997). After that, other Imperial Universities were founded in major cities. Some of them maintained a policy of increasing the number of comprehensive institutions, whereas others were organized in accordance with local citizens' expectations. Until the founding of Nagoya Imperial University in 1939, Japan had nine Imperial Universities, including two institutions abroad (Keijo Imperial University in Seoul and Taipei Imperial University). Even after the Second World War, seven former Imperial Universities comprised the group of the most active and extensive research universities. They also attracted the most talented high-school students in each regional area. All of them have become national public universities. In summary, the national initiatives implemented during the founding era shaped the modern higher education system in Japan.

3.3.2   Higher Education During the Prewar Period

Initially, lectures at the Imperial University were delivered in foreign languages. At the Imperial University of Tokyo, English, French, and German were used depending on the area of expertise. The most urgent task faced by the university was to *import* scientific knowledge from the nations with the most advanced scholarship. Professors were invited from major foreign universities to teach in their mother tongues, and students were required to assimilate their teachings as quickly and accurately as possible. The most important mission of the Imperial Universities was to introduce state-of-the-art science from advanced nations and train personnel who could contribute to building a new empire attempting to catch up with the advancements of the West (Nakayama 1978).

Old high schools provided basic instruction in foreign languages, and language studies allowed specialized teaching in universities. Old high schools primarily aimed to ensure general education at the higher education level. Therefore, they composed a part of the higher education system. (After the Second World War, high schools were placed at the secondary-education level.) Old high schools also required their applicants to pass competitive entrance examinations, which are almost comparable to modern-day competitive entrance examinations for high-ranking universities. In that sense, old high schools were considered foundations for elite training. They were institutions not only for teaching foreign languages and general education but also for cultivating young students' character through residential living and personal interactions between teachers and students. Old high schools could be compared to Japanese-style liberal arts colleges. Elite people living in the prewar era formed their identities under intimate educational settings provided by old high schools. After the Second World War, the old high-school system was integrated into a newly established university system, and most aspects of their original environment were lost (Hata 2003).

In 1918, the Ministry of Education issued the University Ordinance. With the economy booming, the Ministry shifted its restrained higher education policy to an expansionary approach. Under the ordinance, some former vocational training schools upgraded their status to university and were bestowed the authority to award academic degrees. By the end of the Second World War, many public and private colleges and universities emerged. In many cases, the conditions of teaching and learning in these institutions were considerably different from those in the Imperial Universities. Particularly, the business operations and teaching methods in private institutions were usually much more economical and without substantive financial support from the national government. However, staying true to their mission and purpose, private institutions worked hard to handle these severe conditions and played important roles in preparing young students for work (Amano 2009a, b). Private institutions played an even more significant role after the Second World War in expanding higher education opportunities. We can find the emergence of the concept of higher education management in these prewar private institutions.

3.4 Development of Higher Education After the Second World War

3.4.1 Drastic Changes in the Higher Education System

Japanese higher education kept its basic structure until the end of the Second World War. Subsequently, under the guidance of the allied occupation forces, the higher education system experienced a drastic change along with the nation itself. A delegation of experts from the American education system thoroughly reviewed the Japanese education system during wartime. Their report indicated that one of the most serious issues in the Japanese education system was the insufficient number of free-thinking, educated people who could oppose the military-led government from exercising its autocracy. Institutional autonomy and academic freedom were carefully discussed even in prewar era (Terasaki 1979). However, before and during the wartime, they were severely restricted on many occasions.

The first report prepared by the delegation emphasized that the old higher education system had largely been exclusively for the privileged classes and that the new system should be more open and democratic, which meant that the system should provide much more learning opportunities for ordinary citizens (The United States Education Mission to Japan 1946). Accordingly, a large number of reformed or newly organized colleges and universities emerged. Most old colleges and universities were handed a renewed status under the School Education Act enacted in 1947. In addition, mergers, upgrades, and/or new constructions led to the establishment of a large number of national public, local public, and private higher education institutions. In the meantime, a new structure for the higher education system was formulated within 5 years. Most of these newly established institutions were developed from prewar institutions. In that sense, the new higher education system preserved the fundamental attributes of the old system. Postwar higher education owes the prewar system for its underpinnings.

Since the 1950s, the higher education system rapidly expanded in a short period of time. It is plausible to argue that postwar higher education reform succeeded in providing educational opportunities to many citizens. On the other hand, it was difficult to maintain the educational quality of the expanding higher education system, particularly under postwar disorder and unstable socioeconomic conditions.

3.4.2 Adoption of a General Education Curriculum

One of the most fundamental issues for postwar higher education reform was the adoption of a general education curriculum as a requirement for undergraduate studies. During the prewar period, colleges and universities were a type of institution reserved almost exclusively for specialized and/or vocational education, and old high schools and preparatory divisions of universities provided basic instruction in preparation for college studies. After the war, most old high schools were merged into new universities, and high schools were newly established as institutions for the latter part of the secondary-education system. New high schools widely disseminated the provision of education across a broad range of general subjects. This created an issue in the formulation of general education curricula in higher education institutions, which needed to be different from general studies at high schools.

Documents and reports on general education in the United States, including the Harvard Redbook (Harvard University 1945), were widely read in Japan. Japanese academicians involved in discussions on general education visited major universities and liberal arts colleges in the United States. They rigorously studied general education and attempted to understand and adopt its concept and contents for the Japanese context. The basic structure of general education was composed of the distribution requirements of the humanities, social sciences, and natural sciences, along with some foreign language studies, physical education, and, in some cases, interdisciplinary courses. General education proposed that college students should have broad knowledge before they started to study more specific disciplines.

However, this newly conceptualized general education did not very well suit Japanese higher education. Even though general education has become a requirement for undergraduate students in all colleges and universities, both students and faculty members were never satisfied with the real state of affairs. One reason for this was that postwar undergraduate education has still emphasized specialized teaching more than broad studies. In the Japanese system, students usually had already matriculated in specialized schools or colleges in higher education institutions when they were admitted as freshmen. General education was often criticized as a repetition of what students had already learned in high school. Another factor for negative reactions to general education was that the concept of general education was not considered seriously and that teachers taught their own specialties under the guise of general courses (Kaigo and Terasaki 1969; Osaki 1999).

In 1991, still only less than half a century after general education was adopted, it was removed as part of the official national government's university standards. It ceased to be a series of specific courses, and each institution was required to assume responsibility for organizing courses on broad and basic studies. Following this change, the integration of broad education and specialized education has often been discussed both in the national policy arena and in individual institutions. However, as a national trend, in many institutions, specialized studies have been emphasized over and above broad and basic education (Yoshida 2013). Even though there have been concerted efforts across all institutions to actively implement the concept of general education, the widely shared concept of undergraduate education is still unclear.

3.4.3 Graduate Education Under the New System

Another critical issue in higher education after the war was graduate education. As already briefly described, in Japan graduate schools already existed during the prewar era. The first graduate school was created in the Imperial University of Tokyo in 1886, following a small graduate division that existed as a forerunner to the graduate school for a few years. Prewar graduate schools did not function as training schools for academic researchers. Future researchers often studied abroad in countries such as Germany, England, and the United States after their undergraduate studies. Graduate schools in Imperial Universities had few students, and there were no specific curricula or seminars for research training. Only a limited number of students received doctoral degrees. At that time, awarding doctoral degrees had almost no relevance to graduate work. Candidates could submit their dissertation regardless of their enrollment in graduate programs.

After the war, the graduate school system experienced a drastic change and was transferred to a new system. The American graduate school system served as a model for this shift. Two levels of educational programs were clearly set out: masters programs and doctoral programs. Each program had to have a specific curriculum, with the focus placed on awarding graduate degrees. Students were encouraged to complete a coursework and a dissertation (or thesis). This new system was referred to as "graduate schools with degree programs," in contrast to the prewar tradition. The series of national policies on graduate education since the 1950s have been based upon this idea. The main goals of this new system were as follows: enhancement of the quality and quantity of coursework, improving completion rates of doctoral degrees, and adapting graduates to the needs of labor markets both within and beyond academia. Even though the basic format was derived from the American graduate education system, the organization of Japanese graduate schools has some distinctions (Ichikawa and Kitamura (Eds.) 1995). There have been a limited number of professionally oriented programs, except in engineering. Furthermore, masters' programs are usually designed as an early phase of a Ph.D. program (Fukudome 2012). In 2003, a new professional school system was passed into national law. In addition, following national policies in recent years, the Japanese graduate education system has attempted to enhance its flexibility and adaptability. Although the system still faces many continuing issues, increasingly unconventional methods are being adopted in graduate programs.

3.5 Expansion and Disorder Under "Massification"

Postwar higher education commenced with many challenges. Japanese higher education has expanded continuously since the establishment of the new system. The enrollment rate of 18-year-olds in four-year and two-year colleges and universities increased to as high as 40% in the mid-1970s. In the prewar period, opportunities for higher education were severely restricted, and only a small percentage of male students could attend college or university. Since the war, higher education enrollment has dramatically increased, and many non-elite and female students have enjoyed access to higher education.

As in other advanced countries, a student movement opposing the "massified" higher education system emerged in Japan in the late 1960s. Students of this period spiritedly attempted to question the rationale of postwar higher education development. Even though the students' activism largely reflected the social and political contexts at that time, students vehemently protested against bureaucratic university administration and the "mass-production" format of college education. Classes and daily operations were suspended in many institutions, and at the University of Tokyo, one of the campuses that encountered severe hostility decided to cancel its entrance examination. Faced with disarray, many universities made proposals to reform their administration and teaching (Osaki 1994). However, after the turbulence was over, most of these proposals were shelved. Although these campus riots were unable to significantly change the approach of higher education institutions, they created sufficient momentum to encourage a group of academicians to start considering higher education from a different standpoint. For example, in 1972, a few years after the turmoil, the Research Institute for Higher Education was founded in Hiroshima University. It was the first stable research organization devoted to the academic study of higher education and contributed to the enhancement of higher education research in later years.

3.6 Post-1990s Reform Era

The Japanese higher education system has continued to expand. By the early 1990s, nearly 60% of 18-year-olds attended higher education, including those who attended vocational training colleges. The system has greatly matured since then, but issues still exist in many different areas, some of which are inherent in the historical development of Japanese higher education.

Since the 1990s, Japanese higher education has entered an era of reform. The rapid decrease in the youth population in recent decades has had an extremely large impact on higher education reform. The population of 18-year-olds reached its peak in the early 1990s and has rapidly decreased since then. During the last two decades, the number of 18-year-olds has declined by approximately 40%, from about 2 million to 1.2 million. Although the attendance rate in higher education has increased, the number of students has actually decreased from the mid-1990s. Until then, higher education had simply been sustained by the growth of the young generation and their rising attendance rate. Now, higher education institutions have to compete with each other to admit enough students to maintain their business. Institutions can no longer secure their status if they cannot promote their quality and distinctions.

Furthermore, the transition from an industrial society to a knowledge-based society means that people's work and behavior based upon advanced knowledge and skills are becoming increasingly meaningful. Research and development and advanced education in colleges and universities are especially significant for society and the national economy.

Higher education institutions therefore need to adapt to a new environment along with these social changes. Accordingly, in 1991, the national higher education policy changed its approach as the Ministry of Education started to "deregulate" its university standards. It is often claimed by many higher education researchers that this amendment had the largest impact on persuading colleges and universities to independently transform. This policy change served as a wake-up call for the beginning of the reform era. University Council, set up in 1987 in the Ministry of Education as its major advisory board for higher education reform, published a series of reports, some of which had considerable influences on higher education institutions.

3.7 Future Issues for Japanese Higher Education: Sustainability Based on Autonomy

Higher education still faces a myriad of wide-ranging critical issues, including undergraduate education, graduate education and research, community engagement, quality assurance and accreditation, and governance and management. However, I believe that the most significant challenge relates to how higher education institutions can implement their initiatives to address these issues. The trigger for reform was pulled by the national government. The world of higher education, however, has remained passive in almost every aspect. Regardless of nations and cultures, colleges and universities are basically conservative and often resist change. Changes are often externally enforced. Particularly in Japan, government policies have the greatest influence on institutions and compel such institutions to implement reforms.

In more than two decades, autonomous governance and management by higher education institutions has been thought to be critical. However, it is rather difficult to change the mentality of government officials and academicians, both of whom have formulated their traditions over a long period. Governmental control has assured minimum standards of education. At the same time, it has heavily restricted each institution's distinctive development. Compared with elementary and secondary education, Japanese higher education commands relatively low respect internationally. A reason for this is that at the higher education level, the autonomy and uniqueness of institutions are more significant in the dynamic development of the system.

Higher education institutions have gradually and proactively attempted to improve their education and administration. It is all the more critical for the future of Japanese higher education that outcomes of these efforts gradually bear fruition and that they contribute to the creation of a vigorous national higher education system.

References

Altbach, P. G., & Umakoshi, T. (Eds.). (2004). *Asian universities: Historical perspectives and contemporary challenges*. Baltimore: Johns Hopkins University Press.

Amano, I. (1986). *Kouto kyoiku no nihonteki kouzou* [Japanese structure of higher education]. Tokyo: Tamagawa University Press.

Amano, I. (2009a). *Daigaku no tanjo(jo)* [Emergence of Japanese universities, First volume]. Tokyo: Chuo Koron Publishing.

Amano, I. (2009b). *Daigaku no tanjo(ge)* [Emergence of Japanese universities, Second volume]. Tokyo: Chuo-koron Publishing.

Clark, B. R. (1983). *The higher education system: Academic organization in cross-national perspective*. Berkeley: University of California Press.

Fukudome, H. (2012). Daigakuin kyoiku to kenkyusha yousei: Nichi-bei hikaku no shiten kara [Graduate education and research training: Comparative study on Japan and the U.S.]. *Nagoya Journal of Higher Education, 12*, 237–256.

Harvard University, Committee on the Objectives of a General Education in a Free Society. (1945). *General education in a free society*. Cambridge, MA: Harvard University Press.

Hata, I. (2003). *Kyusei koko monogatari* [Old High schools in Japan]. Tokyo: Bungei Shunju Publishing.

Ichikawa, S. & Kitamura, K. (Eds.). (1995). *Gendai no daigakuin kyoiku* [Japanese graduate education in modern times]. Tokyo: Tamagawa University Press.

Kaigo, T. & Terasaki, M. (1969). *Daigaku kyoiku* [University education]. Tokyo: University of Tokyo Press.

MEXT. (2013). *Kyoiku shihyo no kokusai hikaku* [International comparison of indicators of education]. Tokyo: Ministry of Education, Culture, Sports, Science and Technology.

MEXT. (2017). *Gakkou kihon chosa hokokusho: Koutou kyoiku kikan hen* [Basic school survey report: Higher education institutions]. Tokyo: Ministry of Education, Culture, Sports, Science and Technology.

Nakayama, S. (1978). *Teikoku daigaku no tanjo* [The birth of the Imperial University of Tokyo]. Tokyo: Chuo Koron.

Okubo, T. (1997). *Nihon no daigaku* [Universities in Japan]. Tokyo: Tamagawa University Press.

Osaki, H. (1994). *Daigaku funso wo kataru* [Talking about student unrest in Japanese universities]. Tokyo: Yushindo Kobunsha.

Osaki, H. (1999). *Daigaku kaikaku: 1945–1999* [University reform in Japan: 1945–1999]. Tokyo: Yuhikaku Publishing.

Terasaki, M. (1979). *Nihon niokeru daigaku jichi seido no seiritsu* [Establishment of the university autonomy in Japan]. Tokyo: Hyoronsha.

The United States Education Mission to Japan. (1946). *Report of the United States education mission to Japan* (submitted to the Supreme Commander for the Allied Powers), Washington: United States Government Printing Office.

Ushiogi, M. (1997). *Kyoto teikoku daigaku no chosen* [Challenges of the Imperial University of Kyoto]. Tokyo: Kodansha.

Yoshida, A. (2013). *Daigaku to kyoyo kyoiku* [Liberal education in universities in post war Japan]. Tokyo: Iwanami Publishing.

Chapter 4
Restructuring of Social Education and Lifelong Learning and Community Governance

Jeongyun Lee

4.1 Introduction

In Japan, the term "social education" is used, while the equivalent term in America and Europe is "adult education" or "continued education." "Social education" is a term coined by combining "society" with "education." It is an established concept for education that is conscious of society, aimed at society, and involved in society (Matsuda 2014, p. 23). It is said that the term came into use in the 1880s, and social education achieved a major turnaround at the end of World War II. In other words, prior to and during the war, the education system was influenced by nationalism and militarism, with social education conducted under these principles. In the postwar educational reforms based on popular sovereignty, democracy, and pacifism, reforms in social education were implemented, and new legislation for social education was introduced. Facilities, including Kominkan (Japanese-style community learning centers), libraries, and museums were established all over Japan, with various social education programs offered at these facilities, mainly by local governments (Kobayashi 2013, p. 1).

In 1965, the philosophy of lifelong education was proposed by UNESCO and was introduced in Japan around 1970. In the late 1980s, the "Transition to the Lifelong Learning System" was announced as a national policy. However, it was not founded on the harmonized integration of lifelong learning and traditional social education. Specifically, the system of lifelong education was not only poorly structured but also lacked a broad perspective from which to actively position social education, which had been uniquely deployed at the regional and municipal levels. Also, it was a trend in which the measures imposed were implemented in a top-down fashion (ibid., pp. 2–3).

J. Lee (✉)
Graduate School of Education, The University of Tokyo, Tokyo, Japan
e-mail: jylee@p.u-tokyo.ac.jp

© Springer Nature Singapore Pte Ltd. 2019
Y. Kitamura et al. (eds.), *Education in Japan*, Education in the Asia-Pacific
Region: Issues, Concerns and Prospects 47,
https://doi.org/10.1007/978-981-13-2632-5_4

East Asian countries, including Korea, China, and Taiwan, which had been using the term "social education" since their prewar colonization by Japan, not only changed the term from "social education" to "lifelong education" but also proceeded with the integration of these systems. On the other hand, Japan introduced lifelong learning as the concept behind their policies and was not able to develop lifelong education or lifelong learning from the established foundation of social education, with the terms "social education" and "lifelong learning" generally tending to be written side by side. Since the war, systems and facilities unique to Japan have been established, and administrative support that includes allocating specialized personnel to the educational boards of each city and town has been offered. However, the administration of Japanese social education is facing a major turning point due to the recent deregulation and administrative reforms based on market principles.

Lately, due to the rapidly declining birth rate and aging population, sharp declines in population and prolonged economic depression associated with globalization, problems of overconcentration in urban areas, and depopulation in rural areas have emerged. Community renovation through regional regeneration and revitalization is being actively conducted throughout Japan. In this community renovation, the accumulated experience and achievements of social education play a major role, and learning-based community governance is being structured.

In this chapter, I am going to review the restructuring of social education and lifelong learning associated with the administrative reforms of recent years and showcase examples of community governance based on this restructuring, taking into consideration the characteristics of Japanese postwar social education.

4.2 Characteristics of Postwar Social Education

4.2.1 Postwar Educational Reforms and Social Education

After World War II, Japan enacted a Constitution that showed its determination to build a democratic and cultural state and to contribute to world peace and human welfare. In accordance with the spirit of this Constitution, the Basic Act on Education and the School Education Act were passed in 1947 to establish the basis of the new Japanese educational system. In 1949, the Social Education Act was also passed to guarantee voluntary learning and cultural activities for citizens. The Social Education Act defines social education as all organizational educational activities, excluding educational activities conducted as part of the school curriculum, established by the School Education Act. The postwar social education administration had set a top priority of creating an environment in which citizens can learn voluntarily. Japanese social education, which was restructured and deployed after World War II, is based on the three principles of regionalism, citizen autonomy, and facility centrism.

In association with the principle of decentralization in postwar educational reforms, regionalism and citizen autonomy have also been emphasized in social education. In other words, the importance of autonomy and participation by citizens were stressed in accordance with regional needs and in line with actual lives. Regions in this case mainly indicate municipalities comprising cities and towns. The Social Education Act also stipulates that "cities and towns" should play central roles in social education administration. The Act also prescribes rules for establishing organizations to ensure autonomy and participation by citizens, which consist of the Social Education Committee in local municipalities (Article 15 of the Social Education Act), the Community Center Governing Council (Article 29 of the said law), and the Library Governing Council and Museum Governing Council (Article 14 of the Library Act and Article 20 of the Museum Act). Lastly, facility centrism in social educational administration means setting up "facilities," such as Kominkan, libraries, museums, etc., and placing specialist staff at each facility to support citizen learning and other activities. In other words, it is the principle of focusing on "institutional improvement" and "environmental development" in social education (ibid., pp. 5–7). Kominkan consists of social education facilities that are unique to Japan. Until the "Standards for the Establishment and Management of Kominkan" was amended in 2003, Kominkan was specified by law to be located within primary school and junior high school zones. Kominkan is the second most familiar learning environment for citizens following schools.

Postwar social education has been deployed on the basis of the abovementioned three principles. In the 1960s, urban congestion and depopulation in rural areas occurred under the high economic growth policy, bringing drastic changes to people's living environments and problems of pollution that resulted in a deterioration in their health. As these regional and living problems started to become more serious and threaten citizens' lives, local residents themselves started campaigns, as well as learning and cultural activities, to resist these aggravated regional issues. Criticism and a demand for public social education increased against the backdrop of these activities, and a belief in "social education by right" was built up at the same time (Shinkai 2013, p. 46).

4.2.2   Transition to the Lifelong Learning System

The concept of lifelong education was proposed by UNESCO in 1965 and drew the attention of the Japanese industrial world. Companies started life planning and competence development programs for their employees. From 1970 onward, the government adopted lifelong education as their policy for national education restructuring measures following recommendations from various bodies and positioned lifelong education as the basic standpoint for comprehensive municipal educational programs (ibid., p. 50). Specifically, the government actively started implementing concrete policies for lifelong education, as can be seen, for instance, in the reports "The Overall Concept of Social Education to Cope with the Rapidly

Changing Social Structure" published by the Social Education Council (1971) and "Lifelong Education" published by the Central Council for Education (1981).

In 1990, an Act for the improvement of systems, etc., to implement measures for the promotion of lifelong learning (hereinafter collectively called the "Lifelong Learning Promotion Act") was passed based on the Ad Hoc *Council on Education Report* submitted by the Ad Hoc Council on Education in the mid-1980s. However, the passing of the Lifelong Learning Promotion Act did not institutionalize the lifelong learning system by improving the public sectors (Kobayashi, ibid., p. 12). Instead, the government tried to expand learning opportunities by relying on the initiative of the public sector and commercializing social education. In other words, the political perspective on lifelong learning was transformed from "guarantee of the right to learn," on which the traditional social education placed emphasis, to "provision of educational services." As a result, the concepts of resident participation in local communities through learning and education and citizen autonomy were weakened, and the commercial implication focused more on providing motivation in individuals' lives and building fulfilling lives.

4.3 Commercialization, Municipal Reforms, and the Restructuring of Social Education and Lifelong Learning

4.3.1 Propagation of Neoliberalism and Market Principles and the Lifelong Learning Policy

As discussed above, lifelong education was introduced as a public policy in the 1970s. In the education reforms of the 1980s, "learning" was commercialized, and the diversification of service providers was promoted. Specifically speaking, the Ad Hoc Council on Education presented four reports on educational reform (1984–1987). In the third report, the Council proposed the "transition to a lifelong learning system" and a concept of educational reform that would correct society's traditional academic career-based view and advocate the individualization and liberalization of education. In the fourth report, the Council described lifelong learning as something "to be selected freely, and continued throughout your life." The Council also stressed the importance of self-motivation and autonomy as a learning concept and that lifelong learning should be the responsibility of the individual. The Ad Hoc Council on Education also tried to overcome the problem of the academic background-oriented society, which had expanded from the merit-based educational system, by diversifying and individualizing (demassifying) school education. In other words, the Council intended to adopt market principles for education as a means of education administrative reform and rationalization (Shinkai, ibid., pp. 50–51). Under the neoliberal policy, the Lifelong Learning Promotion Act was passed, enabling private businesses to participate in education in the public sector. As a result, lifelong learning was established politically as an extremely personal, commercial commodity (Han and Makino 2013, p. 449).

The designated administrator system was created to promote privatization of lifelong learning in the public sector. This system was established based on the revised Local Autonomy Act of 2003. It enabled public facility management and operation, which were previously run by local public organizations or their affiliated bodies, to be comprehensively delegated to other organizations including business corporations, commercial enterprises, foundations, incorporated nonprofit organizations, and citizen's groups. However, the adoption of this system enabled comprehensive delegation of public facility management from cultural or sport projects, such as Kominkan, libraries, and museums, to business corporations and private businesses. As a result, the public aspects of social education regressed because the budgets and the number of allocated staff members in the public sector could decrease, while the burden on beneficiaries could increase. Besides, the delegation period could be limited, for example, to 3 or 5 years, and this could lead to instability and a deterioration in the expertise of staff members.

4.3.2 Weakened Education Administration System Associated with Decentralization Reforms

After the war, the Japanese Kominkan guaranteed the right of citizens to learn and functioned as a place to give citizens autonomy. The Japanese Kominkan was presented all over the world as an ideal model of regional social education facilities and became a symbolic presence in Japanese social education. However, as part of the administrative and financial reforms, administration of the Kominkan was relegated from the boards of education to the department chiefs, some of the Kominkan was eliminated or consolidated, and the number of staff members was reduced or their work was delegated to contract workers. With reduced budgets and the adoption of the designated administrator system, the autonomous social education system found itself in an extremely difficult situation (Lee 2006, p. 22).

With the "Act on Revisions of Related Acts for Promoting Decentralization" that was passed in 1999 (hereinafter, "Omnibus Decentralization Act") municipal mergers were conducted, and the number of cities and towns was halved (from 3229 in April 1999 to 718 at the end of April 2014) (MIC 2014). Wide-area administration was introduced by integrating cities and towns in order to streamline administration and increase financial efficiency. This led to the elimination or consolidation of Kominkan and reduced numbers of staff members or delegation of their work, and above all, this discouraged citizens from participating in social education. For example, due to the revision of the Social Education Act associated with the introduction of the Omnibus Decentralization Act, the appointment of a Community Center Governing Council became arbitrary, even though the Council played such an important role in citizen participation in community center management.

Hearings for the appointment of community center directors were also abolished, and thus the guarantee to mirror public opinion was no longer ensured.

The Japanese government focused on community administration as a way to minimize public unrest caused by the abovementioned decentralization, the relaxation of regulations, and the commercialization of the public realm. As a result, the government has been restructuring the administration system centering on lifelong learning. Along with lifelong learning now being administered based purely on the initiative of the department chief, many local governments not only changed the department name from Social Education Department to Lifelong Learning Department but also included the enlightenment programs of the general administration in their lifelong learning programs, transcending educational administration boundaries. This administrative system was transformed by integrating lifelong learning and social education administration into general administration, and as a result, the Lifelong Learning Department was separated from the Board of Education and then reorganized. This also encouraged Kominkan to become counter-educational institutions (Lee, ibid.). In other words, the public aspect and expertise of the traditional social education administration were significantly compromised.

A major amendment to the Basic Act on Education was made in 2006, which reinforced the trivialization of social education. In other words, in the revised Act, social education is included in the lifelong learning concept in the narrow sense that promotes individual enjoyment of benefits and cultivation of human resources. Moreover, in the partial amendment to the Social Education Act associated with the revised Basic Act on Education (2008), the administration of social education has been limited to a "school support administration" (Anezaki 2013, pp. 90–91). These legal amendments can thus be seen as denying the history and transition unique to Japanese social education, which had been conducting community-based learning activities and community development practices based on citizen participation and autonomy. In other words, the three principles (regionalism, citizen autonomy, facility centrism) that have been emphasized in postwar Japanese social education are beginning to be broken. In response to such a situation, although organizations such as the Japan Society for the Study of Adult and Community Education (JSSACE) and the Japan Association for Promotion of Social Education (JAPSE) have strongly criticized, it seems to be insufficient to prevent this reform.

4.3.3 Expansion of Participation by and Activities of Citizens and Public Aspects

Lately, due to administrative and financial reforms that include regressive political measures and financial retrenchment, social education and lifelong learning policies have been seen to fluctuate significantly. On the other hand, the activities and practices of citizens, including volunteering activities by nonprofit organizations (NPOs) and other groups, are diversifying, and their spheres of activity are increasingly expanding.

In 1995, more than 1,400,000 volunteers got together to provide aid for recon-struction work after the Great Hanshin-Awaji Earthquake, which drew attention to the capabilities of citizens in Japanese society. At the same time, the incident made society realize the necessity for legal support for volunteers (Sato 2013, p. 224). In 1998, the Act to Promote Specified Nonprofit Activities (NPO Law) was introduced, which further intensified civil activities. In approximately 15 years since the law's enactment, the number of NPO organizations has increased dramatically, and the number of certified organizations in June 2014 reached 49,460 (NPO Homepage of CAO 2014).

NPOs provide opportunities for cultural learning by citizens, aimed at citizens, and focused on the purpose of the activity. More and more NPOs are also acting as consignees in the management of social education facilities that include Kominkan, libraries, museums, and sports facilities, as well as other administrative businesses. In fact, under the designated administrator system, many local governments are assigning educational or cultural public facility management and operations to civil groups and NPOs.

While local government finances deteriorate, NPOs promote citizen-oriented participation and learning and are becoming an indispensable presence and a part-ner in the autonomic administration that is building a citizen-oriented lifelong learn-ing society in Japan (Sato, ibid., p. 223).

4.4 Potential of Learning-Based Community Governance

As I mentioned previously, extreme pressure has been applied to reduce and dis-mantle Japan's social education administration. There is some possibility of devel-oping civil publicness in some aspects through the promotion of autonomic reforms and privatization in recent years. However, it may be difficult to ensure the civil publicness of social education if public spaces are delegated to private business under harsh conditions (Ishiiyama 2013, p. 71). Furthermore, it is highly probable that no guaranteed right to learn will be ensured. However, considering various issues that Japanese society is facing, such as the prolonged financial deficit, a declining birth rate combined with an aging population and depopulation, we can no longer assume that traditional education or a welfare assistance system will con-tinue to be available in this era of the national economy.

As a result of declining birth rates and the aging population, as well as urban migration, especially relocation by young people, rural depopulation is accelerat-ing. If the symptom persists at the current pace, rural communities may disappear. The nation's autonomic administrative and financial circumstances are not promis-ing. In 49.8% of 896 cities and towns, the number of females between the ages of 20 and 39 will decrease by 50% or more between 2010 and 2040. The country is in an extremely serious situation, with approximately 50% of local governments at risk of becoming "extinct cities" in the near future. Even our densely inhabited cit-ies are rapidly aging, and it is said that large cities will also be faced with the problem of aging. If the predicted drastic decline of the country's population becomes a reality, it may be not only "extinct cities" that will struggle to survive but Japanese society itself (Masuda 2015).

How can we prevent symptoms that include "extinct towns," "overconcentration in Tokyo," and a "unipolar society"? Masuda suggests that we can stop the overconcentration of people and resources in Tokyo by creating attractive places to learn and work in rural areas. Also, considering Japan's current financial situation, it is extremely difficult to increase public investment, unlike in the past. Therefore, We need to consider where to allocate our limited finances and also need cooperation and coordination between various organizations, including between national and local governments and between local governments and citizens (ibid.). In other words, we need to make Japan a sustainable society by preventing "extinct towns" though rural regeneration and revitalization efforts as well as by community governance.

In reality, many bodies throughout Japan, including local governments, citizen groups, NPOs, universities, and companies, are making efforts to cooperate and coordinate with each other to solve the problems faced by the individual regions. Noteworthy practices from the social education and lifelong learning perspectives are their efforts to restore the weakening functions of local communities and restructure systems to support each other irrespective of whether they are urban or rural areas. In the following sections, I will cite some case examples of coordination or "community governance" between citizens and local governments or schools (universities) to regenerate and revitalize communities.

4.4.1 Building Autonomous Competence Based on Citizen's Community Centers and Revitalizing Communities: Case Example of Iida City

Iida City is a typical suburban city located in the southern part of Nagano Prefecture with a population of approximately 100,000. Iida City is famous for the extremely lively activities of their Kominkan. These Kominkan are regarded as representative of the social education facilities in Japan. Each administrative district has one community center, and a total of 20 public Kominkan are located in the city. There are also 103 autonomic Kominkan functioning as subordinate civic autonomic facilities called "Bunkan," which are established and managed voluntarily by citizens. At these Kominkan, residents enjoy pursuing hobbies and learning about culture, socializing, passing on the traditions and culture of each region, as well as conducting various community activities and events to resolve the problems and issues faced by each region. They have been actively using these Kominkan to promote local culture, foster next generation resources, help each other, and build trusting relationships.

However, lately this suburban city is also facing depopulation as a result of young people relocating and an aging population. Partly because Iida City does not have a 4-year university, the ratio of young people leaving the city after graduating from high school is high, and the ratio of young people returning to the city is also low. Depopulation, especially by young people, is a serious problem for a community to handle. Because of these problems, the city considers that they needed to foster "local residents who understand, love, and contribute to the community," in order to create an attractive town that young people will want to stay in or return to after leaving. As a result, the Kominkan, a local occupational high school, and a university worked together to implement a new activity they have called "local human resource cultivation" to foster local leaders who can manage and coordinate the area. This "local human resource cultivation" is held during the "research project" class at the high school. During the class, a public community center director suggests various themes related to the local problems for research projects and offers advice and support while working as a mediator between high school students and local residents.

In the Kawaji region of the city, communication and relationships between generations have become diluted as a result of young people relocating to urban cities. To help resolve this problem, the community center, local primary school, and residents are working together to conduct a "school commuting camp," an experience-based activity where primary school children stay away from their parents for 1 week with other children in a local public facility, commuting to school with the help of local residents. This activity is designed to revitalize the community and encourage children to develop a fondness for the community by communicating with various adults from different generations who have been part of the community since childhood, while parents and residents foster new relationships. Through this project, a major change in consciousness can be observed in the local residents who participate in the project, as well as in the children themselves. It also helps to build a community network that connects many different individuals.

To summarize, Iida City has been conducting community center-based activities to solve regional problems through community governance, utilizing accumulated experience and know-how in social education. The city has also been successful in fostering the autonomous competence of its citizens and in revitalizing the community by discovering and encouraging many different actors and establishing networks.

4.4.2 Multigenerational, Interactive Community Built at a Community Café: A Case Example in the Takayanagi Region of Kashiwa City

The Takayanagi region of Kashiwa City in Chiba is one of the commuter towns that surround Tokyo. After the war, the first baby boomers relocated to this area where land prices were reasonable to find an ideal home environment. In spite of their workplaces being located in Tokyo, they did not choose to live in the city because of its high land prices. This generation has now reached mandatory retirement age and has been aging rapidly. But because they did not form relationships with the community during their careers, an increasing number of aged individuals are facing issues with life after retirement. Also, as a consequence of the diluted community relationships resulting from the trend toward nuclear families, reduced birth rate, and the large number of double-income households, more and more young parents are suffering from parenting anxiety, and children are feeling insecure and lonely because they have no adults to talk to other than their parents.

In an attempt to influence the situation, the local volunteer group, schools, and the local government worked together to establish a "multigenerational, interactive community executive committee" in 2010. The aim of this committee was to create a community that would promote community-involved childcare (improve regional competence in child-raising) and encourage aged individuals to participate in local activities (motivating the lives of the aged). Firstly, to create a community-involving structure, the committee opened a "community café" in 2012. This community café can be easily used by multiple generations from children to the aged and provides a place for residents to communicate with each other. It offers opportunities for citizens to find something that they are interested in doing, or something to learn or do, and also holds seminars to explore and foster new resources.

The local government and citizens cooperated in establishing the community café as a community-based facility that promotes communication, learning, and activities by citizens and strengthens their regional capabilities.

4.4.3 Community Network Established by an NPO: A Case Example of the NPO "Matching Hongo" in Bunkyo-ku, Tokyo

Tokyo University is located in the Hongo district of Bunkyo-ku. Traditionally, the merchants' association and the town assembly played central roles in local community activities. However, in recent years, the number of stores is decreasing due to an insufficient number of board members and people to take over the stores. Although the number of new residents is increasing because of falling land prices, the regional community is declining due to a large number of stores and franchisees deciding not to join the merchants' association.

Obligations and restraint by the merchants' association and the town assembly made it harder to challenge these problems and implement new actions. It was therefore necessary to build a new framework to turn the Hongo district into an "energetic town." A nonprofit organization named "Matching Hongo" was established as a participatory community network organization to connect local residents, schools, and shopping arcades.

The aim of "Matching Hongo" is to explore, learn, and share the local history and cultural heritage, so their major activities are creating a town map (of medical facilities, store information, cultural heritage, etc.) that will make residents' lives easier. They are also involved in cleaning activities, holding festivals to promote communication among citizens, and building relationships with other regions. When there are things that citizens want to try, this NPO will work with the local government, various groups, schools, universities, and companies to assist with the project. One of their recent new projects is the "Under the Same Roof Project" which promotes harmonious coexistence between the aged and the young. In this project, undergraduates and graduates are housed in spare rooms in the houses of elderly citizens. The project aims to promote new relationships of mutual assistance between young students and aged citizens and connect the two different generations with the local community, so that the whole community supports each other and finds motivation for their lives (Matching Hongo Homepage).

As mentioned previously, civil activities guided by an NPO in a metropolitan area where community interaction has become diluted enable new activities directed at the changes in society and local needs, as well as the passing on of the traditions and culture unique to the community. They can also help expand the community network to revitalize the community.

4.5   Conclusion

Here I have mainly reviewed the educational reforms of the 1980s and the restructuring of and issues with social education and lifelong learning associated with decentralization in the 2000s. I also focused on learning-based community governance as a way to protect citizens' lives in the harsh living environment, while Japanese society suffers from prolonged economic depression and an aging population combined with a low birth rate. In the 1970s, lifelong learning was adopted as a political concept. Then, rationalization and autonomic administrative and financial reforms were implemented in line with the neoliberal structural reforms. I considered critically the influence on the social education administration and its assistance system. While society is facing the issues of an aging population combined with a low birth rate, drastic depopulation, and prolonged financial deficit, autonomic reforms and privatization are being carried out. Under these circumstances, various actors including local governments, citizens, and NPOs are collaborating to reinvigorate local communities. Educational and cultural facilities play a central role in these activities, including Kominkan, schools, community cafes, and NPOs. I cited case examples of community regeneration and revitalization and considered the significance and potential of learning-based community governance.

In association with municipal mergers and decentralization, the Ministry of Education, Culture, Sports, Science and Technology (MEXT) and the Ministry of Internal Affairs and Communications (MIC) have realized that building a structure of collaboration between local communities and the local government or so-called community governance as well as cultivating human resources are important tasks to encourage citizens themselves to solve regional issues and revitalize their communities (MEXT 2007; MIC 2013).

In either case, a strong civil autonomic capability is required, and this autonomic capability can be fostered in communities as well as in personal lives by "continuous learning and discussions," or in other words, by social education and lifelong learning (Matsuda 2011). The abovementioned three case examples confirm this point. I consider that communities can enhance social education and lifelong learning by fostering the autonomic competence of their citizens and revitalizing their regions through learning and deliberation-based community governance guided by various local actors. They should also avoid being influenced by the restructuring of social education and lifelong learning under autonomic reforms. Our future success depends on the degree to which we can develop this potential.

References

Anezaki, Y. (2013). Shakai Kyoiku Hosei to Shogai Gakusyu Sinko Seibi Ho [Social education legislation and lifelong learning act for improvement of systems, etc. to implement measures for the promotion of lifelong learning]. In B. Kobayashi, O. Ito, & J. Lee (Eds.), *Nihon no Shakai Kyoiku to Shogai Gakusyu: Atarashii Jidai ni Mukete* [Social education and lifelong learning in Japan: To a New Era] (pp. 78–94). Okayama: University Education Press.

Han, S., & Makino, A. (2013). Learning cities in East Asia: Japan, the Republic of Korea and China. *International Review of Education, 59*, 443–468.

Ishiiyama, R. (2013). Shakai Kyoiku to Shogai Gakusyu no Genzai [Current social education and lifelong learning]. In B. Kobayashi, O. Ito, & J. Lee (Eds.), *Social education and lifelong learning in Japan: To a new era* (pp. 58–74). Okayama: University Education Press.

Kobayashi, B. (2013). Nihon no Shakai Kyoiku to Shogai Gakusyu: So no Tokusitsu to Kadai [Japanese social education and lifelong learning: Characteristics and challenges]. In B. Kobayashi, O. Ito, & J. Lee (Eds.), *Social education and lifelong learning in Japan: To a new era* (pp. 1–20). Okayama: University Education Press.

Lee, J. (2006). Nihon no Shogai Gakusyu Seisaku no Genzyo to Kadai [The present conditions and problems of lifelong learning policy in Japan]. *Journal of the Research on Lifelong Learning and Career Education, , 19–27. Nagoya University.

Masuda, H. (2015). Chiho Shometsu: Tokyo Ikkyoku Shuchu ga Maneku Jinko Kyugen [Disappearing local communities: Rapidly declining population caused by overconcentration in Tokyo]. Tokyo: Chuokoron-Shinsya.

Matching Hongo Homepage. Accessed on 25 Feb 2015 from http://matching-h.jp/

Matsuda, T. (2011). Bunken o Naijitsuka suru Shakai Kyoiku no Kanosei [Potentiality of social education to realize decentralization]. *Monthly Social Education, 55*(2), 64–72. Tokyo: Kokudosha.

Matsuda, T. (2014). *Community Governance to Shakai Kyoiku no Saiteigi: Shakai Kyoiku Hukushi no Kanosei* [Redefinition of community governance and social education: Potentiality of social education welfare]. Tokyo: Fukumura Shuppan.

MEXT (Ministry of Education, Culture, Sports, Science and Technology). (2007). *2007 white paper on education, culture, sports, science and technology*. Tokyo: MEXT.

MIC (Ministry of Internal Affairs and Communications All Rights Reserved). (2013). *Chiiki Kasseika no Kyoten toshiteno Gakko o Katsuyo shita Chiiki Zukuri Jirei Chosa* [Case study of community renovation by utilizing schools as local revitalization foundation]. Tokyo: MIC.

MIC (Ministry of Internal Affairs and Communications All Rights Reserved) Homepage. (2014). Accessed 25 Feb 2015 from http://www.soumu.go.jp/gapei/gapei2.html

NPO Homepage of CAO (Cabinet Office, Government of Japan). (2014). Accessed 25 Feb 2015 from https://www.npo-homepage.go.jp/about/npodata/kihon_1.html

Sato, K. (2013). Shimin no Manabi to NPO [Public learning and NPO]. In B. Kobayashi, O. Ito, & J. Lee (Eds.), *Social education and lifelong learning in Japan: To a new era* (pp. 223–235). Okayama: University Education Press.

Shinkai, H. (2013). Sengo Shakai Kyoiku no Seisei to Tenkai [Creation and deployment of postwar social education]. In B. Kobayashi, O. Ito, & J. Lee (Eds.), *Social education and lifelong learning in Japan: To a new era* (pp. 36–57). Okayama: University Education Press.

Chapter 5
National and Local Educational Administration

Yusuke Murakami

5.1 Introduction

Since the 2000s, Japan's educational administration has experienced more changes than ever before.[1] The Japanese administration itself has been in the process of strengthening the powers of its cabinet functions. With these changes, "the core executives"—the Prime Minister at the national level and governors and mayors at the local level—have gained much more power over educational policies, while the so-called educational policy community, the Ministry of Education, Culture, Sports, Science and Technology (MEXT) and educators, has been losing its influence in recent years. As a result of these changes, the core executives have come to heavily influence the educational policies at the national level, compared to those up until the 1990s. At the local level, as the governal or mayoral educational reforms progressed, the Local Educational Administration Act was reformed in 2014 to decrease the authority of the Boards of Education and strengthen the authority of the Chief Executives (governors and mayors).

The purpose of this chapter is to outline the changes that have taken place in Japan relating to the educational administrative systems at both the national and the local level since the 2000s.[2] Section 5.2 of this chapter will deal with the

---

[1] Some examples of English literature on Japanese educational polices are the following: Pempel (1978) analyzed the 1970's higher education in Japan; Schoppa (1991) examined the educational policies of Japan between the 1970s to the 1980s; Hood (2001) studied the reforms conducted by Prime Minister Yasuhiro Nakasone in the 1980s; and in recent years, Nitta (2008) has analyzed and compared Japan's and United States' educational reforms between the 1990s and the early 2000s.

[2] This chapter is based on previously published papers by Murakami (2013, 2014), which have been partially revisioned.

Y. Murakami (✉)
Graduate School of Education, The University of Tokyo, Tokyo, Japan
e-mail: murakami@p.u-tokyo.ac.jp

© Springer Nature Singapore Pte Ltd. 2019
Y. Kitamura et al. (eds.), *Education in Japan*, Education in the Asia-Pacific
Region: Issues, Concerns and Prospects 47,
https://doi.org/10.1007/978-981-13-2632-5_5

circumstances of change in national educational administration, and Sect. 5.3 will cover those concerning the local government. In Sect. 5.2, after briefly reviewing the national educational policies since the Mori administration in the early 2000s to the current second Abe administration, an explanation will be given of how the decision-making processes in national educational policy making have changed. Section 5.3 will present the characteristics of the recent local educational policies and describe both the circumstances and an outline of the 2014 reforms relating to the system of the Board of Education that has been implemented. Understanding these matters, we can hope to gain a better understanding of the trends in Japan's national and local educational administrations.

5.2 The Transformation of Educational Administration

5.2.1 Educational Policies Since the 2000s

The typical understanding of Japan's system of planning and deciding on its educational policies up to the 1990s was that it basically relied on a centralized authority led by the bureaucrats of the Ministry of Education. However, some studies (such as Park 1986) have come to a different understanding, stating that rather than the system being led by the bureaucrats in the Ministry of Education, there was a stronger influence from politicians; and when it came to educational policy at the local level, the local governments had a certain degree of autonomy from the national government, with the national and local governments maintaining a relationship of interdependency (Reed 1986; Aoki 2004).

Compared to the 1990s and earlier, the main characteristic since the 2000s is that the Prime Minister and other ministers have gained greater influence over educational policies. Up to the 1990s, certain members of the Diet who familiarized themselves with the educational policies (who were called the "education zoku" or "education tribe") often had more influence over this matter rather than the Prime Minister or other ministers. However, in the 1990s, the electoral system for the House of Representatives changed from a medium to a small constituency system, and as the powers of the cabinet were strengthened in the early 2000s, the influence of the Prime Minister and ministers increased; and, in turn, the influence of the education zoku and the bureaucrats in the Ministry of Education decreased.

By strengthening the political leadership in a different way from the past, many educational reforms have been implemented since the 2000s. First, the Basic Act on Education, which had not changed once since its enactment in 1947, was revised by Abe's first cabinet in 2006. The new Basic Act on Education stated its educational aim to be one of nurturing an attitude "to foster an attitude to respect our traditions and culture, love the country and region that nurtured them,"[3] which was a reform reflecting conservative forces. Second, the educational policy placing more emphasis on experience, called "yutori-kyōiku" (education that gives children room to grow), changed radically. In the Educational Guidelines of 1998 to 1999 (a curriculum standard set by the national government), a "period for integrated study [sougou teki na gakusyu no jikan]" that emphasized empiricism was introduced, but this was met with the criticism that it led to a decline in academic abilities and increased the disparities in academic achievement. As a result, in 2003, the Ministry of Education, Culture, Sports, Science and Technology (MEXT) revised part of the Educational Guidelines and reversed the *yutori* education. Third, as the process of decentralization of power to the local governments advanced further, as will be discussed later, the governors and the mayors expanded their political leadership. Additionally, up till then, half of the salaries for the faculty of compulsory education were covered by the national government, while the prefectures covered the other half. However, to advance the decentralization of power to the local governments, the national government reduced its portion to one-third from fiscal year 2006. However, with many prefectures facing financial difficulties, about half of the prefectures could not afford the standard number of regular teachers' salaries based on national standards, instead hiring more part-time teachers.

The Democratic Party of Japan (DPJ) was the ruling party from 2009 to 2012. The DPJ had initially planned to (1) reduce the burden of household educational expenses, (2) maintain the quality and quantity of teachers, and (3) reform the educational governance, in that order. Out of the three, the plan to (1) reduce the burden of household educational expenses resulted in paying out a set amount of allowances, regardless of income level, to every family with children; furthermore, it made public high school tuition free (and provided a partial supplement to those entering private high schools). However, with their defeat in the 2010 election of the House of Councilors, they lost their majority in the Upper House, and they were no longer able to pass laws in the National Diet without the support of the opposition parties. Therefore, when it came to (2) maintaining the quality and quantity of educators, and (3) reforming educational governance, for example, they had plans to reform the teacher training system, reevaluate the system of the Board of Education, and establish school boards, but they were unable to accomplish these reforms.

During the DPJ administrations, the Prime Minister's leadership was not seen when it came to educational policy; and in reality, the three highest ranks in the ministry (the minister, vice minister, and the parliamentary secretary, all of them members of the Diet) of MEXT were at the center of policy making (though this was not unique to MEXT as the same situation was seen in other ministries as well). The DPJ held a national strategy meeting and aimed to have the cabinet lead the way in shaping policy, but ultimately this did not work and resulted in the three highest-ranking members in each of the ministries playing a more prominent role.

---

[3] Basic Act on Education (Act number 120 of 2006), Article2 (5), cited from the ministry of education website (an unofficial translation) (http://www.mext.go.jp/b_menu/kihon/data/07080117.htm) (2016.3.1).

5.2.2 The Educational Policy of the Second Abe Administration (2012 to Present)

In the second Abe administration, similar to the Education Rebuilding Council that Abe had created in his first administration, he set up an Education Rebuilding Implementation Council directly under the authority of the Prime Minister. The educational reforms are implemented based on this council's recommendations, and the details of the system designed to implement them are left to MEXT and the Central Council for Education (which is referred to as "education rebuilding" by the Abe administration). Since the Education Rebuilding Implementation Council is under the direct authority of the Prime Minister, we can say that reformation will continue to take place based on political leadership. The following three traits relate to this reformation process.

First, the Education Rebuilding Implementation Council has made eight sets of recommendations within the span of 2 years, recommending large-scale structural changes to the system in many areas. The Council made many recommendations pertaining to educational policies, such as dealing with the issue of bullying (the first set of recommendations); reforming the Board of Education system (the second set), universities (the third set), English education (the third set), and university entrance examinations (the fourth set); implementing a continuous, single educational system between elementary school and junior high school (the fifth set); extending assistance to school truants (the sixth set); reforming the teacher licensing and training system (the seventh set); and providing sufficient funding for education (the eighth set).

With the first set of recommendations, the prevention of bullying was legislated. Since then, what had previously been allocated to "moral education" once per week but had not constituted an official curriculum became one. The second set of recommendations brought about changes in the municipal educational administration laws as well as the strengthening of the authority of the Chief Executives in the municipalities. The third set of recommendations weakened the authority of faculty councils and instead strengthened the authority of the school president. Additionally, English is set to become part of the curriculum for fifth- and sixth-grade students from the fiscal year 2020 (and for some from 2018). The fourth set of recommendations has led to a new test or set of tests currently being drafted to replace the National Center Test for University Admissions, which is to be abolished. With the fifth recommendations, the 6 years of elementary education and 3 years of junior high school became institutionalized as a single compulsory educational system, with the municipalities being able to decide on their own if or when to establish the "unified compulsory schools." The Abe administration has in this way shown that it has much more passion toward educational reform compared to the past administrations and that it has a tendency to make large-scale educational reforms.

Second, from the fact that it has strengthened the textbook review process and reconsidered the courtesy that had been extended to neighboring countries in history education, it is clear that it is aiming at a more conservative educational policy than the DPJ administration that immediately preceded this one. Even compared to the past Liberal Democratic Party (LDP) administrations, Abe's first and second administration have shown a preference for bringing such policies to the forefront; and with it, the Abe administration has often been criticized for its policies, including its educational policies, leaning to the right.

Third, while the Abe administration is passionate about educational reform, since the national economy suffers when it comes to policies requiring expenditure, such as increasing the number of teachers to relieve overworked colleagues or establishing a sufficiently funded scholarship system, there has not been much progress. However, when it comes to nursing and raising children, a 2012 decision was reached to fund the new Comprehensive Support System for Children and Child-rearing, partially to increase the number of care locations and preserve the quality of teachers. Also, as the Abe administration had made it its policy to promote women's success in society when the system was officially established in the fiscal year 2015, approximately 500 billion yen has been allocated to this new system.[4]

In this way, when it comes to the content of the educational policies, we can observe many diversified reforms having taken place during the second Abe administration, especially in comparison to other past administrations. One reason for this is because the second Abe administration finds itself on a relatively stable political foundation.

When we look at the second Abe administration, as with his first administration, he has created a structure in which the core executives take the rein over policy making with the Prime Minister at its center. With the core executives assuming more leadership, it may seem reminiscent of the Koizumi administration, when the LDP led the way; but, when it comes to educational policy, there is a difference in the policy-making stance between the Koizumi administration and that of Abe.

In the Koizumi administration, the educational policy itself was not the target of reforms but rather a result of the strengthening of leadership of the Prime Minister's office (such as in the Council on Economic and Fiscal Policy), with the Cabinet Office of other ministries having gained more influence over educational policy making. In other words, the strengthening of the Prime Minister's office had the effect of boosting the cabinet's influence on overall policy making, and educational policy was no exception in that regard. In comparison, the Abe administration has positioned educational policy as an issue of importance, listing educational reforms as one of the cabinet's priority issues. While in the Koizumi administration, the Council on Economic and Fiscal Policy and other policy-making institutions had a

[4]Originally, 700 billion yen was to be allocated to this program using the increased revenue obtained from the consumption tax, which was to be increased from 8% to 10%. However, the Abe administration decided to postpone the raising of the tax that had been planned for April 2015; consequently, the amount allocated for this program was reduced to 500 billion yen.

certain influence over educational policy, a further contrast in Abe's administration was apparent in the setting up instead of advisory bodies such as the Education Rebuilding Council and Education Rebuilding Implementation Council specializing in educational reform.

5.2.3   The Changes in the National Educational Policy

- One of the changes in Japan's educational administrations since the 2000s could be said to be that political leadership has come to the forefront in both the central and local governments. It is certainly noticeable that the influence of the political leaders such as the Prime Minister and Chief Executives has become much stronger.
- Compared to the current system, Japan's central government's policy decision-making system up to the 1990s had placed much more emphasis on the separation of powers and getting agreements from related parties. For example, the medium constituency system was designed so that one electoral district could produce multiple winners from the LDP, which had resulted in balancing the factions within the LDP itself while at the same time weakening the cabinet. Additionally, when laws were proposed by the LDP, there was a preliminary internal evaluation by the Policy Research Council and the General Council, which basically required unanimous agreement beforehand. Not only did an agreement therefore need be made within the cabinet, but it also emphasized getting agreements within the party.
- However, since the changes in the decision-making process of the 2000s, the consensus building aspect has gradually given way; and, compared to the past, the concentration of power has moved more toward the cabinet.
- In this way, even with parliamentary democracy, there are differences in how consensus is built into decision-making, based on preference and the degree of concentration of powers. With regard to this point, Arend Lijphart, who is a political scientist specializing in comparative politics, has asserted that in a parliamentary democracy there are majoritarian democracies and consensus democracies. After categorizing the two, he looked at the two dimensions that these democracies have: that is to say, the dimension of the government and political parties (the ruling system, party system, and the electoral system), and the federal dimension (central and local relationships and jurisdiction), pointing out that there are such differences based on majoritarian democracies and consensus democracies as seen in the chart below (Lijphart 2012).

Chart: Majoritarian democracies and consensus democracies

	Majoritarian democracies	Consensus democracies
The dimension of government and political parties	Concentration of executive authority to a cabinet comprised of a single majority party	A cabinet with multiple parties participating with shared executive authorities
	Power is centralized with core executives holding absolute power	Balanced core executives, council, or house relationship
	Two-party system	Multiple-party system
	Majority rule, nonproportional representation type of electoral system	Proportional representation system
Federal dimension	Government with singular, centralized concentration of power	Shared powers between the federal system and the municipal systems
	Single house to hold power over legislation	Two levels of houses that hold different electoral bases with divided authority in establishing laws
	An elastic constitution that can be amended with a simple majority	An inelastic or rigid constitution that can only be amended with a super majority
	In passing laws, the councils hold the final say	A system in which a supreme court or a constitutional court holds the final say in the legality of established laws
	A central bank that relies on the government	A central bank that maintains independence from the government

Adapted from Kawade and Taniguchi (2012, p. 80)

From the chart we can see that, up to the 1990s, Japan's central government was more of a consensus democracy in its decision-making process. When it came to political parties, though the LDP had a strong majority, instead of concentration of power in the cabinet, it rather had the characteristics of a coalition administration, as the factions within the LDP were quite strong. It can also be pointed out that, in the past, cabinet posts were given to each of the faction groups within the party. Additionally, when it came to the electoral system for the House of Representatives, it was the medium constituency electoral system that was used, and not the small constituency electoral system, which has a tendency to converge the parties into a two-major-party system. Rather, it was more akin to a proportional representation electoral system, which brings about a multiple-party system and which had created weaker cabinets and strong factions (*habatsu*) within the political parties.

However, in the mid-1990s, the medium constituency electoral system was changed to a combination of single-seat constituencies and proportional representation. Though there was still an element of a multiple-party system based on the existence of proportional representation, gradually a convergence toward a two-major-party system had come about, and by 2009, administrations had finally changed. Additionally, along with the reorganization of the ministries and government offices in the early 2000s, the Cabinet Office was established, and a strengthening of cabinet functions took place. Though there are those who criticize that this has not gone far enough, more power has been concentrated in the cabinet than in the past.

This notwithstanding, there are even now many aspects that represent more of a consensus democracy when it comes to reforms relating to the decentralization of power to the local governments. There are also those who advocate maintenance of an inelastic constitution. However, when it comes to the dimensions of government and political parties, ever since the 1990s, systematic reformation toward majoritarian democracy has taken place. Currently, with regard to the dimensions of the government and political parties (inside the government), majoritarian democracy is dominant, but at the federal dimension (outside of the government), the consensus democracy yet seems to have a strong grip on the system. Therefore, the overall system has resulted in a mixture of both types of characteristics (Sunahara 2015).

Additionally, if we look at recent discussions on reforms and trends, there is a stronger sense of moving toward a majoritarian democracy rather than a desire to return to consensus democracy. For example, the discussion on making amendments to the 96th article of the Constitution is an attempt and argument to move from an inelastic to an elastic constitution. Furthermore, some even question the roles and necessity of having a House of Councilors at all, arguing for a single house system by abolishing it. Additionally, the monetary easing policy by the Bank of Japan (BOJ) and the appointment of the governor of BOJ after Abe's administration came into existence contributed toward weakening the independence of the Central Bank. We could say that each of these essentially represents an attempt to move toward a majoritarian democracy, as described by Lijphart (2012).

As mentioned above, the governance system in the Japanese central government is transitioning from a consensus democracy that focused on the separation or sharing of powers to a majoritarian democracy characterized by the concentration of power.

If we were to compare the two from the perspective of stability and change in policy, the majoritarian democracies basically represent a "winner-takes-all" system, and while this speeds up the process of decision-making, there is also potential for rapid and frequent change in policy. The consensus democracy is the opposite of this, and while it takes longer to make decisions, the speed and degree of change tend to be slower compared to the majoritarian type.

The Japanese central government could be said to have shaped its policies based on the system of consensus democracy up to the 1990s. Especially when it came to the preliminary reviews in the passing of legislation, the LDP and the cabinet acted as the central role of the decision-making process. It has also been pointed out that this tends to lead to immobilism (Schoppa 1991), and the dualistic decision-making process between the ruling party and the cabinet has further been criticized (Nishio 2001). If we look at this from another perspective, it was a system in which the policies put into place were more stable and easier to maintain.

The transition to a majoritarian democracy has the advantage of being able to make quicker decisions and changes in policies based on the exigencies of time, which means that it is not necessarily inferior in all areas to a consensus democracy. However, from the standpoint of the stability and continuity of a policy, it has greater demerits compared to a consensus democracy. Specifically, from the standpoint of educational policies requiring stability and continuity, the adverse effect of frequent and rapid changes accompanying each change of administration, Prime Minister, or ministers cannot be ignored.

Unlike the municipal governments that utilize the Board of Education system to make policy decisions, the central government has not separated its policy-making system from the other administrative systems. What this means is that, just as with the other administrative areas, each minister and agencies are in charge of the jurisdiction of each of their offices. Even in the case of working under a minister, not a committee, the reason why a certain amount of stability and continuity was in existence had a lot to do with the system of consensus democracy, a mechanism and system different from that of "winner-takes-all."

In other words, the stability and continuity of educational policies Japan enjoyed at the central government level was not because of a separate, independent educational administrative committee; the stability and continuity it had experienced had more to do with the policy decision-making system based on a consensus democracy. It can be asserted that while it was not the intended consequence, this became the foundation for the stability and continuity of the educational policies outside of the educational administrative system.

On the other hand, as the transition to a majoritarian democracy has been put in motion since the 2000s, there have been many educational reforms, one after another; and except for the period when the controlling parties of the Houses of Representatives and Councilors were split, the stability and continuity of carrying out educational policies at the central government level has declined (Murakami 2009). It is to be expected that as the nation moves more toward a system of governance reflecting majoritarian democracies, this trend will only get stronger.

Of course, if we consider that if the overall system of governance is not limited to education, and if there is speed in decision-making and instigation of changes in policy at the appropriate timing, then adopting a system based on majoritarian democracy is certainly one option.

The author's perspective on this is that if we were to make such a decision, then there should be a way to soften the blow from the adverse effects of the majoritarian democracies in the areas where stability and continuity are required, such as in the case of educational policies, and we should instead consider putting into place a system that guarantees the stability and continuity of such policies. An example could be a kind of independent administrative committee; but, whatever the system, it must be one that prevents sudden changes in educational policies and guarantees a certain amount of continuity and stability, while it should nevertheless incorporate an element of responsibility to political demands.

5.3   The Change in the Local Educational Administrations

5.3.1   The Educational Reforms Led by Chief Executives

One of the characteristics of Japan's educational administrations in the municipalities since the 2000s has been that as the reforms led by Chief Executives of local government (governors and mayors) have moved forward, more competitive educational policies than in the past have been adopted, based on market principles. These changes have included the rating of schools, freedom of choice in which school to attend, and the adoption of national achievement tests. This section of the chapter will focus mainly on the reforms led by the Chief Executives as well as the reform of the Board of Education system in relation to these reforms.

Japan's municipal governments adopted the Board of Education system imported from the United States in 1948. However, there are no school districts, and each prefecture and its municipalities have a Chief Executive and a Board of Education. The Boards of Education came into existence as a reaction to the highly centralized and bureaucratic system prior to World War II. It is a system which was learned from the United States and implemented in 1948 with the goal of democratization and decentralization of education, allowing the local governments to share in its authority. Originally, the members of the Boards of Education were chosen through popular election (popular election-based Board of Education). However, there were cases in which the Chief Executives and the Boards of Education, who were all elected through popular vote, would clash. Additionally, at the prefectural level, there were many members of the Boards of Education that were backed by the teachers' union, which the Chief Executives felt to be problematic. There were strong opinions stating that the Boards of Education should be abolished. Eventually, in 1956, it was revised to a system in which the Chief Executives appointed the members of the Boards of Education with the approval of their councils (appointment-based Board of Education).[5] Since then and to this day, the basic characteristics of the Boards of Education, a collegial institution somewhat independent of the Chief Executives, have not changed (Ogawa 2010).

Until the 1990s, the national government had been heavily involved in the educational administrations and had more of a centralized system, compared to the present day. For example, the central government was legally required to direct the municipalities, and the standard size per class was decided by the national government (which has been set to 40 students per class since the late 1980s), which did not allow the municipalities to independently offer classes with fewer students per class. Additionally, when appointing the Superintendent, which was considered the position with the greatest influence in the municipal educational administrations, at

---

[5] On one hand, there are opinions that by changing the Board of Education to an appointment-based system from an election-based system, the conservative party and the Ministry of Education turned the Boards of Education into a mere façade (Mikami 2013); on the other hand, some praised the continuance of the system of the Board of Education, while other strong voices called for it to be abolished altogether (Honda 2003).

the prefectural level, education board would require approval from the Minister of Education, while at the municipal level, the prefecture's Boards of Education had to approve the choice.

When the reformation to decentralize power to the local governments took place in 1999, the system of authority delegation that was designed for the national government to be involved in all aspects of policy, including education, was abolished; at the same time within the educational administrations, the requirement for the national government to direct the municipalities as well as the system of national involvement in approving Superintendents was abolished. Since then, we have seen some educational reforms led by Chief Executives within the municipalities.

One well-known case concerns Toru Hashimoto, who was the mayor of Osaka City (2011–2015) after being the governor of Osaka (2008–2011). Hashimoto created a policy in 2011 called the Basic Educational Administration Act and with it gave the Chief Executives the authority to decide on the municipality's educational goals, something that had always been considered the authority of the Boards of Education. This had the potential to go against the Local Educational Administration Act, but eventually the LDP administration approved of this move.

- In addition to this, Hashimoto decided as the governor of Osaka to publish the achievement test results based on each municipality, and while he was the mayor of Osaka, he decided to implement the freedom of choice in selecting what school a child should attend. He had a tendency to adopt educational policies that were based on competitive principles, and they were often met with a negative reaction from the municipalities, schools, and local citizens. While his policies received much opposition due to the level of education in Osaka Prefecture and Osaka City being on the decline, there were some voters who support these policies and the party "Ishin-no-Kai" (The Restoration Party), which Hashimoto led at the time. On the other hand, there were several scandals caused by principals who were selected through an open screening, started by Hashimoto. It also caused a further stir when the number of those desiring to become teachers declined compared to other neighboring municipalities.

There were other active Chief Executives in other municipalities who concerned themselves with offering smaller class sizes. In Yamagata Prefecture, the governor decided to implement a reduction in class sizes to between 30 and 35 students in all grades. In Saitama Prefecture, Shiki City, the municipalities decided to independently hire their own teachers, offering smaller class sizes with a limit of 25–32 students per class for the first- to third-grade level of elementary school. While these policies have changed slightly as the Chief Executives have changed, they are still in place. In Aichi Prefecture's Inuyama City, the mayor and the Boards of Education both objected to the national achievement test that started in 2007, and it became known as the only municipality that did not participate in the test. (Inuyama City later elected a mayor who was for participating in the test; and when the Boards of Education members who were against participating came to the end of their terms, these were not renewed, after which Inuyama City participated in the test in 2009.) In the early 2000s, in larger metropolitan areas, the United Sates had also seen similar situations in which mayors became actively involved in educational policies, as in the case of "education mayors" in Japan in the early 2000s.

The reason why we started to see such educational reforms being led by Chief Executives from the 2000s was likely because of the following two factors. First, they had been influenced by the reforms to decentralize power to the local governments in the late 1990s. Through the reforms that called for the decentralization of power to the local governments, the national government's involvement was reduced, and compared to the past, the self-determination of the municipalities had increased. Up till that point, for example, the class sizes were determined by the national government, and the municipalities were not allowed to choose their own class sizes. With regard to the influence of the Chief Executives and the councils, they were completely cut off from the educational administration (Aoki 2013). When deregulation opened up opportunities, especially concerning policies that involved class sizes that could only be accomplished with a corresponding budget, this allowed for the Chief Executives to exert more influence as they had authority over the educational budget. Second, there was greater political benefit for the Chief Executives to lead the way in educational reforms. Until the early 1990s, the Ministry of Education and the Japan Teacher's Union had clashed quite visibly, and its impact was felt across the local areas. At that time, if any of the Chief Executives became actively involved in educational policies, it could have led to a confrontation with the opposition. It was consequently considered a high-risk move politically. However, as the cold war ended, the ideological confrontation cooled down, and the confrontations between the Ministry of Education and Japan Teacher's Union were practically resolved. Afterward, in order to win the next election, it became a politically more beneficial option for the Chief Executives to get involved in educational policies. Nevertheless, there were plenty of Chief Executives who left educational policy making to the Boards of Education, even after the 2000s. As mentioned earlier, however, we started to see more of the likes of "education mayors" who were actively involved in educational policy matters. As a result, some started to argue that the Boards of Education should be abolished and the Chief Executives should have single-handed control over the educational administrations, which led to the revision and reformation of the system of the Boards of Education.

5.3.2   Revision of the System of the Boards of Education

Approximately 10 years since the emergence of the educational reforms led by the Chief Executives, in 2014, the first major revision in about 60 years to the system of the Boards of Education has taken place. It has been argued that the Boards of Education have since the 1960s and 1970s become just a façade or that the Boards of Education members' jobs have merely become honorary.

This was the direct origin of what caused the second Abe administration to look into revising and reforming the system of the Boards of Education. In April 2013, the Education Rebuilding Implementation Council, which operates directly under the Prime Minister, proposed that the Superintendent should hold the final responsibility, and with this recommendation, from the following month in May, the Central Council for Education started to discuss practical steps in designing a new system in its Educational System Subcommittee.[6] However, the Education Rebuilding Implementation Council had not clarified whether or not the Boards of Education would continue to exist as a legally binding "executive body" (which means they have the authority to make the final decisions) based on the Local Autonomy Act, and the details on the structural design of the system were left to the discussions at the Central Council for Education.

The specifics of the proposal for reformation were to make the Superintendent an executive body based on Local Autonomy Act and to give final authority to him instead of to the Boards of Education. However, there was strong opposition from Chief Executives and from the Ministry of Internal Affairs and Communications, claiming that the Chiefs should hold the final authority on the educational administration. As a result, two plans were proposed. Plan A was to place the Boards of Education under the Chief Executives as its attached institution, to take away its decision-making powers relating to educational administration, and to centralize the final decision-making power to the Chief Executives. Plan B was to maintain the Boards of Education as an executive body but revise its relationship with the Superintendents.

According to media reports, the Chief of the Cabinet and the ministers were in favor of Plan A,[7] and by the end of the meetings at the Central Council for Education, Plan A was considered the majority and Plan B the minority opinion. However, some of the members of the Central Council for Education, including the current author, raised concerns about keeping this position as politically neutral as possible, and the opinion was voiced by some members of the LDP and Komeito that Plan A could not be supported. In the end, in December 2013, the response of the Central Council for Education had uncharacteristically taken a highly irregular move to make the recommendation by listing both plans side by side and pass the discussion of reformation over to the political arena.

Finally, as the ruling party carried out the discussion, the LDP and Komeito set up a working group with the related lawmakers, and a compromise between Plan A and B was considered. As a result, the Boards of Education were given the authority as an executive body, while the Superintendent would assume the role of head of the Boards of Education with added clarity to its responsibilities. On the other hand, with consideration to the Chief Executives who wanted to expand their authority, they were given the authority to set the basic policy on educational administration, and a new "General Education Conference" where the Chief Executives would meet with the Boards of Education to discuss and adjust matters was to be established. In March 2014, the LDP and Komeito came to their ruling party agreement, in June it passed as a bill, and as of April 2015, a new Board of Education system came into existence.

---

[6] The current author also participated as a member in the Educational System Subcommittee discussion.

[7] "Mainichi Shimbun," Morning Edition, December 14, 2013.

Next, we will consider what changes this new system of local educational administration is going to bring. Three key points are listed to provide a general idea of what these reforms will do.

First, the current Boards of Education will continue to have decision-making authority as an executive body, but the current position of head of the Boards of Education will be assumed by the Superintendent, and the full-time Superintendent will become the representative of the Boards of Education with the responsibility for ministering its meetings. Additionally, the Superintendents will be directly appointed by the Chief Executives with the approval of the council[8]; and to allow the Chief Executives to make at least one appointment of a Superintendent while in office, the term of the Superintendents will be reduced to 3 years (though the members of the Boards of Education will retain 4-year terms).

Second, a new General Education Conference will be established as a place for the Boards of Education and the Chief Executives to meet and discuss the basic charter for the educational administration and its necessary conditions for improvement. A General Education Conference will be called by the Chief Executives, and the development of the charter, policies to be implemented with a focus on educational conditions and maintenance, and preparing and planning for any emergencies must be discussed and arranged between the Chief Executives and the Boards of Education. It is further stated that what has been arranged and decided must be respected by the comprising members.

Third, the authority to set the charter, which is the basic policy of the educational administration, is being transferred from the Boards of Education to the Chief Executives. The Chief Executives will discuss the charter in the General Education Conference and make the necessary adjustments. However, while there will be discussion and work toward an agreement, in case the two parties do not come to an agreement, the Chief Executives will have the right to set the charter.

When we look at the above and summarize it, we can see that the current reform has left the Boards of Education as an executive body that has the final decision-making authority, and by increasing the involvement of the Chief Executives with responsibilities such as developing the charters and with the creation of the General Education Conference, there has been an attempt to clarify the responsibilities of educational administration as well as maintaining political neutrality, consistency, and stability. Even as we look at the process in which the reformation proposal was made, the bill that was passed in the National Assembly is indeed a compromise between Plan A and B, as the Central Council for Education had proposed.[9]

---

[8] In the system prior to 2014, the Superintendent was to be appointed by the Board of Education. But in Japan, the Superintendent was also a member of the Board of Education, and it was a rather complicated system. In all practicality, it was customary that when a candidate for the Superintendent was going to be appointed as a member of the Board of Education, the Chief Executive would indicate this to the council before the approval was granted.

[9] While the reform on which the ruling party came to an agreement may look like it came about rather abruptly, the ways in which the Superintendent and the Head of the Board of Education were to be consolidated as one, how the Chief Executives were to create the charter, how the Superintendents were to be directly appointed by the Chief Executives, and the shortening of the

Since the result of the current reform was a political compromise between those who wanted the Boards of Education to remain in existence and those who did not, its evaluation is split among researchers and practitioners. First, there are those who praise the fact that the Boards of Education were allowed to continue to exist as an executive body with decision-making powers and that the full-time Superintendents were to have a responsibility as a head of the Board of Education. It is thought that this will clarify who will ultimately bear responsibility. Second, there are those who claim that if the Chief Executives are creating the charter, and now with the conception of the General Education Conference, the Chief Executives will have too much involvement, and the Boards of Education will become more of a façade than ever before. Third, those who argued that the Chief Executives should hold all the final authority over educational administration matters have criticized that with decision-making power remaining in the Boards of Education, this current reform does not go far enough. Furthermore, other criticism asserts that too much power and authority reside with the Superintendents.

It is not possible at the point of writing (in early 2016) to know how this reform will influence the educational field. Initially, there were worries that perhaps there would be no stopping Chief Executives or a Superintendent who decides to implement a self-righteous educational policy or that with the consolidation of schools or the selection of textbooks, the political views of the Chief Executives may wield too much influence. In either case, as the authorities of the Chief Executives and Superintendents have become much stronger compared to the past, both their influences are expected to increase. Additionally, when the presiding Chief Executive loses an election, it is possible that the new Chief Executive and the Board of Education appointed by the previous Chief Executive could face conflict within the General Education Conference. Therefore, it is necessary to continue to analyze the changes going forward.

5.4   Conclusion

In this chapter, the changes seen in the national and local educational administration since the 2000s were explained by focusing on the changes within the decision-making process when policies were being set. At both the national and local levels, the authority and influence of the political leaders such as the Prime Minister and the Chief Executives of a local government have become stronger, and political leadership has become more pronounced; and with it, the individual leader's intentions now have much more influence over educational policies. This means that when there is a necessity to make changes, with political leadership it is now

Superintendents' terms were all actually points that were discussed within the Central Council for Education. However, when it came to the creation of the General Education Conference, the Central Council for Education hardly discussed the matter, and they are likely ideas that arose from within the leading party discussions.

possible to make a swift change. On the other hand, it also means that the administrations' intentions of the time will be able to influence education more directly, which could cause frequent changes that would adversely affect the schools and the teachers; and at the same time, the specialized field of education may be taken too lightly. Additionally, some point to the fact that as political leadership tends to seek quick results with its educational policies, there is a tendency to rely on competitive principles and market theories, which means that there will likely be an adverse effect on the classrooms as the politicians rely heavily on what can be measured with test scores (and thus the teachers will end up teaching to the test).

How and by whom the educational policies are decided will have a significant effect on the content of educational policy. If we are to help enrich education, it is important to recognize teachers as specialized and skilled workers and respect their autonomy. There may be educational administrations or teachers that take the expertise of education as an excuse to act from a place of self-righteousness. Political controls and competitive market theories may be powerful solutions to avoid such problems, but there is a danger of going too far, and we may end up with politically biased education or create too much competition, which could result in a variety of adverse effects. How to balance the expertise of education and its control mechanism (through citizens or politicians, or through implementations of competitive principles) will remain a challenge for educational administration, as it has been in the past and will continue to be in the future.

Additionally, Japan is experiencing a rapid decline in population through fewer births and an aging population. Currently, the number of births in Japan has been reduced to about 40% (1 million births) of the peak at the end of the 1940s (at 2.7 million births). Under these circumstances, the consolidation of schools in rural areas with declining populations has become a major issue. Additionally, with the worsening of economic conditions since the 1990s, there is an increase in children that fall below the poverty line, and the disparities are becoming a social issue. Furthermore, with globalization and the progress and development of IT, the type of academic abilities that are called for has changed from those of the twentieth century. With all these changes taking place, how will the educational administrations support the schools and children, and how and by whom will such educational policies be decided and implemented? As with the case of other nations, Japan is also facing difficult challenges.

Acknowledgment This work was supported by JSPS KAKENHI Grant Numbers 16K04536, 70242469, 20177140, and 26245075.

References

Aoki, E. (2004). Intergovernmental relations in educational administration [*kyouiku gyousei no seifukan kankei*] : Taga Shuppan (in Japanese).
Aoki, E. (2013). Decentralization and educational administration [*chiho bunken to kyoiku gyousei*]: Keiso Shobo (in Japanese).

Honda, M. (eds.). (2003). Politics and administration in reorganization of Education Board System [*kyouiku iinkai seido seihen no seiji to gyousei*] : Taga Shuppan (in Japanese).

Hood, C. P. (2001). *Japanese education reform: Nakasone's legacy* (The Sheffield Centre for Japanese Studies/Routledge series). London/New York: Routledge.

Kawade, Y., & Taniguchi, M.. (2012). Politics [*seijigaku*] : The University of Tokyo Press (in Japanese).

Lijphart, A. (2012). *Patterns of democracy: Government forms and performance in thirty-six countries* (2nd ed.). New Haven: Yale University Press.

Mikami, A. (2013). The study of The Education Board System [*kyouiku iinkai seidoron*]: Eidell Kenkyusho (in Japanese).

Murakami, Y.. (2009). "Political process in education reform." In H. Okada, & N. Matsuda (Eds.), Theory and situation in Japanese politics [*seijikatei no riron to jissai*], Minerva Shobo (in Japanese).

Murakami, Y. (2013). Education policy changes caused by a change of government and problems of education policymaking in Japan. [seiken koutai ni yoru seisaku henyo to kyouiku seisaku kettei sisutemu no kadai. Review of The Bulletin of The Japan Educational Administration Society [*nihon kyouiku gyousei gakkai nenpo*], *39*:37–52 (in Japanese).

Murakami, Y. (2014). Problems for local autonomy system in Japan from the point of view of the education board reform. [kyouiku iinkai kaikaku kara mita chihou jichi seido no kadai]. *Review of Jichisoken, 430*:75–91 (in Japanese).

Nishio, M. (2001). Public Adminstration[*gyousei gaku*]: Yuhikaku (in Japanese).

Nitta, K. A. (2008). *The politics of structural education reform* (Routledge research in education, Vol. 13). New York: Routledge.

Ogawa, M. (2010). The future of education reform in Japan [*kyouiku kaikaku no yukue*]: Chikuma Shobo (in Japanese).

Park, Y. H. (1986). *Bureaucrats and ministers in contemporary Japanese government* (Vol. 8). Berkeley: University of California Institute of East Asian Studies.

Pempel, T. J. (1978). *Patterns of Japanese policymaking: Experiences from higher education* (Westview replica editions). Boulder: Westview Press.

Reed, S. R. (1986). *Japanese prefectures and policymaking, Pitt series in policy and institutional studies*. Pittsburgh: University of Pittsburgh Press.

Schoppa, L. J. (1991). *Education reform in Japan: A case of immobilist politics* (The Nissan Institute/Routledge Japanese studies series). London: Routledge.

Sunahara, Y. (2015). A condition for democracy [*minsyusyugi no joken*] : Toyo Keizai Shinpo (in Japanese).

Part II
Educational Issues in Japan

Chapter 6
The Relationship Between Teachers' Working Conditions and Teacher Quality

Masaaki Katsuno

6.1 Introduction

In June 2014, when the results of the second round of the Teaching and Learning International Survey (TALIS) were published, some Japanese papers gave significant publicity to the long work hours and low levels of self-efficacy and occupational satisfaction of Japanese teachers (Asahi Shimbun2014b; Mainichi Shimbun 2014). On average, Japanese teachers work 53.9 h per week. This is the longest average work week of the nations and regions participating in the international survey conducted by the Organisation for Economic Co-operation and Development (OECD). Japanese teachers also reported extremely low levels of confidence in their pedagogical competence, such as developing student interest and positive attitudes toward learning, classroom management, and effective use of different teaching and assessment methods. A paper cited Professor Yuki Honda's comment that more teachers and other professional staff are definitely needed to alleviate the intensity of teaching and to improve the quality of teaching (Asahi Shimbun 2014a).

The Ministry of Education, Culture, Sports, Science and Technology (MEXT) responded promptly to the publication of the TALIS results (Monbukagakusho 2014). MEXT significantly emphasized improving teacher quality by reforming the systems of initial education, recruitment, and in-service education for teachers. MEXT also demanded complete implementation of the Course of Study, which it compiles to indicate authoritatively what and how teachers should teach and students should learn. MEXT confirmed the need to address the issues of teachers' working conditions, but it placed more emphasis on pursuing its policies regarding quality and outcomes of the educational system.

M. Katsuno (✉)
Graduate School of Education, The University of Tokyo, Tokyo, Japan
e-mail: mkatsuno@p.u-tokyo.ac.jp

© Springer Nature Singapore Pte Ltd. 2019 87
Y. Kitamura et al. (eds.), *Education in Japan*, Education in the Asia-Pacific
Region: Issues, Concerns and Prospects 47,
https://doi.org/10.1007/978-981-13-2632-5_6

Over the last few decades, MEXT has been advancing such policies as ability-based grouping, team teaching, and smaller class sizes to ensure more individualized instruction. More recently, the Ministry has stressed active and collaborative learning for problem-solving in line with the global shift in the emphasis on learning (e.g., the OECD's key competencies and twenty-first century skills). It also has been emphasizing the need to address urgent challenges, such as special needs education, bullying, and prolonged student truancy. If not entirely, MEXT has succeeded in securing additional school staff for local implementation of these policy initiatives. MEXT can effectively control the number of school staff that prefectural governments can employ because of its significant role in educational funding, as the Ministry funds part of the local school staff's remuneration. The number of regular and extra positions for school staff is calculated centrally for each prefecture. The number of regular positions is set to meet the general needs of prefectural education, and the number of extra positions is used to advance national policies. Extra positions provide local governments with earmarked budgets to meet national priorities.

MEXT has also demanded increases in the number of regular teaching positions, but it has rarely succeeded. In August 2010, MEXT developed the plan to increase the number of teachers and school staff and demanded an increase in regular positions by 51,800 over the years from 2011 to 2018 to gradually reduce class sizes, beginning with the first grade in elementary schools and eventually through the third grade in junior high schools. In 2012, the related law was revised to the effect that the number of students per first grade class should not exceed 35 (previously 40). In 2013, the maximum class size was reduced from 40 to 35 for the second grade, but this was not through a revision to the law, but by budgetary measures, which provide less stability. Since then, however, further reductions in class size have not been enacted by law or provided through budgeting. The government finally rejected this MEXT plan completely, claiming that the beneficial effects of smaller class sizes had not been confirmed and that budgets for civil service personnel needed to be cut further. Hence, the average number of students per class continues to be high in Japan, 28 in elementary schools and 33 in junior high schools. These class sizes are well above the OECD averages of 21 and 24, respectively (OECD 2014a).

As the present government of Japan, particularly the Ministry of Finance, adheres to austerity measures in public sector spending, MEXT seems to have little chance of increasing the number of regular positions for teachers and other school staff. The best that MEXT can hope for is to increase the number of extra positions. For the 2014 fiscal year budget, MEXT succeeded in securing 703 extra positions for teachers in order to address its prioritized policies, such as addressing bullying, intensifying moral education, developing special needs education, and preparing for the institutionalization of English as a subject in the elementary school curriculum. However, the government cut 800 regular positions under the rationale that the overall number of students is declining. For the first time in the postwar period, the total number of positions for teachers and other school staff was set below the number for the previous year. This is also true for fiscal 2015, which had an even larger decrease. While 900 extra positions were secured, 4000 regular positions were cut.

In addition to the cuts in the number of regular teaching positions, the casualization of the teaching profession has become a serious issue affecting both the working conditions of teachers and the quality of teaching. The general labor market in Japan is rapidly becoming precarious with no less than 38.2% of workers employed as irregular employees as of 2012. The teaching profession is no exception. The rate of irregular employment in teaching, including short-term contracts and working part-time, has increased from 8.7% in 2005 to 16.1% in 2012 (Monbukagakusho 2012). In the context of the overall casualization of the labor force, pressure has increased on local public finances, and the discretion of local governments regarding the usage of central grants for payment of school staff has resulted in an increase in the number of teachers with an unstable employment status. Although irregular employment can help some teachers who want more flexible ways to work, many teachers have no alternative to enduring irregular employment, which places them at a significant disadvantage in many ways. A significant result of this type of employment status is that teachers have lesser opportunity for professional development compared with their colleagues who have regular employment status. They have less time to engage in collaborative work on planning and studying lessons with colleagues. They also have limited time to engage with students and their parents or guardians. These limitations can have negative effects on the quality of their teaching.

The stabilization of teacher employment is necessary not just to secure better working conditions but also to improve the quality of education. Casualization of the teaching profession is now a worldwide trend (ILO 2012). Behind this movement is an increase in the demand for teachers in line with the increase in the number of students in Asian and African regions, the adoption of austerity measures in the field of education, and the introduction of the New Public Management policies that provide increased flexibility in teacher employment. Advocates of the New Public Management assume that giving more power to employing authorities to oversee the hiring, evaluation, and dismissal of teachers will lead to improved student achievement. However, the outcomes of this assumption are not guaranteed. What the effects of the casualization of the teaching force coupled with cuts in the number of teachers are having on the quality of teaching and learning in Japanese schools needs to be investigated, and the findings should be used as evidence to form the rationale for reconsidering current policies.

6.2   Working Conditions for Teachers

6.2.1   Misleading Response

Under the demographic circumstances and fiscal policies of austerity in the public sector, MEXT seems to be obliged to prefer enhancing teacher quality over improving the working conditions of teachers. To ensure the quality of education, MEXT has been pursuing reforms in the curriculum and teacher education. However, can teacher quality, and eventually student learning, be improved unless conditions in which teachers' work are more seriously taken into consideration?

It is universally understood that improving teacher quality significantly impacts the improvement of student learning. However, improving teacher quality does not render efforts to improve working conditions for teachers unnecessary. Indeed, both aspects are necessary. For example, the success of educational reforms in Ontario, Canada, that began in 2003 has generated new opportunities and significantly improved the quality of learning. This success is at least partially attributable to also improving the working conditions of teachers, including reducing class size, increasing the number of teachers, and providing more time for lesson preparation (Barber and Mourshed 2007). Further evidence of assuring quality working conditions for teachers is that even in nations that have implemented austerity measures amid the worldwide economic downturn that began in 2008, these countries have seldom reduced teachers' pay. Among the OECD nations, only France, Greece, and Japan have reduced the pay level of teachers over the years from 2000 to 2012 (OECD 2014a).

According to TALIS, Japanese teachers teach and look after more students than those in most of the other participating countries and regions. In Japan, the ratio of students to teachers at the lower secondary level (grades 7, 8, and 9) is 20.3:1. Regarding this ratio, Japan is second only to Chile at 20.4:1, and the average ratio for the participating nations and regions is 14.9 students to each teacher. Some countries in Asia have larger class sizes than in Japan, but their teachers attend to a smaller number of students. For example, in lower secondary education in Malaysia, the average class size is 32.1, and the ratio of students to teacher is 13.6:1. In Korea, the average class size is 32.4 and the ratio of students to teacher is 15.5:1. In Singapore, the average class size is 35.5 and the ratio of students to teacher is 14.9:1. In refusing the MEXT demand that class sizes should be reduced, the Ministry of Finance claims that the ratio of students to teachers matters more significantly than the average class size, but this international index also reveals that Japanese teachers work in rather disadvantaged conditions, even when seen from this perspective.

Although Japanese teachers work long hours, they do not spend a significant part of their work hours actually teaching. Indeed, on average, they teach for 17.7 h a week, while teachers in other nations and regions teach for 19.3 h on average. Compared with their colleagues in other nations and regions, Japanese teachers spend a little more time on planning and preparing lessons (8.7 h) and collaborating with their colleagues (3.9 h). School management tasks, general administrative work, and extra curriculum work (notably, supervision of club activities) are most responsible for their higher work intensity (OECD 2014b).

Japanese head teachers report more frequently than their counterparts in all of the other nations and regions participating in TALIS that a shortage of competent teachers prevents their schools from providing quality teaching. Apparently, this justifies the eagerness of MEXT to improve teacher quality and to advocate full implementation of the Course of Study as mentioned above. However, a closer examination of the ways teachers are working suggests that this kind of response, based on a kind of deficit model thinking, is rather misleading. Teachers may well be aware of the new directions of teaching and learning that the Course of Study

Table 6.1 Teachers leaving the profession due to sickness (percentage of all teachers leaving the profession)

	2000	2003	2006	2009	2012
Elementary	2.3%	2.4%	2.6%	3.7% (2.1%)	3.3% (1.9%)
Junior High	2.0%	2.4%	3.4%	3.9% (2.2%)	4.1% (2.4%)
Senior High	2.0%	2.1%	2.3%	2.7% (1.3%)	5.0% (2.3%)
Special Education	2.6%	2.5%	4.4%	5.1% (2.9%)	4.7% (2.9%)

Sources: *Statistics on School Teachers* compiled by MEXT every 3 years. Percentages in brackets are teachers leaving the profession due to mental illness

suggests. They may also be applying their best efforts to implement the required changes, almost at the limits of their physical and mental abilities. If so, is it necessary to push teachers harder to accomplish policy mandates rather than to empower them by improving their working conditions?

As Table 6.1 shows, recently, the number of teachers leaving the profession due to physical or mental illness has been on the rise compared with those who cite other reasons, such as taking up another job, educational or familial matters, or occupational problems. The chart also indicates an increase in the percentages of all teachers who are taking leave due to sickness (see Fig. 6.1). This trend has plateaued in recent years but is still high compared with a decade ago. Even considering the fact that the teaching workforce is aging, it is clear that the ways Japanese teachers are working may well be negatively affecting their health.

Besides the negative impacts on their health, adverse working conditions prevent teachers from adequately carrying out their professional responsibilities. Japanese teachers' low self-efficacy as revealed by TALIS must be considered in this light and explored in more depth from the firsthand experiences of teachers.

To this end, this study analyzed writings by a group of teachers where they described their perceptions of the gap between their ideals and the reality of their work. These teachers were participants in a license renewal course provided by a university in 2011. The author was in charge of one of the classes on contemporary issues of education and asked the teachers to reflect on the so-called reality gap ("Ideally what do you, as a teacher, want to do?" and "What prevents you from realizing your ideals?"). Having written down their responses to these questions, they spoke in groups reflecting further on this topic. During and after the discussion, they were given opportunities to revise their writings. After this session, in response to the author's invitation, almost all of the teachers (143 out of 147, i.e., 97.3%) volunteered to submit their writings for analysis.

6.2.2   Dissatisfaction

Three top themes emerged from the analysis: dissatisfaction, changing attributes of students, and restrictive national and local policy mandates. Dissatisfaction was by far the most often mentioned factor that the teachers said prevents them from

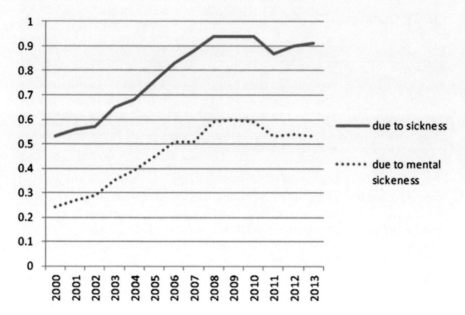

Fig. 6.1 Teachers taking sick leave (percentage of all teachers taking leave). (Sources: *Basic Statics on Schools* compiled by MEXT every year)

pursuing their professional responsibilities. Of these teachers, 77.6% wrote about it. Typical response examples are as follows:

- I wish I could do more preparing and improving my lessons, but I cannot have enough time to study the materials. Consequently, I cannot be satisfied with the quality of my teaching. I am desperate to teach better.
- I wish, with a smaller class of students, I could take more meticulous care of them, but I am too busy. I have to give lessons immediately after administrating tests, and I am busy marking tests and giving supplementary lessons. I have neither the time nor strength left to take care of my students. I also wish I had more time to mix with them, to be among them. In reality, I spend long hours at my desk doing paperwork. In my school, every teacher has a personal computer on their desk. Ironically, as a result, we are always tied to the desk and separated from the students.
- I want to practice more of things like learning by experience and activities in my classes. I want to use student-centered learning. I want to make my teaching more engaging and inspiring so that every student can understand deeply, but I simply can't because I do not have enough time. On the contrary, I am always hurrying up my students. I feel sad.

As these writings illustrate, dissatisfaction and intensified work are not just impacting their health but are also deteriorating the quality of education that they can provide. To truly ensure authentic teaching and development for all students, teacher work hours need to be reorganized both in terms of total hours and the composition of what type of work they do within those hours. Although they work well beyond the statutory 40 h per week, Japanese teachers are only granted a small amount of overtime pay (4% of the regular pay) based on a "comprehensive evaluation" of their work hours. It is true that teachers volunteer to work for such long hours, but they are not content with the ways in which they are working. The teachers quoted above want to spend more time preparing lessons, studying materials, and being with their students. The discrepancies between how they want to spend their time and how they actually spend it are very likely related to their low levels of self-efficacy and job satisfaction recorded by TALIS.

6.2.3   Changing Attributes of Students

After dissatisfaction, the second most often mentioned factor attributed to the reality gap was the changing attributes of students. Of the participating teachers, 23.8% identified it to be a kind of hurdle for successfully teaching and instructing to their satisfaction. Typical comments are as follows:

- I can see a bipolarization among students. Some students are eager to learn. They move steadily, and indeed they learn much. Other students are distracted from learning and consequently fail to learn. I see this gap widening year by year. I feel it is hindering my efforts.
- In elementary school, students are supposed to learn basic academic knowledge and skills, but some of them are not ready to do even this work. They simply fail to gain basic living habits. They don't eat regularly. They don't sleep well. As a result, they are distracted in class. Other students are hyperactive and hang around after class. I am concerned that these students are not properly cared for by their parents.

The bipolarization mentioned by one of these teachers confirms what Kariya (2001) called the "incentive divide." The point of this concept is that the socioeconomic status of the family affects students' academic achievements because it differentiates their incentive to learn. Disadvantages in family background have adverse effects on students' willingness to learn and learning outcomes. Despite the image of a rich and equal society, Japanese society now contains significant segments of deprived populations. As of 2013, the relative poverty rate in Japan was 13.6%, marking the highest recorded since 1985. For reference, the average rate for the other OECD countries and regions was 11.3% in 2010. Poverty particularly afflicts children and adolescents. The relative poverty rate for children under 18 years has been increasing over the last three decades, and it reached 16.3% in 2012, well above the average rate for the OECD countries and regions. The same rate for children reared in households supported by a single adult was 54.6% in the same year, the highest in the OECD countries and regions (Naikakufu 2015). Accordingly, the number of elementary and junior high school students who receive financial assistance for attending school has also increased from 6.1% in 1995 to

15.64% in 2012 (Naikakufu 2015). Over the years, the number of reported incidents of child abuse has also risen dramatically from 2722 reports in 1995 to 66,701 in 2012 (Koseirodosho 2015). Recently, child poverty and its related issues have drawn attention not just at home but also abroad. In June 2013, the act on measurements to counter child poverty was enacted. The Committee on the Rights of the Child (2010), a body that monitors the implementation of the United Nations Convention on the Rights of the Child by member states, has expressed deep concern for the increasing number of Japanese children in poor living conditions, including child–parent relations, and how they have been deteriorating, which has negative effects on a child's emotional and psychological well-being. Children in such disadvantaged living conditions bring these negative effects to school. As suggested by the teacher comments, these changing student attributes are making it difficult for some teachers to fulfil their professional responsibilities.

6.2.4 Restrictive National and Local Policy Mandates

The third most often mentioned factor contributing to the gap between teacher ideals and reality was restrictive national and local policy mandates. 21.6% of teachers wrote about it. The following comments reveal the teachers' thoughts:

- Students will discover what they want to learn about, what they want to inquire about spontaneously, and then they will actually discover something. In doing so, they will actually acquire the knowledge and skills that they need. My ideal is to encourage this type of learning in classrooms. In reality, however, I am desperate not to be behind schedule and just deliver the required things to students. The local board of education and the school direct me on how I should teach. They also set goals for how much students learn measured by tests. These policies drive me, leaving me little room to pursue what I would ideally like to do.

This particular teacher wrote about dissatisfaction as many of the teachers did. However, for her, very restrictive policy mandates are the root cause of the dissatisfaction. As indicated by the last sentence in her comments, policy mandates decrease teacher self-efficacy and occupational satisfaction. Furthermore, very restrictive policy mandates coupled with dissatisfaction may be contributing to the deskilling of teachers. Such restrictions leave little discretion for teachers to study and try other ways of instruction and assessment than those designated by authorities. Dissatisfied teachers have no other choice than to rely on lesson plans and tests developed elsewhere, thus reducing the room for discretion further. Indeed, according to the TALIS results, Japanese teachers are far less likely to develop and implement their own methods of assessment; only 29.1% of them do so, while on average, 67.9% of teachers in other nations and regions who participated in the international survey do so. In recent years, an increasing number of local authorities, both prefectural and municipal, have implemented their own educational achievement tests. Often, the creation of the tests is contracted out to the educational industry along with the scoring and analysis of the tests. While this procedure can help reduce the workload on teachers, it may deskill them (Katsuno 2014). TALIS also shows that Japanese head teachers report less discretion granted to schools for selecting textbooks and other educational materials compared with their counterparts abroad.

The teachers in this study confirm that test accountability is harming the professional autonomy and mentality of teachers. Public perceptions that academic standards in Japanese schools have declined helped MEXT introduce national testing in 2007. All students from the last grades of both elementary and junior high schools that are run by national and local governments take these tests in mathematics and Japanese annually and in science every 3 years. Increasing numbers of local education authorities and schools now set targets for student performance measured by these tests. Some of them publish authoritative guidance that elaborates on how teachers should teach to reach the targets. In this context, individual teachers are also supposed to set targets for student achievement, which comprises part of the teacher's own performance evaluation (Katsuno 2010).

The recent move to testing accountability is a result of the politicization of education. The more widespread public concerns over the issues of bullying, violence, and suicide, as well as low achievement, have become more interesting and engaging to local policymakers running local schools. While the politicization can help effectively resolve some issues, it very likely promotes the policies that appeal to the general interests of voters and produces outcomes that can be clearly presented, such as school choice, tests, and publication of school test results. Indeed, some local governments publicly announce local test results by school. Very often in these cases, prefectural governors or municipal mayors, in collaboration with like-minded local politicians, enforce policies against the will of education authority officers and school teachers. They have also urged MEXT to change its non-publishing policy. In 2014, MEXT finally compromised. It allowed local governments to publish the national test results by school, if accompanied by plans on how to improve the results. In 2014, the politicization of education also led to a comprehensive restructuring of local educational governance with the effect that prefectural governors and municipal mayors now hold stronger power over educational policy. This echoes the development of more mayoral control seen in American cities. The educational mayors also very likely pursue policies that hold schools and teachers accountable for test results, but according to the available evidence, it is questionable whether the policies have produced the intended effects. On the contrary, negative effects have been reported, such as the demoralization of teachers, the narrowing of curricular scope, and the loss of creativity in teaching (teaching to the test) (Ravitch 2011).

In Japan too, national tests, local tests, and the related accountability policies have been implemented supposedly to ensure quality education. However, according to a recent survey conducted by an independent panel of learned people, called "The Committee of Ten on Japanese Education" [*Nihon no Kyoiku wo Kangaeru Junin Iinkai*], a majority (66.5%) of teachers approached through the Internet felt pressured to raise student achievements. 75.5% of the same teachers expressed perceptions that they are under tighter control since the introduction and implementation of national testing (Asahi Shimbun Digital 2015).

6.3 Teacher Quality

6.3.1 Problematized Teacher Quality

To ensure quality in education, both the working conditions of teachers and teacher quality matter. The last section reviewed issues related to the conditions that teachers work in, and an argument was made that such conditions should be considered more seriously and carefully. In this section, the focus moves on to policies that MEXT has been pursuing in recent years to address teacher quality.

On balance, in Japan, the institutional framework of teacher education was relatively stable until the 1980s. Initial teacher education was implemented based on a tenet of "openness," established by postwar reformers with the goal to democratize, decentralize, and liberalize education (Horio 1994; Kaigo 1971). These reformers deeply regretted the way education in the past had been so strongly influenced by nationalism, patriotism, and imperialism. They regarded academic freedom as a necessary condition for liberating education from political and administrative control. The particular tenet of "openness" that was a corollary of academic freedom set out that any university or college should be able to engage in preparing teachers as long as it could provide quality education for both subject and pedagogical matters.

Thus, general universities and colleges, as well as purpose-built institutions, began providing teacher training courses, even though few of them could afford a sufficient number of teacher education specialists to adequately educate teachers. They simply did not have the personnel or material resources required to provide quality training for prospective teachers. Meanwhile, the demand for teachers continued to increase as birth rates rose along with school enrolment from the 1950s to the 1970s (Yamasaki 1997). General universities and colleges engaged in initial teacher education did play a significant role in meeting the rising demand for teachers, even though they failed to provide fully integrated initial teacher education programs. Still, the quality of new teachers had not been openly regarded as problematic. Generally, people trusted teachers. Since the era of postwar education reform, being a university or college graduate has been a minimum requirement to obtain a teaching license. Teachers were well-regarded elites in a society where only a minority of people had a higher education. The supply of teacher candidates (i.e., license holders) always surpassed the demand for teachers. Consequently, the recruitment of teachers was more or less competitive. This competitiveness, together with the high academic status of teachers, helped maintain teacher quality (Sato 2015). The national government's policy implemented in 1973 to maintain a higher salary for teachers compared with other general civil servants' salaries continued to attract well-qualified graduates to the teaching profession.

In the 1980s, the increase in demand for teachers stabilized (Yamasaki 1997), and teachers no longer enjoyed the same high academic status as before as more people acquired a higher education. Japanese society's participation rate in higher education was 10.1% in 1955 and by 1975 had increased to 38.4%. At the same time, public awareness of educational issues increased, such as prolonged student truancy, bullying, and violence in schools. These problems were taken to imply teacher incompetence, as well as school malfunctions. These perceptions caused policymakers to begin to address teacher quality in terms of practical competence. Indeed, by the late 1980s, the Ministry of Education began to frame teacher quality using the phrase "practical competence for instruction."

6.3.2   Policy Development

In 1987, the Council on Educational Personnel Training, an advisory body reporting to the Minister of Education, officially demanded that a practical competence for instruction be developed. There were other demands for cultivating other qualities and abilities in prospective teachers, such as a sense of mission for teaching, a deep understanding of human development, a pedagogical love for children and students, sound knowledge about the content to be taught, and an understanding of a wide and rich culture. By 1989, this pronounced emphasis on practicality effectively led to changes in teacher education, including the introduction of induction programs for newly hired teachers.

About 10 years later, in 1997, the Council again articulated the qualities and abilities that it wanted teachers to develop, and these qualities and abilities were categorized as follows:

- The qualities and abilities to act from a global perspective
- The qualities and abilities to live as a citizen in a changing society
- The qualities and abilities to carry out the work of a teacher

While this articulation included the need for teachers to develop personal attributes and general culture, it continued to emphasize a practical competence to instruct and lead students. Indeed, the council emphasized the practical rather than theoretical side of teaching and proposed that initial teacher education programs at universities and colleges should be reorganized to teach these subjects and to train teachers on how to communicate with students. It also made a proposal to extend the period of the practicum experience. All of these proposals were enacted and implemented.

In 2000, the Council on Educational Personnel Training merged with the Central Council for Education and continued to formulate teacher professional competences and requirements for more general qualities and abilities. In 2006, the Council proposed several significant changes to teacher education, notably the introduction of a teaching license renewal system and the establishment of professional schools for teacher education.

Introduced in 2009 to ensure that teachers continuously update their professional knowledge and skills, the teaching license renewal system requires teachers to complete a set of designated courses every 10 years in order to renew their licenses. Before the introduction of this system, licenses were granted without any terms of validation. MEXT broadly defines the content of the courses. It states that teachers will spend 12 h learning about teaching in general, child or adolescent development, and recent education policies. They will also be required to spend 18 h on acquiring more specific knowledge and skills about the subject that they teach, guidance, and more. Only universities and other teacher training institutions that are accredited by MEXT can provide these courses.

Professional schools for teacher education have been existing since 2008 to address the need to improve graduate teacher education programs. These schools educate both prospective and practicing teachers, thus providing both initial education and continuing education at the graduate level. Before the introduction of these professional schools for teachers, graduate teacher education programs were provided by two types of institutions: graduate schools of arts and sciences and graduate schools of education. Graduate schools of arts and sciences impart advanced content knowledge in particular fields to prospective teachers, but they do not provide pedagogical training. On the other hand, graduate schools of education do educate students on teaching methods or pedagogy, but critics contend that their programs are very theoretical. To redress these shortcomings, professional schools for teacher education are supposed to provide programs that can better integrate theory and practice. The curriculum is composed of these five common areas in addition to elective subjects: (1) design and implementation of curriculum, (2) practical methods to teach subjects, (3) guidance and counseling, (4) classroom and school management, and (5) schooling and teaching. Obviously, practicality is emphasized in the curriculum. Practical teaching methods such as case methods, lesson observation and analysis, and fieldwork are also supposed to be used. Students must earn no less than 10 credits for school practicum out of the 45 required for completion of the program. Furthermore, MEXT requires that clinical tutors who have significant experience in the field and high practical abilities should compose no less than 40% of the entire faculty.

The introduction of professional schools for teacher education was a breakthrough in graduate teacher education, but it did not change the licensure system. To obtain a license, prospective teachers are required to take teacher preparation courses normally related to the subjects they will teach in addition to their undergraduate degree courses in arts and sciences. Professional schools for teacher education provide professional master's degrees in education and advanced licenses for teaching. Advanced licenses are granted to students who have successfully completed graduate courses either in arts and sciences or education. Even today, professional schools for teacher education are not the sole providers of graduate teacher education.

In 2007, the Central Council for Education proposed to upgrade initial teacher education programs to the graduate level. Following the examples of other countries, notably Finland, the Council intended to extend the minimum period of teacher preparation from 4 to 5 or 6 years to professionalize teachers. This proposal drew criticism. Some critics argued that such a prolonged period of teacher preparation would cause students to incur significant costs, which could consequently lead to a decrease in the number of prospective teachers (Kita and Miura 2010). The change of the government in 2009 from Democratic to Liberal Democratic also contributed to the failure to enact the proposal. However, the need to professionalize teachers through graduate programs has since been increasingly recognized. In 2013, MEXT asked national university corporations to convert their graduate schools of education into professional schools for teacher education, expressing an official preference for practicality over theory in teacher education.

6.3.3 Practicality As a Policy Driver

As this brief review suggests, concern regarding practicality has been a driving force in teacher education policy over the last few decades. Sensational incidents, such as violence, bullying, suicides, classroom breakdowns, and more recently, the alleged decline in academic achievement, have fueled the impetus of this concern. Teachers have often been arbitrarily blamed for their inability to effectively deal with these types of incidences and problems. The concern has given cause to a series of new policy initiatives in teacher education, such as induction programs, the teaching license renewal system, professional schools for teacher education, and others.

A problem with this policy development is that practicality is not well defined (Yoshioka and Yagi 2007). Practicality as a policy driver is reactive, and as a concept on which to judge teaching ability, it is not well grounded in robust research on how a teacher effectively helps students learn and develop. Practicality has been studied in education research in terms of practical knowledge, practical wisdom, and practical inquiry of teachers. Overall, following the seminal work of Schwab (1971), it is generally understood that practicality requires deliberation, high-order thinking, and decision-making in complex contexts, and thus, it is a moral as well as rational process (Calderhead 1989). This implies that practicality is much more than just performing given tasks effectively.

Despite (or due to) its vague conceptualization, practicality has been legitimizing intervention in teacher education. As already stated, following the recommendations of the Council on Educational Personnel Training Council in 1987, MEXT revised the laws and regulations regarding initial teacher education programs so that prospective teachers could learn more about pedagogical matters. Since then, reforms with the same intention and effects have been repeated. This development opens up possibilities to improve the curriculum by promoting individual and institutional reflection on what and how prospective teachers should learn. However, general universities and colleges have found this emphasis on the pedagogical side of teaching difficult to cope with, considering their lack of resources. Furthermore, MEXT has taken to using its accreditation process to tighten its control over the initial teacher education curriculum that is provided by individual institutions, consequently leaving little room for the providers to develop original programs (Katsuno 2006; Yoshioka and Yagi 2007). There is a need to examine whether the emphasis on practicality has led to the enrichment or stereotyping of programs and prospective teachers' learning experiences.

Since the teaching license renewal system was recommended by the Central Council for Education in 2006 and implemented in 2009, critics have repeatedly identified the possibilities of arbitrarily dismissing teachers (Kubo 2007; Tsuchiya 2008). The concern about the increase in the instability of employment is justified, although only a very few teachers have been refused license renewal thus far. Another problem is again concern with the lack of well-defined criteria for evaluating eligibility for teaching jobs (Tsuchiya 2008). Although this system can provide opportunities in professional learning to reflect on teaching and updating knowledge and skills (Akiba 2013), they are still subject to the official procedures that teachers are supposed to undergo to continue teaching. Without proper criteria or standards for teacher quality, any decision on renewal is arbitrary. Simultaneously, as stated above, MEXT sets the framework and content of renewal courses, and thus, it can more or less prescribe what teachers should know and be able to do. In a similar vein, under the name of practicality, MEXT also can exercise strong control over the provision of professional schools for teacher education through accreditation, evaluation, and resource allocation.

It should be noted that practicality has increasingly come to be conceived of as the delivery of the Course of Study, what policymakers want teachers to do. Policymakers proclaim their intention that practicality throughout teacher education and training should be emphasized more. Their assumption is that university and colleges are not ready to provide prospective teachers with practically useful knowledge and skills unless forced to do so and that practicing teachers are not keen on updating their practical knowledge and skills unless forced to do so. However, policy intervention addressing teacher quality based on these perceptions may well threaten both the professional autonomy of teachers and the institutional autonomy of universities and colleges that have been enshrined in Japan's teacher education system, with the consequence of causing serious damage to the quality of teaching and learning.

6.4 Conclusion

Recently, Japanese policymakers have come to like to see the body of knowledge for teachers more clearly defined regarding what they should know and be able to do in their jobs, including subject teaching and instruction, classroom management, and administrative work. MEXT has begun to consider articulating levels of professional competence that teachers should have gained by each stage of their careers from novice to veteran teacher status (Asahi Shimbun 2015). Some local boards of education have already published their own standards for teachers to promote professional development. MEXT intends to encourage this kind of policy and practice further by developing model standards.

Professional standards for teachers are needed, given the lack of a well-defined concept of practicality. Standards can help teachers rethink and improve their practice and can also improve the ways in which teachers are selected, evaluated, promoted, and rewarded. They also can help universities and colleges, including recently introduced professional schools for teacher education, develop original and effective programs. For example, the standards developed by the National Board for Professional Teaching Standards in the USA are grounded in the best available research on effective teaching and are prepared by the teaching profession in partnership with other educators, researchers, and members of the public, hence, contributing to the enhancement of teacher professionalism (Darling-Hammond et al. 1999). However, professional standards of questionable quality can harm teaching as a profession. It should also be noted that standards can become a powerful control lever over teachers by aligning their practices to what policymakers want them to do (i.e., policy goals), with the consequence of reducing teacher autonomy. Furthermore, it is easy for teachers to be disempowered unless they play a significant role in defining and implementing the standards (Down 2012).

The move to articulating professional standards in Japan needs to be carefully monitored in a broader policy context with regard to professionalizing teaching. As stated earlier, intensified workloads leave teachers with less professional autonomy concerning their teaching content and pedagogy. For professional standards to contribute to professionalizing teaching, related policies should be aligned in their goals and effects. Part of this policy alignment process should include a much stronger focus on improving the working conditions of teachers, such as class size reduction, the ratio of the number of students to teachers, and, in particular, providing time for reflection on teaching and understanding students from a socioeconomic point of view. Finally, restrictive policies must be identified and eliminated to advance teaching as a profession.

References

Akiba, M. (2013). Teacher license renewal policy in Japan. In M. Akiba (Ed.), *Teacher reforms around the world: Implementaions and outcomes* (pp. 123–146). Bingley: Emerald.

Asahi Shimbun. (2014a, June 24). *Kocho shigoto ni manzoku saitei: OECD kokusai kyoin chosa* [Our headteachers are the least content with their work, the OECD international teacher survey reveals] (p. 35).

Asahi Shimbun. (2014b, June 24). *Nihon no sensei jishin saitei: OECD chugakko kyoin chosa: Kinmu jikan ha saicho* [OECD survey reveals that Japan's teachers are the least confident but they work the longest] (p. 2).

Asahi Shimbun. (2015, May 6). *Kyouin noryoku kojo he shihyou kento: Monkasho shin shido yoryo ni taio* [MEXT considers the standards for improving teachers' abilities in accordance with new Course of Study] (p. 1).

Asahi Shimbun Digital. (2015, July 2). *Gakuryoku chosa kyoin ni atsuryoku? Kyoikugakusha ra ga kyoin 1044 nin chosa* [Do achievement tests pressurize teachers? Educationalists and others surveyed 1044 teachers].

Barber, M., & Mourshed, M. (2007). *How the world's best-performing school systems come out on top*. London: Mckinsey & Company.

Calderhead, J. (1989). Reflective teaching and teacher education. *Teaching and Teacher Education, 5*(1), 43–51.

Darling-Hammond, L., Wise, A. E., & Klein, S. P. (1999). *A license to teach: Raising standards for teaching*. San Francisco: Jossey-Bass.

Down, B. (2012). Reconceptualising teacher standards: Authentic, critical and creative. In B. Down & J. Smyth (Eds.), *Critical voices in teacher education: Teaching for social justice in conservative times* (pp. 63–80). Dordrecht: Springer.

Horio, T. (1994). *Educational thought and ideology in modern Japan: State authority and intellectual freedom* (S. Platzer, Trans.). Tokyo: University of Tokyo Press.

ILO. (2012). *Joint ILO-UNESCO Committee of experts on the application of the recommendations concerning teaching personnel* (Geneva, 8–12 October 2012). Geneva: International Labour Office.

Kaigo, T. (1971). *Kyoin yosei* [Initial teacher education]. Tokyo: University of Tokyo Press.

Kariya, T. (2001). *Kaisoka nihon to kyoiku kiki: Hubyodo saiseisan kara iyoku kakusa shakai he* [Stratified Japan and educational crisis: Inequality reproduction and incentive divide]. Tokyo: Toshindo.

Katsuno, M. (2006). Kyoshokukatei no nintei to hyoka wo meguru saikin no seisaku ni tsuite [On recent policies regarding accreditation and evaluation of initial teacher education programmes]. *Nihon Kyoshi Kyouiku Gakkai Nenpo* [Annual Bulletin of the Japanese Society for the Study on Teacher Education], *15*, 26–32.

Katsuno, M. (2010). Teacher evaluation in Japanese schools: An examination from a micro-political or relational viewpoint. *Journal of Education Policy, 25*(3), 293–307.

Katsuno, M. (2014). Kyouiku no gabanasu kaikaku to kyosi no senmonshokusei [The educational governance reform and teacher professionalism]. *Kyoiku Ho Gakkai Nenpo* [Education Law Review], *43*, 72–80.

Kita, A., & Miura, T. (2010). *Menkyo koshinsei deha kyosi ha sodatanai: Kyosi kyouiku kaikaku heno teigen* [Teaching license renewal system does not develop teachers: Proposals for reforming teacher education]. Tokyo: Iwanami Shoten.

Koseirodosho. (2015). *Jido gyakutai taisaku no genjo to kongo no hokosei* [Present measures to counter child abuses and their future directions]. Tokyo: Author.

Kubo, F. (2007). Menkyo koshinsei to genshoku kenshu kaikaku [The teacher certification renewal system and the reforms of the professional development system]. *Nihon Kyoshi Kyouiku Gakkai Nenpo* [Annual Bulletin of the Japanese Society for the Study on Teacher Education], *16*, 25–32.

Mainichi Shimbun. (2014, June 24). *Kokusai kyoin shido kankyo chosa: Sekai no chugaku OECD chosa, Nihon no kyoin kinmujikan saicho, shu 53.9 jikan, bukatsu de jimu de* [TALIS finds Japan's junior high school teachers work the longest, 53.9 hours per week, spending many hours on supervision of club activities and administrative work] (p. 1).

Monbukagakusho. (2012). *Kyoshokuin teisu gaizen no hitsuyosei* [The nened to increase teacher places]. Tokyo: Author Retrieved from http://www.mext.go.jp/component/a_menu/education/micro_detail/__icsFiles/afieldfile/2012/09/18/1325940_03.pdf.

Monbukagakusho. (2014). *OECD kokusai kyoin shido kankyo chosa (TALIS 2013) no pointo* [Important findings from the OECD International Teaching and Learning Survey]. Tokyo: Author Retrieved from http://www.mext.go.jp/component/b_menu/other/__icsFiles/afieldfile/2014/06/30/1349189_2.pdf

Naikakufu. (2015). *Heisei 27 nendo-ban kodomo seinen hakusho* [Whitepapers on children and adolescents 2015]. Tokyo: Author.

OECD. (Ed.). (2014a). *Education at a glance 2014: OECD indicators*. Pais: OECD Publishing.

OECD. (Ed.). (2014b). *TALIS 2013 results: An international perspective on teaching and learning*. Paris: OECD Publishing.

Ravitch, D. (2011). *The death and life of the great American school system: How testing and choice are undermining education*. New York: Basic Books.

Sato, M. (2015). *Snemonka toshite Kyosi wo Sodateru* [Developing teachers as a profession]. Tokyo: Iwanami Shoten.

Schwab, J. J. (1971). The practical: Arts of eclectic. *The School Review, 79*(4), 493–542. https://doi.org/10.2307/1084342.

Tsuchiya, M. (2008). Kyoin menkyo koshinseido no kento [Critical analysis of teaching license renewal system]. *Kyoiku Ho Gakkai Nenpo* [Education Law Review], *37*, 84–92.

United Nations. (2010). *The Committee on the Rights of the Child fifty-fourth session: Consideration of reports submitted by States parties under Article 44 of the Convention.* Retrieved from http://tbinternet.ohchr.org/_layouts/treatybodyexternal/Download.aspx?symbolno=CRC%2fC%2fJPN%2fCO%2f3&Lang=en

Yamasaki, H. (1997). *Kyoin saiyo no kako to mirai* [The past and future of teacher recruitment]. Tokyo: Tamagawa Daigaku Shuppanbu.

Yoshioka, M., & Yagi, H. (2007). Kyoin menkyo shikaku no genriteki kento: Jissenteki shidoryoku to senmonsei kijun wo megutte [Certification and qualification of teachers based on professional standards and "practical teaching ability": Some considerations]. *Nihon Kyoshi Kyouiku Gakkai Nenpo* [Annual Bulletin of the Japanese Society for the Study on Teacher Education], *16*, 38–54.

Chapter 7
Lesson Study

Yasuhiko Fujie

7.1 Introduction

Lesson Study, a form of research on teaching by teachers, creates learning opportunities for teachers. Lesson Study is a collaborative process in which teachers observe, analyze, and evaluate each other's actual classroom lessons mainly with the objective of improving their lessons. In a typical flow of Lesson Study, a classroom lesson is observed by other teachers, and this is followed by a conference in which the observers present their analyses and interpretations of lesson elements such as the teacher's and students' specific actions during the lesson, lesson content and teaching materials, learning style, and educational goals. The teacher who administered the lesson reflects on the lesson, his or her professional competencies, and other relevant matters. One cycle of Lesson Study is completed when both the observed and observer teachers apply findings from the conference to designing their respective future lessons. This indicates that Lesson Study serves as a learning opportunity for teachers, as it is said that teachers learn by example (Shulman 2004). Lesson Study in Japan is primarily characterized by its school-based organization. Defining Lesson Study as an organizational learning opportunity, we present in this chapter an overview of Lesson Study as practiced in Japan and explain its actual situation through the example of an elementary school.

Y. Fujie (✉)
Graduate School of Education, The University of Tokyo, Tokyo, Japan
e-mail: yfujie@p.u-tokyo.ac.jp

© Springer Nature Singapore Pte Ltd. 2019
Y. Kitamura et al. (eds.), *Education in Japan*, Education in the Asia-Pacific
Region: Issues, Concerns and Prospects 47,
https://doi.org/10.1007/978-981-13-2632-5_7

7.2   Present Situation Surrounding Lesson Study in Japan

Schools where organizational learning is conducted effectively share some characteristics with regard to Lesson Study. Firstly, in these schools, Lesson Study is placed at the heart of school administration. While schoolteachers' main occupation is administering lessons, they are also charged with myriad responsibilities including student guidance, communication with parents, and attendance at various meetings in and outside their schools. As for the role of school education in society, it is first and foremost the provision of an environment in which students can partake of deep learning. In this sense, it is only natural that Lesson Study should occupy the central place in school administration, since it urges teachers, who design the learning environment, to endeavor to improve themselves as professionals.

Secondly, in these schools, Lesson Study serves not as a process for teachers to learn about pedagogy, but as a process to design students' learning and reflect on their designing. Teachers are not merely required to improve their teaching skills; they must continue their day-to-day project of discerning and organizing the specific and individual classroom experiences of their students, who always remain unknown to them. To discern and organize students' learning experiences, teachers need to understand the students' learning in qualitative terms and interpret the uncertainties of the learning experiences positively. To this end, Lesson Study is expected to lead teachers to share a viewpoint for discerning students' learning experiences.

Thirdly, in schools with effective organizational learning, Lesson Study is viewed as a platform for collaborative learning by professionals. Unlike teaching skills, the professional qualities that enable teachers to engage in creative practices while negotiating a somewhat unstable and changeable situation as reflective practitioners and adaptable experts, the image of which has become generalized in recent years, cannot be improved through teachers' individual efforts alone. Teachers need to share their lesson experiences among themselves in a specifically created person-oriented environment in which they can visualize their teaching practices and recontextualization through the representations of their practices through students' learning. That is to say, in Japan, Lesson Study is premised on the formation of an organization that supports teachers' learning, that is, a learning community of professionals.

Let us now examine the trends in Lesson Study in Japan. The National Institute for Educational Policy Research (NIER) conducted a survey on the implementation of Lesson Study in schools, involving 705 public elementary schools, 665 public middle schools, 254 full-time general-track public high schools, and 77 full-time general-track private high schools (NIER 2011). The survey items included research theme selection, school-wide organization for in-house research, evaluation methods for instruction plans, the invitation of external instructors, daily instruction by the school principal, and visits by the educational supervisor of the board of education. Following is an overview of Lesson Policy in Japan based on the NIER report (NIER 2011).

The survey revealed the following about the implementation of Lesson Study in schools. Firstly, a school-wide organization was established for Lesson Study in 90.5% of the elementary schools, 79.1% of the middle schools, 26.8% of the public high schools, and 16.9% of the private high schools. There was a statistically significant correlation between the establishment of a school-wide Lesson Study organization and faculty communication in the middle schools. Secondly, Lesson Study was implemented following the selection of a single school-wide research theme in 98.7% of the elementary schools, 90.7% of the middle schools, 35% of the public high schools, and 20.8% of the private high schools. There was a statistically significant correlation between the selection of a uniform research theme for the entire school and lesson standards in the middle schools. Thirdly, a certain number of teachers were placed in charge of promoting Lesson Study in 94.4% of the elementary schools, 89.3% of the middle schools, 37.4% of the public high schools, and 18.2% of the private high schools. The teachers in charge of promoting Lesson Study had reduced teaching duties in 16.5% and 10.4% of these elementary and middle schools, respectively. To summarize these findings, the following can be stated: Almost all the elementary schools surveyed had a school-wide Lesson Study organization with a staff of teachers in charge, and Lesson Study was implemented on a uniform theme for each school. Comparing the elementary and middle schools in terms of survey responses under the same items, the elementary schools were far more involved in, and organized for, Lesson Study. In the middle schools, the school-wide Lesson Study organization impacted communication among the teachers positively, while the selection of a uniform theme led to qualitative improvement in lessons. It can be surmised that the more involved and organized the middle schools were for Lesson Study implementation, the more qualitative improvement was attained for their lessons.

The survey revealed the following about the structure of Lesson Study: Firstly, at all school levels, the most widely adopted Lesson Study structure at 99.3% of the elementary schools, 93.5% of the middle schools, 81.5% of the public high schools, and 72.7% of the private high schools consisted of the observation of a research lesson (lesson taught by a designated teacher, usually observed by all the other teachers) by several teachers, followed by a critical review. At the same time, in many high schools, (71.3% of the public high schools and 44.2% of the private high schools), teachers also observed one another's lessons on an "open lesson day" or during an "open lesson week." Secondly, with regard to teacher participation, in 72.1% of the elementary schools, all teachers taught lessons to be observed, while in many of the middle and high schools, teachers representing an academic subject or school year (grade) taught research lessons (46.9% of the middle schools, 47.3% of the public high schools, and 48.2% of the private high schools). To sum up, it can be said that Lesson Study is widely practiced regardless of school levels and types. However, just as expected, it is most actively carried out in elementary schools, and its practice diminishes as the school level advances. It is necessary to build or reinforce relationships among teachers that would enable teachers to observe and learn from each other's lessons in secondary education.

Based on all the NIER survey results, including those mentioned above, the characteristics of Lesson Study in Japan at each school level can be summarized as below (NIER 2011).

At the elementary school level, a statistically significant correlation was found between the four indicators of Lesson Study efficacy (faculty communication, lesson standards, academic performance compared with the local average, and academic performance compared with the national average, established based on statistical analysis using NIER's indicators of the school situation) and the following particulars of Lesson Study practice: (1) the establishment of a substructure or substructures under the school-wide Lesson Study organization, (2) the setting of individual research themes by teachers, (3) annual review and compilation of research results, (4) the adoption of an annual schedule drawn up in the previous school year, (5) the organization of an open lesson during a regulatory visit of the educational supervisor from the board of education, (6) the school principal's guidance on instruction plans, and (7) the educational supervisor's guidance on instruction plans. These particulars are actions that lead to lesson quality improvement, which in turn improves a school's quality.

At the middle school level, a statistically significant correlation was found between the same four indicators of school quality and the following particulars of Lesson Study practice: (1) the establishment of a school-wide Lesson Study organization, (2) the setting of a single school-wide research theme, (3) the examination of instruction plans by academic subject-specific groups of teachers, (4) the examination of instruction plans by the entire faculty, (5) the organization of advance lessons or model lessons, (6) the recording of lesson progression during a research lesson, and (7) the use of lesson records and video images during the conference after a research lesson. These particulars are organizational actions, which seem to influence school quality. It should be noted that all of these actions were also found in the elementary schools, which also showed a higher ratio of implementation than the middle schools.

With the elementary and middle schools combined, a statistically significant correlation was found between the indicators of school quality and the following: (1) the organization of a research meeting to present research results, (2) the implementation of research lessons by all teachers, and (3) the invitation of external lecturers. It can be said that the presentation of activities relating to daily lessons and Lesson Study to external parties has a part in improving school quality.

At the high school level, no significant correlation was found between the particulars of Lesson Study practice and the four indicators of school quality. The findings suggest that not only is Lesson Study less actively practiced at this school level but also Lesson Study is not implemented in a manner that leads to school quality improvement.

Among the findings presented above, let us focus our attention on one particular point: at the elementary school level, there was a significant correlation between school quality improvement and the setting of individual research themes by teachers. Basically, it is considered preferable to implement Lesson Study first by adopting a school-wide research theme and then establishing a school-wide organization to operate Lesson Study on an annual basis, followed by the adoption of sub-themes and the formation of sub-organizations as deemed necessary in view of each school's objectives and challenges. The school-wide implementation of Lesson Study can be hindered by teachers' individual research themes. They are necessary, however, because it is essential that individual teachers actively take part in educational activities not only as members of an organization but also as autonomous professionals. This is especially true in consideration of the Japanese school situation in which relatively frequent change of school is an institutionalized part of a teacher's career. Teachers' growth as professionals is largely supported by the learning opportunities that materialize in teachers' reflection on their own classroom lessons and peer support for that reflection (Sato 2015). Their learning is premised on their autonomy as professionals. School must therefore function as communities that enable teachers to mutually respect and learn from each other while sharing a sense of belonging and being assured that the opportunity for their individual professional development is not compromised.

In this regard, the conceptual diagram by Shulman et al. is highly indicative (Shulman and Shulman 2004). The elements in the inner cycle constitute individual-level learning. These elements interact with one another and are also closely connected with the elements in the outer cycle of community-level learning. What is important is at the core: individual and institutionalized reflection. The diagram indicates that individual and institutionalized reflection overlap. They are mutually complementary in that the former influences the latter and vice versa. Teachers must therefore set their individual research themes by linking them organically with the school-wide theme, without assuming that individual and organizational learning are independent of each other. This does not mean that teachers' individual themes must closely follow the school-wide research theme. It would be necessary, though, to carefully support teachers in their theme setting through workshop-type training so that their personal career development objectives and classroom realities surrounding their students can be harmoniously incorporated into their research themes. In the following section, we will examine the case of an elementary school in which a single school-wide research theme was adopted while the teachers set their individual themes (Fig. 7.1).

7.3 Case of an Elementary School

The school that we study here ("School X") is a public elementary school that was established about 15 years ago. It is located in a city accessible in about an hour by train from Tokyo, in a residential neighborhood that is calm despite being only about 500 meters from the beach, in a district developed a long time ago as a coastal resort. The school has 6 grades (school years), each with 2 classes, giving 12 classes in total. The school has a total student population of about 300.

Since its foundation, School X has pursued research on teaching principally based on teachers' individual themes. The reason for this practice is explained in the

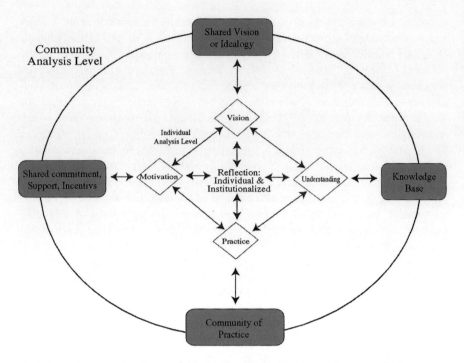

Fig. 7.1 Learning community at individual and institutional levels. (Shulman and Shulman 2004)

school's administration concept. It states that the ultimate purpose of Lesson Study is to improve individual teachers' ability. For an individual teacher to improve his or her intellect and general culture, teaching qualities, and expertise, it is necessary to share with other teachers the efforts made and difficulties encountered in the process of individual research and its results in a formal and structured manner because each teacher has different convictions as a teacher, values regarding educational practices, and background experience. At School X, it is believed that it is essential for teachers to establish themselves as individuals for their professional development as well as the formation of camaraderie among the teachers. Needless to say, the school also adopts school-wide research themes. They are always oriented toward achieving the "target image of the pupil," adopted by the school as the embodiment of its ultimate educational goals. This clearly differs from the majority of Japanese elementary schools that set their school-wide research themes in connection with specific academic subjects.

1. Multiple Learning Platforms for Teachers

School X provides its teachers with multiple learning platforms, as indicated in Table 7.1.

When organizing a research lesson, School X invites teachers from other schools in the same city to join its faculty. The grade-specific meeting is conducted in units of "grade blocs," which are explained below. This can be considered one of the two

Table 7.1 Learning platforms at School X

Research lesson	A teacher administers a lesson, which is observed by the other teachers. All the teachers eventually take turns in teaching a research lesson
	Teachers in the other schools in the same city are invited for collaborative learning
Grade-bloc meeting	Conducted by the teachers of the grade bloc (group of two adjoining grades) to which a teacher assigned to a research lesson belongs, to collect views to present at the plenary meeting in preparation for the research lesson
Plenary meeting	Held to discuss teacher training planning, confirm its orientation, and summarize general relevant matters to deepen the faculty's understanding about Lesson Study
In-house teacher training	Various teacher training programs are carried out as deemed appropriate in consideration of the situation surrounding teachers

pillars of this school's learning platforms for teachers, along with research lessons. The plenary meeting is held about five times a year to collectively examine and determine how research lessons should be carried out. Other in-house teacher training programs are organized about three times a year on themes that are deemed necessary on each of the occasions.

2. Teachers Learning Division

School X has a Teachers Learning Division, charged with the formulation of an annual in-house training plan based on the school administration plan established by the school principal. While the Teachers Learning Division is responsible for the management of the four learning platforms listed above and coordination for each research lesson, the Division is not merely a leader, for it also represents model learning teachers.

The Teachers Learning Division has five members who are all teachers with their respective homeroom classes. They are selected roughly evenly from the three grade blocs: the low-grade bloc (first and second grades), the middle-grade bloc (third and fourth grades), and the high-grade bloc (the fifth and sixth grades). Their appointment as members of the Division can be considered reasonable in that all of them have a relatively short teaching experience and are highly motivated at the individual level and their learning results are likely to be easily visible.

At the outset of each academic year, the Teachers Learning Division distributes a written statement of the school's annual teacher training policy to the entire faculty. The one we studied explains the significance of the school's in-house teacher training system centering on research lessons as follows:

Our in-house teacher training system centering on research lessons is intended for teachers to learn. A teacher undertaking a research lesson is expected to improve, through this experience, his or her lesson delivery ability and teaching skills, learn to better understand student behavior, and acquire creative lesson design competences based on his or her expertise. The other teachers who observe the research lesson are expected to learn how to observe a lesson while cultivating their ability to discern student learning (capture the moments when pupils make connections among themselves and with teaching materials and deepen their understanding) and share composed and confident classroom lesson styles. Furthermore, both the observed and observer teachers can acquire an attitude for learning through research on educational materials and solidify the basics for lesson design.

In our Lesson Study, all the teachers are involved in research, acquiring and improving various abilities in pursuit of our target image of the pupil. We aim at the kind of Lesson Study that we can pursue while enjoying the process, sharing our views, ideas, and feelings among ourselves regardless of our age and experience, and that prompts us to feel really glad that we have done it.

In this document, Lesson Study is clearly defined as a platform for teachers' learning. The document stipulates the objectives of this learning program: the acquisition of "creative lesson design competences" for the teacher who undertakes the research lesson; the cultivation of the "ability to discern student learning," learning "how to observe a lesson," and sharing "composed and confident classroom lesson styles" for the observer teachers; and the acquisition of an "attitude for learning through research on educational materials" for both. Finally, the document recalls the fundamental role of school education in society by referring to the school's "target image of the pupil" as the realization of its educational goals manifested in its students. It is suggested that schools can fulfill their role in society when teachers' learning is pursued successfully.

A teacher's learning is centered around reflection on his or her lesson experiences (Sakamoto and Akita 2008). The reflection in this context is a process that involves reviewing factual matter and reexamining one's framework for perception and thought. In Lesson Study, a teacher pursues this process in collaboration with other teachers. In this process, a teacher acquires a new way of looking at things, a point view of "the other," leading to reconstructing the framework for perceiving lessons, which is premised on each individual teacher's views on lessons, learning, and learners. It is for this reason that the framework is individualized. According to the social constructionist theory of learning that respects differences among the members of a group and seeks the possibility of attaining greater consistency and consensus formation in dialogue and interaction, individuality is the very starting point for learning. Why? Sakamoto and Akita (2008), who research teachers' collaborative learning, attempt to explain this with the concept of "problematizing." Problematizing refers to the process of questioning anew what has come to be regarded as self-evident. For example, for a teacher, how to view classroom lessons and contemplate them might have become self-evident. A teacher can then use reflection to "problematize" these preconceived ideas. Furthermore, in collaborative reflection, each teacher comes into contact with the way other teachers view lessons, thus being led to reexamine, expand or modify their own views of lessons, and acquire new ones. At School X, the process of school-wide Lesson Study begins with the explicit written communication of its objectives to the whole faculty at the beginning of each academic year. Once the annual Lesson Study policy is proposed and approved in a faculty meeting in early April (the first month of the school year in Japan), a year-long plan is drawn up as summarized in Table 7.2.

Table 7.2 Lesson Study schedule (April–May, excerpt)

Date	Activity	Focus/content	Description
April 8	Faculty meeting	Policy proposal	
April 11	Faculty meeting	Annual plan proposal	Annual plan and schedule are confirmed
April 15	Grade-bloc meeting	Call for research lesson teachers	Call for volunteers for monthly research lessons
April 22	Grade-bloc meeting	Selection of research lesson teachers	Coordination of candidate research lesson teacher's schedule by grade bloc → research lesson teachers are selected for regular in-house teacher training
April 27	Plenary meeting	Sharing of understanding	Training policy and content are confirmed
May 1	Grade-bloc meeting	Selection of individual themes	Compilation and reporting by grade bloc of "individual research record (1)" (to be submitted to Teachers Learning (TL) Division)
		Study of research lesson #1	
May 7	TL Division meeting	Study of instruction plan for research lesson #1	Study of instruction plan submitted by grade-bloc meeting
May 11	Grade-bloc meeting	Study of research lesson #1	Further study by grade bloc if necessary after study by TL Division
May 15	Research lesson #1	6th-grade Science	5th period (open lesson) → Lesson Study conference
May 18	Grade-bloc meeting	Review meeting	Compilation of review meeting results by grade bloc
		Study of research lesson #2	Study of instruction plan for next research lesson in June
May 28	Two weeks after research lesson		Submission of "individual research record (2)" to TL Division
May 29	TL Division meeting	Study of instruction plan for research lesson #2	Study of instruction plan for research lesson #2 scheduled for June

While the above table only shows the early part of the academic year, it clearly illustrates how the schedule is drawn up in detail, on a daily basis. For well-organized in-house Lesson Study, a thorough yearlong plan and its execution according to schedule are important. Teachers usually have a large workload of numerous duties and are often called on to deal with unexpected incidents, for each of which they must reshuffle their priorities. It is therefore essential that Lesson Study activities be scheduled, not as all-time top priority, but in a manner that enables implementation in parallel with eventualities. In other words, Lesson Study should be positioned, not as a specific problem-solving project or action research, but as an integral part of regular operation (Wolf and Akita 2008). The research lesson cycle shown in Table 7.3 is the basic unit of an annual schedule.

Table 7.3 Research lesson cycle

	Grade-bloc meeting #1	Study of first draft of instruction plan
Two weeks before research lesson		Submission of revised instruction plan to TL Division
Following day	TL Division meeting	Study of instruction plan by TL Division, selection of moderator (person in charge)
	Grade-bloc meeting #2	Further study of instruction plan
One week before research lesson		Distribution of final instruction plan to entire faculty
	School-wide research week	Grade-bloc meeting if necessary
Research lesson	Research lesson	Research lesson followed by conference
Following day	Grade-bloc meeting #3	Review of research lesson (*If necessary, other grade blocs also hold a meeting to compile views)
Two weeks after research lesson		Submission of "individual research record (2)" to TL Division
Faculty meeting, debriefing		Distribution of a compilation of "individual research record (2)" and Lesson Study newsletter

School X's Lesson Study is supported by the assured repetition of this cycle. The cycle is routinized in that a pattern of actions following the cycle is regularly repeated. The routinization controls actions by persons involved, whose integration constitutes in turn the routine, which is, so to speak, a cultural product of the group of persons involved. The existence of the routine thus makes Lesson Study also part of the school's culture.

Once the annual plan is drawn up, a call for volunteers is made for research lessons, and assignment begins. While this concerns teachers who will teach research lessons, all the other teachers will also be involved in the research lessons in one way or another. Since not all teachers willingly volunteer to undertake a research lesson, the Teachers Learning Division sends out a message, an excerpt of which is cited below, to entice teachers. For teachers, teaching an open lesson for others to observe is tantamount to exposing themselves to their critical eyes, and teachers are often tempted to avoid the experience. In view of this, the message is focused on the advantages of teaching a research lesson for the teacher, in an attempt to create an environment in which teachers can feel at ease about the experience:

"Advantages of teaching an open research lesson"

"I can't stand the idea of teaching in front of my colleagues!" "A research lesson requires so much preparation …" So, "I don't want to do an open lesson!" … we think we can almost hear you murmuring these days.
But why don't you try to think about it differently?
Teaching in front of your colleagues means that you can get advice from many people about your teaching, learning what improvements are needed and finding out what you are doing right or wrong in the classroom.

> It is true that a research lesson requires a lot of preparation. But this also means that you can enrich your experience in lesson design (essential for a quality lesson) through your research on educational materials.

We have looked at School X's Lesson Study with a focus on the Teachers Learning Division's activities. The Division also introduced various material and institutional instruments to construct the school's Lesson Study framework, while at the same time contributing to developing the school's organizational culture through the sharing of the framework.

3. Material and Institutional Instruments

One material instrument that the Teachers Learning Division has introduced into School X is a format for drafting an instruction plan. An instruction plan is drawn up for Lesson Study by the teacher assigned to administer the research lesson. It is composed of the following elements: (1) basic information such as the date, grade, subject, unit, and theme of the research lesson, (2) the situation surrounding the pupils in the class attending the research lesson, (3) the objectives and plan of the unit that includes the research lesson and criteria for evaluation, and (4) the objectives of the lesson held as research lesson, an evaluation plan, and a lesson development plan. These elements are usually found in a lesson plan that is in general use in Japan, although there is no nationwide standardized lesson plan format, and most schools have an arbitrary format. School X, on the other hand, has adopted a unified model format to be used by all the teachers in writing their instruction plans. This is not an attempt to unify their lesson styles. The teachers are allowed to have their own lesson styles. The purpose of introducing a uniform format for the instruction plan is to promote the teachers' learning. An instruction plan is not a simple lesson plan; it comprises a lesson plan, as well as an observation of the pupils and the results of research on the educational materials—in other words, a written statement of the research lesson teacher's professional convictions through his or her views on pupils, educational materials, and classroom lessons, to be disclosed to others. As the teacher writes down the pupils' situation and aspects of research on educational materials, the teacher generates knowledge about the pupils and educational materials and how they should be brought into contact, that is, knowledge about the educational materials in the realistic context of an anticipated lesson (pedagogical content knowledge). On the other hand, observer teachers attend the research lesson with the knowledge of the research lesson teacher's views and convictions as expressed in the instruction plan. For the observers, such knowledge is a semi-contextualized representation of the research lesson teacher's educational practice, which should lead the observers to complete the remainder of contextualization by observing the actual lesson and based on their own experience. In a document distributed to the teachers, School X provides the following pointers for the use of instruction plans:

- The research lesson teacher must clearly indicate his or her "wishes" and "devices" in the instruction plan. Any reference documents and materials consulted in preparation for the research lesson must be mentioned in the instruction plan to share the information with the observers.

- Copies of the final version of the instruction plan must be distributed to the observers at least 1 week before the research lesson. At the same time, the textbook and worksheets to be used in the research lesson, seating chart, lesson schedule, etc. must also be put together for distribution.

The "wishes" are not lesson aims; they express the teacher's values attributed to the pupils' learning. They express, so to speak, the teacher's self-realization objectives as reflected in the pupils' learning because the wishes describe how the teacher wants the pupils to develop through this learning experience and receive and respond to the educational materials. The term "devices" can be defined as "instruments prepared in advance to fulfill a specific purpose" (Kage 2008). Devices are characterized by their intentionality (including the developer's and user's designs and objectives), artificiality (man-made tool), and anteriority (prepared prior to use). One device can perform several functions: intellectually stimulating pupils to learn, orienting learning, and visualizing information necessary for learning. At School X, a final instruction plan, with "wishes" and "devices" clearly indicated, must be distributed to the observers at least 1 week before the research lesson, together with the textbook to be used, work sheets to be provided to the pupils, a classroom seating chart, a lesson schedule, etc.

The observer teachers are expected to come to the research lesson after having carefully read the instruction plan, thus grasping the research lesson teacher's viewpoint and intention. They are also expected to observe the lesson in consideration of the intention, "wishes," and other matters that can be learned from the instruction plan.

Regarding the open research lesson and subsequent conference and instruction plans and research records, the Teachers Learning Division has established sets of common rules for the entire faculty. The rules concerning the research lesson and conference include the following (an excerpt from a document distributed to the faculty):

- During a research lesson, the observers must try to discern the facts of learning, seeking out the moments when connections are made among the pupils, understanding is shared, and their learning is deepened.
- The conference following a research lesson begins with group discussions, in which participants engage in an active exchange, freely expressing their impressions, views, ideas, and questions.
- The research lesson teacher must circulate from one group to another and participate in the group discussions.
- The participants freely take notes of keywords, impressions, and so forth during the group discussions. Each group then writes the contents of its discussions on the whiteboard to inform the other groups.
- In the subsequent plenary discussion, the observer teachers provide the research lesson teacher with feedback on the facts of learning, centering on the connections

that the pupils made and their deepening of understanding, using what has been written on the whiteboard and based on the group discussions. The discussion must be based on these facts and cover how the lesson design and practice influenced learning, to contemplate what should be done to realize better learning.

- The moderator must serve as facilitator, creating an atmosphere that enables all participants to speak out with ease regardless of their age and experience.
- At the end of the meeting, the research lesson teacher speaks about what he or she has learned from the research lesson and conference and how to link it with future lessons and instruction.

The rules presented above indicate in a detailed manner what the observers should watch during the research lesson (moments of interactions among pupils, deepening of learning, and other aspects of learning in detail), how to organize a post-research lesson conference (group discussions followed by a plenary discussion), contents of discussion, and so forth.

In the group discussions, the observers share their impressions, views, and questions and exchange ideas. The contents of the discussions are written, thus visualized, on the whiteboard for all the participants in the subsequent plenary discussion. The participants then exchange their perceptions of the research lesson, that is, representations of a practice. Each representation is an interpretation of the actions of the teacher and pupils based on each observer's convictions, experience, and other factors. Through the discussions, the participants share with one another the path they took to arrive at their interpretations of what they observed. In the plenary discussion, the facts of learning that took place in the research lesson are communicated to the teacher, with a focus on the pupils' interactions and their deepening of understanding. Representations of the practice generated through observation, particularly those judged to be valid, and representations of past practices by the observers are integrated and presented to be shared by the entire faculty.

The teacher who undertook the research lesson participates in group discussions and listens to remarks by the group representatives during the plenary discussion. In addition to the teacher's views on the pupils and educational materials already evident in the instruction plan, the research lesson teacher further discloses other aspects of his or her lesson design, including decisions made on the spot and responses to changes in situation during the lesson, in a direct exchange with the observers. In the plenary meeting, the teacher receives the observers' representations of the practice in the form of the facts of the lesson.

The moderator (who should be a member of the Teachers Learning Division) works rather as a facilitator and tries to create an atmosphere conducive to carefree discussions. This is where the representations of the practice as perceived by the individuals, both the observers and the observed, are brought together. For this process to succeed, it is essential that the moderator serve as a meta-observer, who is able to reflect on the research lesson beyond all the representations by the individual observers.

4. Grade Blocs

School X adopts units of grade blocs for research lesson preparation, implementation, and review. A grade bloc is obtained by dividing the six grades of elementary school into three groups of two adjoining grades. The teacher in charge of a research lesson and the grade bloc to which he or she belongs is expected to form a relationship of role sharing summarized below, as described in a document distributed to the teachers:

Research Lesson Teacher

- *Clarify what you intend to obtain* from this research and lesson.
- Necessary to have the *ability to select those with which you agree* from among various opinions and *put them into practice*.

Grade-Bloc Members/Observers

- Necessary to have an *attitude to design a lesson* while *staying close to the research lesson teacher's intention* and from the *same viewpoint as the teacher* (as if you are teaching the lesson).
- Discern connections made by pupils, deepening of their understanding, and give feedback to the teacher on the facts of learning.

As mentioned above, at School X, research lesson preparation, instruction plan study, and post-research lesson reviews are carried out in grade blocs. Each bloc is composed of the teachers in charge of two adjoining grades. In the process of instruction plan study, in some cases, a draft instruction plan is revised in consideration of responses by the pupils in trial lessons: the draft instruction plan is used to teach two or more classes before the instruction plan is finalized. Since the classrooms are arranged in such a way that two adjoining grades share the same floor at School X, it is relatively easy to hold grade-specific meetings. While this grade bloc-based mechanism of assisting teachers in lesson design is well established, teachers in charge of research lessons are at the same time required to be autonomous in their lesson design. This means that School X's organizational Lesson Study is not always pursued on a school-wide basis. The grade blocs are established as intermediary units, and their Lesson Study activities serve to maintain a balance between individual teachers' autonomous research and organizational Lesson Study implementation, which creates and reinforces the school's culture.

5. Individual Themes and Individual Research Records

At School X, the smallest unit of action for Lesson Study is the individual teacher. As already mentioned, the teachers set their individual research themes.

At the outset of each academic year, led by the Teachers Learning Division, the teachers select individual research themes and academic subjects in which they intend to carry out research. They present their decisions in front of the entire faculty in early May. The research themes selected in an academic year are summarized in Table 7.4.

Table 7.4 Individual research themes (examples; excerpt)

Grade-class	Name	Subject	Research theme
1 – 1		Math	Thinking together, with everyone
2 – 2		Math	Children mutually communicating "my ideas"
3 – 1		Art	Creating objects while looking at oneself and interacting with others
4 – 2		Japanese	For lessons for speaking one's ideas, actively listening to others, and deepening one's ideas as a result
5 – 1		Japanese	Practice of lessons for learning how to observe something and deepening thought: nurturing children who learn independently and communicate with one another
6 – 2		Social Studies	For a deep learning attitude with interaction with others and mutual acceptance
3rd–5th grades		Science	Toward lessons that enable vivid experiences of new discoveries

Since School X is an elementary school, each teacher basically teaches his or her homeroom class in all the academic subjects. The teachers choose one to three subjects that they wish to research and focus more attention and effort than on the others each year. Different teachers will want to work on different subjects with extra effort. Since they are allowed to select a subject or subjects that the teachers and/or their classes wish to focus on each year, the teachers are usually highly motivated for, and proactively involved in, Lesson Study. They also feel more responsible for their involvement in and execution of Lesson Study.

The teachers' individual research themes shown in Table 7.4 are only some of the themes adopted in that year. They describe the lessons that the teachers want to realize, activities that they want to be given extra importance, and target images of the pupils. Unlike typical research themes composed by professional researchers, these themes are more like a declaration of a teacher's ideals, remarks addressed to pupils or something else written from the standpoint of the teacher and/or pupils as the main actors in the lessons. Rather than research questions, these themes can be viewed as a statement of a teacher's weaknesses, a pedagogical challenge, or a problem-solving policy regarding school administration. Composed in this manner, they help Lesson Study to become integrated into the teachers' day-to-day duties.

The teacher's individual research is recorded in writing in the form of an "individual research record" to be shared and stored. There are two types of individual research record, (1) and (2), whose entry is regulated as below (an excerpt from the school's guide on individual research record entry):

Individual Research Record (1)
- Outline of your individual research

- Enter why you have chosen this subject or theme (your intentions and wishes), what kind of research you want this to be, and other important matters.

- Enter the actions, means, devices, and concrete methods that you intend to use to pursue the research theme.

- Enter what you wish to emphasize in daily lessons in pursuing the theme, what you wish to continue instructing, etc.

Individual Research Record (2)

Grade __ Class __ Date _____ Subject _____ Unit _____

Conference

The Teachers Learning Division summarizes the contents of the plenary discussion and general comments by the external instructor.

Review by the Teacher

(Example)

I designed and taught the lesson based on the idea that… (past)

↓

As a result, during the open lesson, [enter what happened, how pupils responded, etc.], and I felt that… At the conference, I learned that … I couldn't agree more with the comments by [the external instructor] that … (present)

[Enter your impressions of and findings from the Lesson Study as shown above.]

↓

Therefore, I decided to do…, try … in the following day's lesson and … (future)

[Enter your concrete decision and practice.]

↓

Consequently, I noticed that the pupils have changed in that …, and something about me has also changed because…

[Describe the changes that you have perceived.]

↓

[After the end of the unit, describe whether or not the pupils learned what the teacher had intended; describe visible positive results and challenges for the future.]

*Attach the materials used in the lesson, photographs that give a good idea of the ambiance of the class, if any, and other objects, and make a visually accessible record.

As illustrated above, individual research records (2) are characterized by the use of a single-person narrative style (see Chap. 7) by the teacher. Many teachers who come to School X after having taught at other schools can feel at a loss if they had little experience of preparing a document for Lesson Study. In such a case, they can refer to the past individual research records that are kept and are available for viewing, to see what items of information should be entered and what format to follow. It may seem that individual research records (2) are all written in a similar style for this reason. In reality, however, it is because of this particular style that keeping individual research records is meaningful for the whole implementation of Lesson Study. The starting point of individual research is an individual teacher's interest in a certain issue or awareness of a challenge to overcome. Priority is given to the pursuit of individual research, although the grade blocs basically lead the process.

Individual research themes, freely selected by the teachers, have the possibility of adversely affecting the organizational side of Lesson Study. Yet, it is particularly thanks to individual research themes that the teachers can vividly experience and record Lesson Study, from preparatory actions to results, at the personal level, to be shared, accumulated, and transmitted. The unified style of the individual research record (2) provides an organizational framework for personal narratives of educational practices. As they are accumulated over time, the format of the individual research record (2) has developed into a cultural tool. Acquiring the use of this tool is also part of learning for the teachers at School X.

7.4 Conclusion

We have surveyed the situation of Lesson Study in Japan, defining it as an organizational learning opportunity for schoolteachers. We have also studied the example of an elementary school, surveying how the school's in-house Lesson Study system is constructed and functions and what significance it has.

In the case study of School X, the following eight conditions are fulfilled so that Lesson Study functions as an effective instrument that enables teachers to grow as professionals.

First, the autonomy of teachers as professionals is respected and emphasized. At School X, the teachers have their individual research themes concerning lesson development or class administration, which they work on throughout the school year. Second, the development of teachers' autonomy as professionals enjoys organizational support. At School X, Lesson Study has a pivotal place in the school administration policy. Under the leadership of the Teachers Learning Division, an annual plan for Lesson Study-related activities is drawn up at the beginning of each school year and shared by all the teachers.

Third, one or more teachers are put in charge of managing the organization and implementation of Lesson Study, serving as model learning teachers. At School X, teachers with relatively short teaching experience are selected to form the Teachers Learning Division. They read research literature and attend Lesson Study sessions held at other schools, demonstrating to their colleagues an autonomous and proactive attitude toward learning as professionals. Fourth, Lesson Study is positioned as a learning platform for teachers. At School X, the process of Lesson Study, from preparation including educational material research to actual classroom lesson and post-research lesson reflection, is clearly defined as learning opportunities for teachers.

Fifth, emphasis is placed on sharing viewpoints of lessons through post-research lesson discussions among teachers rather than on preparing lessons. Teachers have their individualized frameworks for perceiving lessons, based on their differing views of classroom lessons, learning, and learners. Such diverse frameworks becoming visible to one another in discussions enable teachers to reexamine their frameworks, expanding or revising them while incorporating elements from the other teachers' frameworks. Sixth, material and institutional instruments are developed to better enable Lesson Study to function as a learning platform for teachers. School X has a unified-format instruction plan, in which teachers express their views on lessons, learning, learners, and educational materials, to be consulted by other teachers. School X also has rules for observing research lessons, thereby enabling teachers who observe a research lesson to express their representations of the practice as facts of learning. The mutual disclosure of the research lesson teacher's convictions and the observer teachers' representations of the practice promotes learning by example.

Seventh, Lesson Study is promoted by an organization that intermediates between the school and individual teachers. School X has units called "grade blocs," groups of two adjoining grades (school years), ensuring that Lesson Study serves as a pillar of both proactive learning by individual teachers and overall school operation. Eighth, the process of an individual's learning is visualized so that teachers can obtain a meta-observer's perspective of their own change and growth. At School X, all teachers fill out individual research records with their individual experiences. This enables them to realize their personal development, thereby further empowering themselves and identifying their problem areas. Through this tool, they also acquire School X's unique style of narratives of educational practices.

At School X, these eight conditions are fulfilled on the premise of a school culture in which learning through Lesson Study is highly valued. Sharing narratives of lesson experiences in both content and form over a long period has helped nurture a stable school culture.

At School X, school-wide Lesson Study is organized under the Teachers Learning Division's leadership, with various mechanisms and rules in place. The Division's "leadership," however, is not definitive in determining teachers' practices.

In preparation for teaching a story that has appeared in textbooks of Japanese for many years, one teacher at School X visited the birthplace of the author where the story was also set. Her purpose was to understand the story within a broader context. She had already handled the story in class many times. Still, by taking this field trip, she further deepened her understanding of the story. She said, "I learned through this story that a true masterpiece continues to provide the reader with a proposition that makes reading worthwhile in accordance with the reader's situation and maturity."

In the actual lesson, the reading of the story that the pupils found valid differed from the teacher's reading based on her personal interpretation. Receiving the teacher's reading as possible, the pupils addressed it squarely. Some tried to adopt it as their own, while others found it incongruous until the end. In this lesson, the pupils were able to produce their own reading that was different from both the teacher's and the canonical reading of a canonical educational material, probably because the teacher had introduced her own reading, challenging the pupils. The teacher was able to do this because of her in-depth research on the educational material.

As this example indicates, Lesson Study primarily enables teachers' proactive learning, and a dialogue-oriented mechanism must be constructed for Lesson Study implementation, for such a process is also beneficial for teachers' autonomy as professionals.

Finally, a few words about the school principal's leadership, for which this chapter has no space: the school principal's leadership is naturally indispensable for realizing the kind of in-house Lesson Study presented in this chapter. At School X, the school principal appoints the members of the Teachers Learning Division, empowering them to lead the activities. Governance by school administrators can be found in another chapter.

References

Kage, M. 2008. *"Jugyo zukuri niokeru 'shikake'"* [Devices for lesson design]. In K. Akita, & C. Lewis (Eds.), *Jugyo no kenkyu kyoshi no gakushu: Lesson study eno izanai* [Study of lessons teacher's learning: An invitation to lesson study] (pp. 152–168). Tokyo: Akashi Shoten.

National Institute for Educational Policy Research, The (NIER). (2011). *Kyoin no shitsu no kojo nikansuru chosa kenkyu houkokusho* [Report of the survey on the qualitative improvement of school teachers].

Sakamoto, A., & Akita, K. (2008). *"Jugyo kenkyu kyogikai deno kyoshi no gakushu: Shogakko kyoshi no shiko katei no bunseki"* [Teachers' learning in lesson study conference: Analysis of elementary school teachers' thought process]. In K. Akita, & C. Lewis (Eds.), *Jugyo no kenkyu kyoshi no gakushu: Lesson study eno izanai* [Study of lessons teacher's learning: An invitation to lesson study] (pp. 98–113). Tokyo: Akashi Shoten.

Sato, M. 2015. *Senmonka toshite kyoshi o sodateru: kyoshi kyoiku kaikaku no grand design* [Training teachers as professionals: A grand design for teacher training reform]. Tokyo: Iwanami Shoten.

Shulman, L. (2004). *The wisdom of practice: Essays on teaching, learning, and learning to teach.* San Francisco: Jossey-Bass.

Shulman, L., & Shulman, J. H. (2004). How and what teachers learn: A shifting perspective. *Journal of Curriculum Studies, 36*(2), 257–271.

Wolf, J., & Akita, K. (2008). *"Lesson Study no kokusai doko to jugyo kenkyu eno toi: Nippon, America, Hong Kong ni okeru Lesson Study no hikaku kenkyu"* [International trends of lesson study and questions about lesson study: a comparative study of lesson study in Japan, America, and Hong Kong]. In K. Akita and C. Lewis (Eds.), *Jugyo no kenkyu kyoshi no gakushu: Lesson study eno izanai* [Study of lessons teacher's learning: An invitation to lesson study] (pp. 24–42). Tokyo: Akashi Shoten.

Chapter 8
Teacher Narrative Description

Sachiko Asai

8.1 Introduction

My classroom was flooded with morning light. The second grade children were learning either manual arts or arithmetic. Then one piped up, "They're the same"; another replied, "No, they aren't," and still a third said, "They're identical." I don't know how they started the discussion. I listened to them in silence, while dealing with first grade children. I continued to listen to the children, anticipating how the discussion would develop, where the discussion would break down, and whether the children would achieve a breakthrough. As they were talking, they were completely ignoring the manual arts or arithmetic they were supposed to be studying. They were all standing up. It had been Tetsu who raised the subject for the discussion. He made an assertion with a pout, sputtering with a pair of scissors still in his hand: "That's what you say, but two things are never the same. Look, this *origami* paper and that one are the same, but their colors are different." Hearing Tetsu's words, Tamura could not help but comment, "That's what you say, but they are totally the same. How is the color of this one different from that one? This leaf and that leaf are the same. You just have to look at one through the other, and you'll agree with me. Look, they're the same as you can see. Come on, they're the same!" Then Rei broke in on, "That's right. I can buy two or three of the same sheets of *origami* paper at a store. You can't say that they aren't identical." (Kobayashi 1926: 130–131)

These are the opening sentences of a narrative description written by a young primary teacher, Kaneyo Kobayashi, in 1926. She is describing an event that happened one morning in her classroom using a narrative style, as in a novel.

S. Asai (✉)
Graduate School of Education, The University of Tokyo, Tokyo, Japan
e-mail: asai@p.u-tokyo.ac.jp

© Springer Nature Singapore Pte Ltd. 2019   125
Y. Kitamura et al. (eds.), *Education in Japan*, Education in the Asia-Pacific
Region: Issues, Concerns and Prospects 47,
https://doi.org/10.1007/978-981-13-2632-5_8

Traditionally in Japan, teachers wrote many such narrative descriptions called *jissen kiroku* (narrative teaching records), from about the 1920s onward. Narrative records written by teachers have been one of the main discourses used to represent teaching practices (Asai 2008).

Narrative teaching records have three important features. First, teachers tell classroom stories in the first-person narrative. The style of teacher narrative records arose from private journals and "I" novels.[1] Therefore teachers continue to shape and reshape their identity through writing narrative records. Second, teachers address children using their own names in the narrative descriptions. The relationship between the teacher and the children is intimate, as expressed using "I" and "you," as opposed to "teacher" and "student" as in the systematized school education. Third, the teachers illustrate the experiences of themselves and the children as stories. The teachers describe their day-to-day experiences as singular and at least partially accidental in a narrative style. Through reading them, we learn how the teachers pursue their identity, how the teachers build relationships with the children in the classroom, and how the teachers give meaning to the daily events and activities in their classrooms.

The important point is that such teacher narrative descriptions have been one of the means of lesson study in Japan. Lesson study is a form of practice for teachers' professional learning and the development of teaching material. There are two main methods on how to study lessons. One is lesson study through observation and reflection on a lesson. The other is lesson study through collaborative reading of teaching records written by the teacher who taught the lesson. Teachers have written narrative teaching records to be shared with other teachers, for the development of their teaching ability, curricula, teaching methods, and teaching materials. In this chapter, I will try to trace the developing process of teacher narratives in modern Japan to delve into the historical meaning of narrative teaching records.

Teacher narratives in novel form have their origin in the educational novels of the 1900s. At first, educational novels were written in a fictional form to present the image of the ideal teacher. However, educational novels gave way to autobiographical nonfiction aimed at pursuing teachers' identities in the 1910s. In the next decade, teachers started to use narrative styles to represent and study their teaching experiences. This style became widely used among schoolteachers as a means of reflecting on their own practices and lessons from the 1930s to the 1950s. Since around 1955, the scientific validity of narrative styles has been questioned by academic discourses due to their subjectivity. Therefore, lesson study through observation and reflection became mainstream, but quite a few teachers have continued to write narrative teaching records to this day. Furthermore, the style of such records has led to school education in Japan being characterized as holistic.

[1] An "I" novel is a novel based on the author's own life.

8.2   The Educational Novel: From Third-Person Narratives to First-Person Narratives

8.2.1   Pestalozzi and the Educational Novel

Narrative teaching records have their origin in the educational novel. What is an educational novel? To answer this question, we need to examine the process of the acceptance of Pestalozzi's works in Japan.

During the late nineteenth century, Pestalozzi was a well-known figure in relation to the teaching method known as "developmentalism." There were three steps in the acceptance of Pestalozzi's pedagogy in Japan. First, when the modern school system in Japan started in 1872, "object teaching" influenced by Pestalozzi's pedagogy was introduced simply in terms of form. Second, around 1877, books about "object lessons" were translated into Japanese. Third, in the late 1870s, "developmentalism" as Pestalozzi's theory of teaching was introduced to the teacher education at Tokyo Normal School by Hideo Takamine, who studied at Oswego Normal School in the United States (Inagaki 1966).

It was in the early twentieth century that the ways of acceptance of Pestalozzi's works began to vary. Pestalozzi came to be considered as a person who represented and embodied the ideal of a teacher. In 1906, a commemoration ceremony marking the 160th anniversary of Pestalozzi's birth in praise of Pestalozzi's life and accomplishment was held by the Association to Commemorate Pestalozzi. At the ceremony, Masataro Sawayanagi, an undersecretary of the Ministry of Education, gave the opening speech. Mataichi Koizumi, a professor at Tokyo Higher Normal School, also gave a lecture. They talked about Pestalozzi's life in order to determine "the teaching mind" (Teraoka 2006).

How did the way of acceptance of Pestalozzi's works change in this way? The turning point was the publication of the Japanese version of *Leonard and Gertrude*, an educational novel written by Pestalozzi from 1781 to 1787. In 1901, the novel was published in Japan with the title, *Wife of a Drunken Man*. Educators read the novel as a story that provided the very picture of an ideal teacher and tried to write such novels themselves in the context of the teacher culture in Japan. Koizumi wrote a book titled *Sacrificed Stone* (1907). He explained the background to writing the book as follows. When the Association to Commemorate Pestalozzi was founded the year before, he noticed the lack of "educational novels" that described the life story of an ideal teacher. He thought that educational novels would encourage teachers just as *Wife of a Drunken Man* had encouraged parents. So he wrote *Sacrificed Stone*.

In the latter 1900s, several other educational novels were published. They were also written to depict the ideal life of a schoolteacher (Wada 2002). Eiji Ishikawa, who was an editor of the *Journal of Educational Experimentation*,[2] wrote *An Ideal*

---

[2] The *Journal of Educational Experimentation* was a specialized journal devoted to practical studies on teaching mainly by primary teachers. It was first published in 1898.

Primary Teacher in 1906. It is obvious that this book was also influenced by Pestalozzi's *Wife of a Drunken Man*. *An Ideal Primary Teacher* was accompanied by an illustration of "Pestalozzi in Neuhof." In addition to it, *Wife of a Drunken Man* and *An Ideal Primary Teacher* appeared together as "educational novels" in an advertisement appearing in the *Journal of Educational Experimentation*. In the advertisement, we can also see the title of another book, *Small-town Intellectual* (Hasumi 1909), written by Hasumi Kasen.

We shall examine, through *Sacrificed Stone*, the characteristics of the ideal teacher described by educational novels in the latter half of the 1900s decade. Seiichi, the main character in the story, studies at a normal school and becomes a village teacher. He has the opportunity to be the head teacher of a primary school attached to a normal school[3] and to go on to a higher normal school[4] with the aim of being a secondary teacher but rejects these opportunities in order to work among village children and village people. In other words, Seiichi sacrifices his desire to be successful in the world of the teaching profession and devotes himself to national education without social prestige. That is what the title *Sacrificed Stone* means. Strangely enough, even though the novel is intended to depict an ideal teacher, there are no descriptions of Seiichi's actual lessons. By reading the book, we learn that Seiichi is well-liked by the students, parents, and people in the community, but we remain completely in the dark as to whether or not he excels at teaching. Ishikawa's *An Ideal Primary Teacher* and Hasumi's *Small-town Intellectual* have similar plots and features to *Sacrificed Stone*. We might say that the "ideal teacher" in the educational novels of the 1900s was not so much expected to excel at teaching but rather to be a person of high moral character.

An identity crisis among schoolteachers lay behind the rise of such educational novels. In turn, economic factors lay behind the identity crisis. With prices continually rising since around 1900, teachers could barely get by each month in the latter half of the 1900s decade (Kadowaki 2004). Ideal teachers in the educational novels often chose to remain small-town teachers, but that was not always the case. School education had a serious shortage of the teachers at that time.

Small-town Teacher (1909) written by Katai Tayama, who was well known as an "I"-novel writer, reflected the real sentiment of the teachers of the day. This story was similar to educational novels, but it differed from them in that it did not aim to describe an ideal teacher. *Small-town Teacher* is a work of imagination based on the life of a real character named Shuzo Kobayashi. In his private journal, to which Katai referred, Kobayashi actually wrote about his desire to change his career (Kobayashi 1963). Therefore Seizo, the main character of *Small-town Teacher*, is also dissatisfied with small-town life as a teacher. He hopes to be a writer but meets with a setback; he then takes an entrance exam for a music academy, but this ends in failure. There were thus teachers who were simply unable to be teachers. For this reason, educators wrote stories of ideal teachers who continued to be small-town teachers.

---

[3] A "normal school" was a school for training elementary teachers.

[4] A "higher normal school" was a school for training secondary teachers including normal schoolteachers.

8.2.2 Former Teachers' Autobiographies

Educational novels in the 1900s described the ideal teacher's life in order to encourage teachers. By contrast, educational novels in the 1910s portrayed stories of teachers' promotions and career changes, which candidly described the negative side of teachers' lives.

The main characteristic of educational novels written in the 1910s is that they were semiautobiographical novels. Educational journalists who were former schoolteachers described their teaching days in such novels. Some educational novels were still written in the third person, but they were narrated from a first-person perspective. In addition, nonfictional autobiographies were written in first-person narrative form. What it meant to be a teacher was called into question in such narrative form—the first-person narrative forced teachers to face up to the existential questions.

The most characteristic change over the years around 1910 was the emergence of positive descriptions of resignation from a vocation in order to pursue one's own identity. In 1912, *Self-awareness and Confessions of a Young Teacher* written by Sofu Inage, who later became an editor of the *Journal of Educational Experimentation*, was published. Inage looks back over half his lifetime using a first-person narrative. In the story, the protagonist becomes a teacher of a primary school in his hometown and chooses to resign to go to college in Tokyo. Several other similar stories were written. Hiroshi Shigaki wrote one of the stories titled *A Teacher's Story* (1919) in an analogous fashion to *Self-awareness and Confessions of a Young Teacher*. Shigaki was also an educational journalist who used to be a schoolteacher. In *A Teacher's Story*, the protagonist becomes a teacher of a school in a small town, transfers to a primary school attached to a normal school, again transfers to a primary school attached to a higher normal school, and finally resigns to become a journalist. What he wants is an "enhanced living standard" and to "achieve his own identity." Shigaki frequently describes the financial straits in which he found himself. This reflects the serious economic situation facing schoolteachers in the 1910s.

Many other educational journalists who had been schoolteachers wrote semiautobiographies and autobiographies around 1920. For example, the *Journal of Educational Society* started a series titled "Up-and-Coming Teachers in Educational Society," consisting of biographical introductions of educational journalists, in 1921. In 1922, *Creation* carried a similar feature article under the title "The reason why I resigned as a teacher." Journalists narrated their experiences as schoolteachers who had been too creative or too sensitive to fit into the teaching culture. Journalists' semiautobiographies and autobiographies increased as teachers' lives and personalities became educational issues in the debate on teachers' poverty, the reform of education at normal schools, and school reform as part of New Education.

The important point regarding former teachers' autobiographical narratives is that narratives in the first person made it possible to question the ethics of a teacher from the inside, in keeping with the reality of teaching. Regarding his resignation as a teacher, Tohsaku Miura said, "I find that teaching other peoples' children is too demanding for me" because "I reflect on myself very sensitively" (Miura 1922). Goro Tamefuji said that when he chased a student who was smoking, he felt "a sense of pain" regarding "the shameful act" (Tamefuji 1922). In a round-table talk among former teachers, Yasaburo Shimonaka said that students straightened their clothes all in a fluster when they met him in the corridor, and that made him feel bad. Tamefuji responded by criticizing the representation of a teacher as an inflexible incarnation of morality, in other words, a double-faced hypocrite (Tamefuji 1923). Narratives of teacher's experiences around 1920 seemed to dwell on the identity crises teachers felt as teachers.

8.3 Narrative Teaching Records

8.3.1 New Education in Modern Japan

In the 1920s, a style of teacher narrative description called *jissen kiroku* emerged from the narratives of teachers' identity crisis. Some teachers began to write teaching records for reflection of their teaching experiences in narrative styles. The style of narratives resembled novels with their use of the first person "I" and actual children's names. We shall gain a vivid picture of the development of teacher narratives leading to narrative teaching records as we trace the process of teachers' pursuits of their identities at Ikebukuro-Jido-no-Mura ("children's village in the city of Ikebukuro"), a private primary school established in 1924. Jido-no-Mura was an experimental school for New Education. To understand the characteristics of Jido-no-Mura, we first need to review New Education in modern Japan.

Since about 1900, some educators started to criticize the existing education with its uniformity and to advocate new styles of education in reference to Euro-American pedagogy (Nakano 1968). The focus of the criticism was Herbartian pedagogy, which was understood formally as an instruction method. The educational philosophy of Tomeri Tanimoto, a professor at the Imperial University of Kyoto, symbolically encapsulated the change. In the 1890s, he had led the diffusion of Herbartian pedagogy, but he changed his concept of education and described the principle of teaching with the expression "guidance of self-instruction" in the 1910s (Tanimoto 1906). He believed that active and creative individuals ought to be cultivated in schools for imperialistic national development (Inaba 2004). Several private schools holding analogous ideals were also established around 1910.

In the 1910s, the themes of discussion concerning New Education started to change. As nationalistic views had not disappeared but had begun to recede into the background, experimental aspects of New Education came to the foreground. Many schoolteachers at primary schools tried to create a new style of education guided by each school director. Their teaching styles varied greatly.[5]

What is the historical significance of the school reform movement? Previous studies had focused on lesson reform; New Education developed new teaching methods (Nakano 1968). In contrast, recent researchers have focused on the lesson studies adopted in New Education. They point out that lesson studies as a means of school reform, lesson improvement, and curriculum development had their origins in New Education in around 1920 (Inagaki and Sato 1996; Mori 2004). At experimental primary schools, teachers practiced intramural lesson studies nearly every month and open lesson studies every year. They observed each other's lessons and discussed teaching methods and educational materials. On the one hand, it was against the backdrop of these teachers' research and experiments that narrative teaching records were generated, but on the other hand, at the same time, these two styles of lesson study represented different levels of teacher experiences. Lesson study through observation and reflection transformed the style of teaching. The narrative teaching records represented changes in teacher identity on an existential level.

Jido-no-Mura was established as a private experimental school in 1924. It was the school that pursued freedom radically. The people who established the school were educational journalists, the most strident critics of existing schools, and teachers. In 1923, they formed an association for education reform, launched a new journal named *The Century of Education*, and announced a bold plan to establish an experimental primary school, "Jido-no-Mura." The school was presented in the plan as follows:

> Without sticking to the conventional relationship between teachers and children, and without being restricted by institutional subjects, timetables or teaching methods—a new school where children live childlike lives, where we live our lives together, which is our laboratory, which is our working place, which is our entertainment venue, which is our playing field, which is our rest station giving us comfort and enjoyment—this is our Jido-no-Mura. (Kyoiku-no-Seiki-Sha 1923)

This plan creates a vision of Jido-no-Mura using the word "without." It in fact negates the very systems that make schools into schools. This means that Jido-no-Mura was planned as an ideal school but by denying the systems and relationships that conventionally defined schools.

---

[5] Heiji Oikawa introduced the ability grouping approach and the project method to the primary school attached to the Akashi Women's Normal School. Kishie Tezuka led an experiment on "Education of Liberty," characterized by individualized learning and self-government. Takeji Kinoshita, the director of the primary school attached to Nara Women's Higher Normal School, advocated the importance of children's autonomous learning. He composed lessons at the school based on individualized learning and cooperative learning. At Seijo Primary School founded by Masataro Sawayanagi in 1917 for experiments of education, the Dalton Laboratory Plan was set up. The school had the basic principles of respect for individuality and scientific research in education.

8.3.2 Names of Children

The teachers who gathered at Jido-no-Mura had been facing identity crises as teachers. At first, Yoshibe Nomura and Nobu Hirata were assigned as teachers. In the articles describing their arrival at their new posts published in *The Century of Education*, they did not talk about teaching or children. Rather, they devoted their thoughts to themselves. Nomura expressed self-distrust. He wrote an internal conversation to himself: "What are you going to do at Jido-no-Mura? I only want to help myself. If I live vigorously, I can fill the whole world with vigor. But I feel absolutely dead inside." Hirata, for her part, wrote, "I want to be a mistress of myself. Then I hope to live my life with total authority."

The narratives of Nomura and Hirata in the first-person style, through which they pursued their own identities, were quite similar to the narratives of educational journalists in autobiographical educational novels around 1920. However, the narratives of Jido-no-Mura primary schoolteachers came to differ from journalists' narratives. The difference between the two arose in the style of naming children. Children's own names, which never appeared in autobiographical narratives written by journalists, made a symbolic showing in Nomura's description in the first-person narrative. The following is an extract from an article written by Nomura in July 1924.

> This morning, the children are studying in an unsettling manner and are simply not in the mood. I have been discontent for the past few days. Is this right? I just keep silent with a frown on my face... [omission]. I was sitting in my chair gazing at Toshimitsu, one of the children. Toshimitsu seemed to notice my look—he gazed back at me and said, "You haven't smiled this morning." Then Kushiro, who was around, said, "Why the sour face?" "I am depressed about this tedious way of studying." "Please smile. When you have a sour face, we can't study very well," Kushiro replied. (Nomura 1924)

This narrative description shows little sign of the institutional relationship between "teacher" and "student" employed at schools. The intimate relationship between the children and Nomura can be expressed by the words "you" and "I." Since writing this article, Nomura basically addressed children using their own names in his narrative descriptions. And when Nomura started to describe children by their own names in his narrative with the first person "I," the narrative came to illustrate the experiences of the teacher and the children as a story. This is what we call *jissen kiroku* (narrative teaching record).

Narrative teaching records described educational practices just as typical teachers' articles did, but not as the consequences of teaching plans. Rather, narrative records represented experiences with uncertainty. Nomura even said that education had no goal or purpose. He considered the day-to-day experiences of himself and the children to be educational experiences. He thought that daily life with the children could be an education in itself.

> I have discovered the education of truth. The education of truth is education without educational purpose. It is inappropriate to call "education," what is in fact the education of collaborative relationships between children and me. Independent people live in a community together there. People are linked only in friendship there. Friendship makes the community lively and creates collaborative lives. This is the best way to live. And this is the best education. I shall be a good friend of the children from today on. (Nomura 1926a, b)

This representation by Nomura of his education is consistent with the ethical values of the narrative style with "I" and children's own names.

Nomura was not alone in writing teaching records in the narrative style. His colleagues at Jido-no-Mura elementary school also used "I" and children's names in their narratives and described their experiences with uncertainty. I would like to remind you of Kobayashi's beautiful narrative description titled "Philosophy of Tetsu" at the beginning of this chapter. Teachers at Jido-no-Mura developed unique ideas of education through writing narrative teaching records.

8.3.3 Widespread Use of the Narrative Style

From the 1930s to the 1950s, narrative teaching records were disseminated to common schoolteachers who engaged in "seikatsu tsuzurikata" ("life composition education"). Life composition education was a particular style of composition education developed in Japan. Children wrote about their everyday lives in detail in the form of a daily journal. The compositions depicted lives of poverty in many cases. Teachers read the compositions, instructed ways of expression, and guided the children's recognitions and actions represented in the compositions. Sometimes teachers edited children's compositions to be shared in classroom magazines. It was pointed out that teachers of life composition education "let children observe and represent the reality of their everyday lives to cultivate their scientific recognition and subjective motivation to reform the real world" (Funabashi 2001).

Life composition education had its origin in education at Jido-no-Mura. In 1929, teachers of the school launched a new monthly journal called *Composition Life*. Later, in 1935, they began a new journal titled *Life School*. Life composition education was developed in these journals with teacher narrative descriptions. Teachers at Jido-no-Mura used narrative styles of description to represent their classroom experiences, and some teachers among the readers wrote narrative descriptions as contributions. Fumiko Hirano, a young female teacher who was a reader of *Life School*, wrote a teaching record titled *Records of a Women Teacher* in 1940. Hirano aimed at the realization of a learning community to which the children, parents, and she herself all belonged (Hirano 1940). The book became a bestseller and was made into a movie in 1942.

During the years 1940–1942, composition education was subject to harsh repression by the Special Higher Police. The police authorities under the situation of total war considered teachers of composition education to be communists who aimed to overthrow the Imperial system. Many teachers, including Hirano, were forced out of their schools, and some were arrested.

After World War II, the publication of classroom writing under the title *Echo School* (1951) by Seikyo Muchaku, a teacher at a common junior high school in an impoverished village, led to the reemergence of life composition education. He said that children had to study composition to discuss and think about their real lives in order to reform their lives. In connection with the reemergence of life composition education, teachers came to write narrative teaching records in a proactive manner. In the 1950s, a number of books on teaching practices in the narrative style were published.[6] Some educational researchers of the day who belonged to the Association of Scientific Research for Education (ASRE),[7] such as Shuichi Katsuta and Takashi Ohta, encouraged teachers to write narrative records.

It is noteworthy that Kihaku Saito, the principal of Shima Primary School, and his staff drove school reform by writing narrative teaching records from 1952 to 1963. Saito requested that teachers write teaching records in the form of novels in his first year at the school. He considered that writing records cultivated teachers' capacities to interpret events, discover new meanings, question, and be moved by children's expression. Funato Sakiko, a young female teacher of Shima Primary School, wrote a narrative record titled "Living Children." Here I will quote a passage from her records:

> There are 17 children in my classroom. One of them did not talk aloud with me. He just nodded or shook his head. One day I said him, "Let's have a talk in private." Then I talked with him for the first time. "Tadashi, do you like this school?" "Yes, I like it." "How about me?" "I like you." I noticed that Tadashi had a very good voice. Since then, Tadashi and I have had private talks from time to time. Tadashi seems to enjoy them... [omission] Now he can sing alone. When he is learning in a small group, he cheerfully comments, "My answer is correct," or "Oh, I found a mistake." I am delighted to see his progress. And I thank the children in the class for sharing my delight. (Funato 1953)

Funato says that she did not know how to write a teaching record at first. She handed the first draft to Saito and received comments from him. Saito advised her to describe things clearly, such as the expression on a child's face, a math problem that the children were trying to solve, or an idea in her own mind (Saito 1963).

The important feature of teacher narrative descriptions at Shima Primary School was their focus on actual classes. Saito and his staff published a book of narrative teaching records titled *Academic Abilities for the Future* in 1958 (Saito 1958). Concerning the book, Saito made the following statement: "Many books written by teachers are the narrative records of experiences of life guidance written by teachers of composition education. In contrast, the teachers at Shima Primary School have written about their own classes in *Academic Abilities for the Future*" (Saito 1964).

---

[6] *New Geography and History Education* (Aikawa 1954), *Revolution of the Classroom* (Konishi, 1955), *First-grade Children in a Village* (Tsuchida 1955), *Academic Ability for the Development of a Village* (Toi 1957), and *Records of the Classroom for Bringing Up Fine People* (Miyazaki 1957) are well known examples.

[7] The Association of Scientific Research for Education (ASRE) was established in 1952 to develop science of education and realize a democratic society.

8.4   Teacher Narratives and Science of Education

8.4.1   *From Narrative Records* (jissen kiroku) *to Verbatim Records* (jyugyo kiroku)

In the latter half of the 1950s, the style of narrative teaching records was questioned through academic discourse in debates over the scientific nature of educational research. On the one hand, the debates contributed to clarification of the features of the narrative records and understanding of the significance of the style. However, on the other hand, it brought about a reduction in narrative teaching records and an increase in verbatim teaching records to emphasize objectivity in teaching records.

The initial question of the debates began with the way of evaluating the narrative teaching records. The narrative teaching records had been afforded high value in a monthly journal titled *Education* by ASRE, since its launch in 1951. In 1954, "narrative teaching records" were featured in the journal. Five academic figures including Katsuta and Ohta criticized several records from teachers in a round-table talk featured in the magazine. They pointed out the defects of the teaching practice and its record (Igarashi et al. 1954a, b). Teachers in a local circle of ASRE offered rebuttals to criticism of the round-table talk. They pointed out two problems: First, the academicians had no objective criteria with which to evaluate narrative teaching records. Second, the academicians tended to adopt a haughty attitude.

Katsuta and his colleagues discussed the teachers' rebuttals, and Katsuta wrote a paper on behalf of them titled "How can we evaluate narrative teaching records?" (Katsuta 1955). This paper is important because it constitutes one of the basic understandings of narrative teaching records up to the present date. Katsuta accepts that academicians had the irreverent idea of steering teaching practices, even if unwittingly. He also writes, "We think that narrative teaching records (*jissen kiroku*) are life compositions (*seikatsu tsuzurikata*) written by teachers." The narrative teaching records were brought into the act as a medium for the teacher community through the use of this analogy. Katsuta points out that narrative teaching records were the common property of teachers. That is to say, narrative teaching records should be appreciated by other teachers, not be assessed by an absolute standard.

Another criticism of "the science of education" of ASRE relying on teacher narrative records came from Yoshihiro Shimizu (1955), one of the earliest educational sociologists in Japan. He doubted the scientific validity of the narrative records based on the following three points. First, the narrative descriptions were invariably incomplete or subjective. It was impossible to validate whether or not a story represented a real event in a classroom with accuracy. Second, the narrative style was too literary to be subjected to the science of education. Third, teachers tended to consider themselves as heroes or models and romanticize their works in their narrative descriptions. To this criticism, Katsuta and his colleagues made rebuttal statements and stressed the importance of the narrative teaching records for the teachers themselves. However, narrative teaching records appearing in *Education* became fewer in number for several years. Especially from the mid-1960s, academicians expected to construct "the science of education" by relying on verbatim teaching records and critical study of lessons through round-table talks.

What were the characteristics of the new style of lesson study using verbatim teaching records? It was pointed out that the good points of the style upon sharing a lesson plan in an educational research group of teachers were the following two points. First, only the teacher who have taught would not be criticized about the lesson. Second, the same lesson can be done by other teachers (Toyama 1965). That is to say, a teaching plan was created as the development of subject content and teaching materials without careful consideration of the characteristics of the particular children or the particular teacher. That is, new questions on the integration of teaching materials with children's cognition were raised, and such questions led to the establishment of practice-based lesson study (Inagaki 1964).

8.4.2   Narrative Descriptions in Teachers' Voluntary Study Groups

In the 1960s, the agencies of lesson studies became diversified. There were three main agencies of lesson studies: educational researchers who promoted scientific lesson studies under the influence of foreign theories, teachers in voluntary study groups who attempted a scientific approach to educational contents, and the administrations of the Ministry of Education and local educational boards (National Association for the Study of Educational Methods 2011, pp. 142–143). The styles of teaching records varied, but often followed a scientific approach, with "T" (teacher) and "C" (child) used to generalize individual cases, in contrast to narrative teaching records. It was pointed out that the "T-C style" used at the time undermined "teachers' narratives written in the first person using children's own names" (Inagaki and Sato 1996).

However, some teachers' groups continued to follow in the tradition of the narrative teaching record. Teachers in the Japanese Society for Life Guidance Studies, an association studying the organization of classroom groups, wrote narrative teaching records focusing on the guidance of children's school and family lives. It was said that the records "go so far as to encompass not only the actual conditions faced by the children and the teachers' actual efforts at guidance, but also the changes in the children (and children's groups) that emerged out of those efforts at guidance" (National Association for the Study of Educational Methods 2011, p.82). On the other hand, new styles of teaching records were developed. For example, the style of the lesson study and teaching record of the Society for Carrying Out the Original Intention of Social Studies, one of the teachers' voluntary study groups, was affected by the scientific lesson study. The teaching records of the society were basically written in the narrative style and were characterized by attention to the thinking processes of several selected children.

Teachers who belonged to the voluntary research group named the Society for Research on the Problems of ECEC (Early Child Education and Care) intentionally developed their style of teacher narrative records. ECEC teachers wrote many teaching records and contributed to their journal titled *Research on the Problems of ECEC*. The following part of a story is cited from a book titled *Inquiry into ECEC* written by Keiko Takase, a nursery teacher. She wrote the following extract from an episode where she and some 5-year-olds were trying to plant and cultivate seeds:

> One day, I heard an interesting story from the mother of a boy, Yoshinobu. She said, "Yoshinobu is interested in planting, and he buries anything he can think of in the ground. Yesterday, he buried a crayon and watered it to grow a crayon tree." She let the whole thing pass and buried a bean next to it. She said that Yoshinobu would come to know the difference between a crayon and a bean in good time. If she was a mother who didn't understand the child's idea, she would scold Yoshinobu for being naughty. I admired her response.
>   [omission]
> I talked to the children in my classroom about the episode of Yoshinobu and the crayon.
> Yoshinobu: I don't know what's going to happen. It won't come out.
> Teacher: I hope everything will come out.
> Shinji: Rice crackers, too?
> I draw a crayon tree and a rice cracker tree to arouse the children's interest.
> (Takase 1974)

After this conversation, the children and Takase buried a candy, a rice cracker, some coins, and a bean. A few days later, only the bean came out. The children and Takase dug up the soil and discussed the difference between the bean and the other objects. In this story, Takase developed a curriculum with the children. She and her colleagues called their practices "ECEC as Dialogue." They referred to the phrase "Narrative teaching records (*jissen kiroku*) are teachers' life compositions (*seikatsu tsuzurikata*)" uttered by Katsuta (Honjo 1995).

8.4.3 Current State of Teacher Narratives

Nowadays, there are noteworthy developments in narrative teaching records.

Teachers in ECEC and in special-needs education have been actively writing narrative teaching records. Kiyoshi Takezawa, who devoted his professional attention to special-needs education for many years, wrote several books about teacher narrative records. He inquired into the method of looking at children through writing teacher narrative records and points a few things out about "good" teaching narrative records. First, he makes a suggestion to write teacher narrative records in the first person to allow recognition of the difference between the intention of the teacher and the experiences of the children. Second, he proposes the idea of letting the facts speak for themselves. He comments on what "facts" mean: "I think that a typical child's facts are those that help us discover a new aspect of the child." Third, he advocates the importance of dialogue with empathetic colleagues (Takezawa 2005). There have also been several other trials for teacher development or teaching reform through the writing of teacher narrative descriptions. Shun Kujiraoka (2005), who is a developmental psychologist working with nursery and kindergarten teachers, advocates the implementation of "Episode Records" to appreciate the subjectivity of teachers. Isao Ohmiya (2010), a researcher on ECEC, tried to write "Leaning Stories" with nursery and kindergarten teachers, with reference to *Assessment in Early Childhood Settings* by Margaret Carr (2001).

There are several historical approaches to narrative teaching records. Hiroshi Ohizumi (2005) takes a brief look at the history of the teacher narrative description for the development of narrative teaching records. He points out the problem of the idea at ASRE that academicians examine teaching records and generalize the model cases. He makes the following suggestions on how to read narrative teaching records. Educational researchers have to abandon their intention to assess, respect the singularity of each narrative record, examine the basis of each teacher's practice, and inquire about the universal value of education in each practice. Koji Tanaka (2009) writes that children's own names became eliminated from teaching records as teachers and researchers sought scientific teaching records in the 1960s and 1970s. He proposes the idea of promoting teaching records with both a scientific and a literary nature. Ohizumi and Tanaka agree with the view that it is important to remember Katsuta's words: "Narrative teaching records (*jissen kiroku*) are teachers' life compositions (*seikatsu tsuzurikata*)."

There have been some trials aimed at interweaving narrative teaching records in Japan and narrative approaches to teacher's experiences developed in curriculum studies overseas since around the 1980s. Yoshiya Tanaka (2011) looks for a way to interweave the narrative teaching records with the idea of narrative inquiry developed mainly in Canada by Jean Clandinin, her colleagues, and schoolteachers (Clandinin et al. 2006). Tanaka says, "Researches on educational practice in Japan have analyzed each practice carefully, but have not sufficiently developed the concepts necessary to understand such practices with any level of consistency due to emphasis on the singularity of each practice." He pays attention to the concept of the "story" in narrative inquiry, which enables understanding of both the uniqueness of each practice and the social relationships surrounding the practices. Tanaka points out that the idea of narrative inquiry had the potential to give rise to the concept of understanding teacher narrative descriptions philosophically, and the idea of narrative inquiry would be developed still further from the reading of narrative teaching records, the heritage of teacher narratives in Japan.

8.5   Conclusion

Teacher narrative description as a professional teaching culture in Japan boasts a history of over 100 years. In particular from the 1950s, narrative teaching records have been one of the main discourses used to represent and inquire into teaching practice in Japan.

Historically, lesson study by narrative teaching records had a different meaning from lesson study through observation and reflection on lessons. Narrative teaching records were primarily for the personal and subjective inquiry of the teacher who wrote the record. A narrative teaching record shows us how the teacher identifies himself/herself, the relationship between the teacher and the children, and the educational meaning attributed to the events by the teacher. It is particularly for this reason that teacher narrative descriptions are to be appreciated and not generalized. At the same time, it is important that teachers read each other's narrative teaching records and share their values and visions on educational practices. Using the educational journals of the narrative teaching records, teachers have created professional learning communities throughout their schools and developed new ways of looking at educational contents and children's learning processes. Of course, a learning community at a school aimed at fostering collegiality and sharing values is also important.

Recently, lesson study through observation and reflection has been actively pursued, but lesson study through narrative teaching records is falling into decline due to teachers' busyness and increasing demands for privacy protection. However, lesson study using narrative teaching records is needed to gain a holistic, careful, and responsible perspective of school education. The narrative style of teaching records needs to be more vivid and fresh through multiple inquiries into teacher narrative descriptions, as heritages from the past.

References

Aikawa, H. (1954). *New geography and history education [Atarashii-Chireki-Kyoiku]*. Tokyo: Kokudosha.

Asai, S. (2008). *Teacher narrative descriptions and new education [Kyoshi-no-Shigoto-to-Shinkyoiku]*. Tokyo: University of Tokyo Press.

Carr, M. (2001). *Assessment in early childhood settings: Learning stories*. London: Sage.

Clandinin, J., Huber, J., Huber, M., Murphy, M. S., Orr, A. M., Pearce, M., & Steeves, P. (2006). *Composing diverse identities: Narrative inquiries into the interwoven lives of children and teachers*. New York: Routledge.

Funabashi, K. (2001). Seikatsu-tsuzurikata. In Y. Kubo, T. Yoneda, T. Komagome, & K. Komikawa (Eds.), *Modern history of education [Gendai Kyoikushi Jiten]* (pp. 440–441). Tokyo: Tokyoshoseki.

Funato, S. (1953). Living children [Ikiteiru-Kodomo]. *Study Reports at Shima Primary School [Shimasho-Kenkyu-Houkoku], 1*, 25–30.

Hasumi, K. (1909). *Small-town teacher [Inaka-kyoshi]*. Tokyo: Ikuseikai.

Hirano, F. (1940). *Record of a Woman Teacher [Jokyoshi-no-Kiroku]*. Tokyo: Nishimurashoten.

Honjo, M. (1995). *When I Encounter New Myself [Aratana Jibun-ni Deau Toki]*. Tokyo: Shindokushosha.

Igarashi, K., Ohta, T., Otsuki, K., Miyasaka, T., & Katsuta, S. (1954a). About teaching narrative records 1 [Kyoshino-jissenkiroku-wo-megutte I]. *Education [Kyoiku], 40*, 72–99.

Igarashi, K., Ohta, T., Otsuki, K., Miyasaka, T., & Katsuta, S. (1954b). About teaching narrative records 2 [Kyoshino-jissenkiroku-wo-megutte II]. *Education [Kyoiku], 41*, 58–68.

Inaba, H. (2004). *Pedagogy in modern Japan [Kindainihon-no-Kyoikugaku]*. Kyoto: Sekaishisosha.

Inagaki, T. (1964). Working memo for the history of lesson study after the war. *Education [Kyoiku]*, *169*, 54–63.

Inagaki, T. (1966). *A historical research on teaching theory in the Meiji Era [Meiji-Kyojyuriron-Shi-Kenkyu]*. Tokyo: Hyoronsha.

Inagaki, T., & Sato, M. (1996). *Introduction to lesson study [Jugyokenkyu-Nyumon]*. Tokyo: Iwanamishoten.

Ishikawa, E. (1906). *An ideal primary teacher [Riso-no-shogaku-kyoshi]*. Tokyo: Ikuseikai.

Kadowaki, A. (2004). *Historical study on teachers' lives in Tokyo [Tokyo-Kyoin-Seikatsushi-Kenkyu]*. Tokyo: Gakubunsha.

Katsuta, S. (1955). How to evaluate teacher narrative descriptions? [jissen-kiroku-wo-dou-Hyoka--Suruka]. *Education [Kyoiku]*, *49*, 82–86.

Konishi, K. (1955). Revolution of the classroom *[Gakkyu-Kakumei]*. Tokyo: Makishoten.

Kobayashi, K. (1926). Philosophy of Tetsu [Tetsu-chan-no-Tetsugaku]. *The Century of Education [Kyoiku-no-seiki]*, *4*(2), 130–134.

Kobayashi, I. (1963). *Tayama Katai*. Tokyo: Asahisha.

Koizumi, M. (1907). *Sacrificed stone [Suteishi]*. Tokyo: Dobunkan.

Kujiraoka, S. (2005). *Introduction to episode records [Episodo-Kiroku-Nyumon]*. Tokyo: University of Tokyo Press.

Kyoiku-no-Seikisha. (1923). A plan of 'Jido-no-Mura' [Jido-no-Mura-no-Puran]. *The Century of Education [Kyoikuno-Seiki]*, *1*(1), 6–11.

Miura, T. (1922). *Teaching is not my Life Work [Sei-wo-Kyoiku-ni-Motomeezushite]*. Creation *[Sozo]*, *4*(4), 63–64.

Miyazaki, N. (1957). *Records of the classroom for bringing up fine people [Ningenzukuri-no-gakkyu-kiroku]*. Tokyo: Mugishobo.

Mori, T. (2004). Research notes on the history of educational practice. *Memoirs of the Faculty of Education and Regional Studies*, Fukui University, Series IV. *Science of Education, 60*, 53–62.

Nakano, A. (1968). *Study on Taisho liberal education [Taisho-Jiyukyoiku-no-Kenkyu]*. Nagoya: Reimeishobo.

National Association for the Study of Educational Methods. (2011). *Lesson study in Japan*. Hiroshima: Keisuisha.

Nomura, Y. (1924). From my life [Watashi-no-Seikatsu-Kara]. *The Century of Education [Kyoiku-no-Seiki]*, *2*(8), 82–88.

Nomura, Y. (1926a). I am burying the old education [Kyu-Kyoiku-wo-Maisosuruhi-no-Watashi]. *The Century of Education [Kyoiku-no-Seiki]*, *4*(10), 12–27.

Nomura, Y. (1926b). Educational renaissance from the viewpoint of motive [Doki-yori-mitaru-Kyoiku-no-Sosei]. *The Century of Education [Kyoiku-no-Seiki]*, *4*(11), 64–71.

Ohizumi, H. (2005). *For the theoretical development of narrative records [Jissenkirokuron-heno-tenkai]*. Shiga: Sangakushuppan.

Ohmiya, I. (2010). *Learning story for the practice of ECEC [Manabi-no-Monogatari-no-Hoiku--Jissen]*. Tokyo: Hitonarushobo.

Saito, K. (Ed.). (1958). *Academic abilities for the future [Mirai-ni-Tsunagaru-Gakuryoku]*. Tokyo: Mugishobo.

Saito, K. (Ed.). (1963). *Women teachers at Shima Primary School [Shimasho-no-jyokyoshi]*. Tokyo: Meijitosho.

Saito, K. (1964). *Story of Shima Primary School [Shimasho-monogatari]*. Tokyo: Mugishobo.

Shigaki, H. (1919). *A teacher's story [Kyoin-monogatari]*. Tokyo: Kodokan.

Shimizu, Y. (1955). *Structure of educational sociology [Kyoiku-Shakaigaku-no-Kozo]*. Tokyo: Tokyokan.

Sofu, I. (1912). *Self-awareness and confessions of a young teacher [Wakaki-kyoikusha-no-jikaku-to-kokuhaku]*. Tokyo: Naigaikyoikuhyoronsha.

Takase, K. (1974). *Inquiry into ECEC [Hoiku-no-tankyu]*. Tokyo: Shindokushosha.

Takezawa, K. (2005). *Records of practice to open teachers' eyes to children [Kodomo-ga-mietekuru-jissen-nokiroku]*. Tokyo: Zenshokensyuppanbu.

Tamefuji, G. (1922). *Why did I Leave the Teacher? [Yo-wa-Nazeni-Kyoshoku-wo-Jishitaka].* *Creation [Sozo], 4*(6), 68–75.

Tamefuji, G. (Ed.). (1923). *Thrown Pebble [Suteishi]: Memoir of teaching.* Tokyo: Shuseisha.

Tanaka, K. (Ed.). (2009). *Teachers who opened a new chapter in education II [Jidai-wo-Hiraita-Kyoshitachi II].* Tokyo: Nihonhyojyun.

Tanaka, Y. (2011). Potential of narrative inquiry as a methodology for Japanese educational research. *The Japanese Journal of Educational Research, 78*(4), 77–88.

Tanimoto, T. (1906). *Lecture on the New Education [Shinkyoiku-Kogi].* Tokyo: Rokumeikan.

Tayama, K. (1909). *Small-town teacher [Inaka-kyoshi].* Tokyo: Sakurashobo.

Teraoka, S. (2006). The influence of Pestalozzi's educational thought between 1920 and 1930 in Japan. Bulletin of Fukuoka University of Education. *Part IV, Education and Psychology, 55,* 79–94.

Toi, Y. (1957). *Academic ability for the development of a village [Mura-wo-sodateru-gakuryoku].* Tokyo: Meijitosyoshuppan.

Toyama, H. (1965). Problem Posed by the Natural Geography Class, [shizenchiri-no-Jyugyo-ga-Nagekaketamono]. *Education [Kyoiku], 15*(7), 16–21.

Tsuchida, S. (1955). *First-grade children in a village [Mura-no-ichinensei].* Tokyo: Shinhyoronsha.

Wada, A. (2002). *About reading [Yomukoto-ni-tsuite].* Tokyo: Hituzishobo.

Chapter 9
A History of Schools and Local Communities in Modern Japan

Yoshihiro Kokuni

9.1 Introduction

How do schools interact with their local communities in modern Japan (1867-present)? This essay briefly examines the history of the relationship between these two entities over the course of the past one and a half centuries. Historical records show that many local schools relied heavily on their communities for the financial and human resources they needed. Most schools, however, were also under the strict control of the state, which was interested in "national education" (*kokumin kyoiku*)—turning its people into ethnically homogenized yet supposedly voluntary members of a modern nation state—through an institutionalized educational system and a standardized curriculum. This national project, on the one hand, increased the possibility of social mobility through school credentials and thus contributed to a democratic ideal that guarantees each member of the society equal opportunity. On the other hand, national education, through its intrinsic attributes, flattened and effaced the distinctive features of each regional community, to be replaced and represented by the supposedly homogeneous Japanese culture. Thus, the history of school education in modern Japan cannot be understood without looking at the history of local communities and their unique, complex identities, as well as the process in which such uniqueness and complexity disappeared in the name of the homogenized national culture. In the analysis below, by focusing on the role local uniqueness played in classroom at school, I will show how the relationship between local schools and regional communities changed since the late nineteenth century.

Y. Kokuni (✉)
Graduate School of Education, The University of Tokyo, Tokyo, Japan
e-mail: kokuni@p.u-tokyo.ac.jp

© Springer Nature Singapore Pte Ltd. 2019   143
Y. Kitamura et al. (eds.), *Education in Japan*, Education in the Asia-Pacific
Region: Issues, Concerns and Prospects 47,
https://doi.org/10.1007/978-981-13-2632-5_9

9.2   School Education in Early Modern Japan

Historians of Japanese education generally agree that 1872 is the year when an incipient modern educational system emerged. They also agree that, even prior to the introduction of modern school system, namely, in the late Tokugawa period (1603–1867), many people in Japan were fairly well educated. The literacy rate reached as high as 80–90% among townsmen with enough financial resources to own family homes in big cities like Nagasaki and Kyoto. Literacy was also common in rural areas. As the Japanese society was highly bureaucratized by this time, most of the quotidian communication and administration was conducted through documentation. This required a wide variety of the population, from officials to tax-paying peasants, to be at least functionally literate.

Many people learned how to read and write at what they called temple school (*terakoya*). Temple schools were informal private institutions with little or no state intervention, where educated adults such as priests, monks, and lower-class samurai taught practical subjects like reading, writing, arithmetic, and daily moral lessons. Classes consisted of a group of a handful to a few dozen children, the number of which would vary depending on how fast each pupil mastered the desired materials. Lessons were often conducted in public places like temples (hence, "temple school") or at a teacher's residence. There was no standardized curriculum or pre-arranged academic schedule applicable to all pupils. There was also no fixed tuition, so some teachers accepted remuneration from poor peasant families in kind, like produce. Thus, temple schools in early modern Japan served a wide range of the local communities' populations, responding flexibly to the needs of a given regional community and people living there. In other words, denizens of a local community could freely choose what school to go to and what to learn there (Fig. 9.1).

9.3   The Founding of Modern Schools

After the Tokugawa regime was abolished, the Meiji government took the reins of the country and initiated a variety of modernization projects. Educational modernization started in 1872, when the Meiji government issued the first law regarding a new school system. The law announced that no village should have any illiterate inhabitants and held parents responsible for sending their children to school. It also stipulated that local communities were solely responsible for providing the money necessary to establish and manage schools. The national government had no part in financing schools, the law asserted, as school education should serve the interests of individual citizens rather than those of the nation.

Let us take a look at an example of how schools were established. In Kyoto, where emperors resided in pre-modern Japan, it was primarily the wealthy elite of each community who provided funding for communal elementary schools. Of particular interest is the fact that the local communities in Kyoto went beyond simply

Fig. 9.1 The illustration here is a snapshot of a temple school classroom from the 1800s. In the image, one can see the girls learning the shamisen and the boys engaged in reading and writing practices. It was common for a temple school to give a variety of education in the same classroom. (Reproduced from Emori 1990, p. 19)

paying for schools and even conceived of the idea of giving schools banking functions. That is to say that schools in Kyoto at the time were also expected to serve as foundations that lent pooled money to those in need. The interest debtors would pay on their loans would then keep the schools financially independent and sustainable. Furthermore, many such schools "served as the center of local governments" (Naka 1962, p. 123) and therefore shared their facilities with other communal factions such as fire departments, police departments, and town offices. People who helped build schools in Kyoto hoped that they would become "indispensable" to those in their respective local communities. Responsiveness to this desire is evident in the curricula at elementary schools that included classes for designing kimonos—a reflection of the fact that many families in Kyoto engaged in traditional textile known as *nishijin ori* (lit. "fabric in western encampment"). As these examples show, it was common for hopeful denizens of regional communities in the early years of Meiji to make generous and crucial contributions to the establishment of schools (Fig. 9.2).

This changed rapidly, however, as the central government stepped in. The Ministry of Education—the agency of the central government in charge of education, hereafter the "Ministry"—increased its influence and intervened in local administration in ways that gave little or no regard to local situations. One example

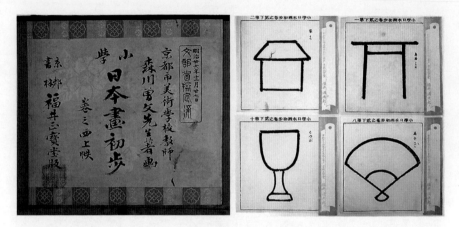

Fig. 9.2 During the Meiji period, teachers and locals prepared teaching materials independently from the central authorities. The images here were geared toward helping pupils learn the skills needed to generate patterns for pottery and kimono. (Reproduced from Kyoto Municipal Museum of School History and Kyoto Municipal Board of Education 2006, p. 52)

of this is the school district system set by the Ministry, which divided the archipelago into 53,760 school administrative districts, each with one elementary school. This measure was both highly impractical and arbitrary: the Ministry drew boundary lines for school districts that did not necessarily coincide with the traditional borders between the 80,000 or so communities existing at the time. In fact, part of the reason for this arbitrary measure was to weaken communal ties and identities so as to effectively integrate local communities under the centralized power structure of the Meiji government (Chiba 1962).

Aside from the above reason, most people did not welcome the Ministry's intervention as they believed that the knowledge learned at modern school had no practical use in daily life and instead simply created an onerous financial burden. One Ministry bureaucrat named Nishimura Shigeki confessed that it cost ten times more to have a Ministry-led modern school run than a temple school, and yet they "did much worse than temple schools in terms of convenience and effectiveness." Pupils were taught, for instance, how to do fractional calculations in their heads and how to write in embellished and stylized ways uncommon in daily writing, which people condemned as draining kids of "brain energy" (*noryoku*) (Nishimura 1876, pp. 44–46). To cap it all, local people and communities had to bear the full financial strain of both that ineffectual education and the school administration. The burden was bearable to highly commercialized and affluent districts like the abovementioned communities in Kyoto, where people showed proactive cooperation in building and managing schools. Many other communities, however, found the whole school business far beyond their means and sometimes staged violent protests, requesting measures such as the "removal of the financial encumbrance of elementary schools" and asserting that "[the Ministry] should abolish elementary schools and allow us to open temple schools at our own discretion" (Tamaki 1954; Tsuchiya 1953).

9.4 National Education Established; Local Cultures and Identities Suppressed

As discussed in the preceding section, the initial years of Meiji saw a huge gap between what the state-led school education offered and what most people in regional communities wanted and needed. The rift narrowed, however, as the state successfully initiated modernization projects in various aspects of people's lives and as the school education system grounded upon the dynamics of modernization was also gradually incorporated into people's lives. At the turn of the twentieth century—roughly three decades after the introduction of the modern education system of 1872—the attendance rate at elementary school almost reached at 100%. Nonetheless, this did not stop the Ministry from tightening its reins on the administration of local education. The Third Elementary School Order (*Daisanji kyoikurei*) in 1900 enjoined all elementary schools to only use textbooks published by the Ministry. Subsequently, children throughout the country studied the same materials almost simultaneously (Fig. 9.3).

The new subject in 1900, the "national language" (*kokugo*, i.e., Japanese), was representative of this trend of knowledge homogenization. It sought to standardize Japanese pronunciation and vocabulary that had previously been so varied, and with so many regional dialects, that even people from two neighboring villages often spoke with noticeable differences. Such disparities had manifested themselves even more in interlocutions between people from different prefectures. The "national language," then, was meant to tackle this problem systematically through education. As phonographs were not yet easily available at the turn of the century, the Ministry made posters with images of palates that showed the "correct" forms and shapes of the mouth and tongue during enunciation, as seen below.

A few decades later, this project on the standardization of pronunciation took an even more aggressive turn with the introduction of "punishment tablets" (*bassatsu* or *batsufuda*) in schools in the 1930s. Sometimes also referred to as "dialect tablets" (*hogenfuda*), each punishment tablet had a cross mark, "X," on it that denoted disgrace or rejection. Schoolteachers hung this tablet around a pupil's neck as a punitive measure if he or she was caught speaking a dialect. The humiliated child then had to keep it dangling around his or her neck until the teacher heard another boy or girl talking in a dialect and passed the tablet to them. The punishment tablet was a very effective tool with which schoolteachers forced children to internalize a sense of shame toward speaking their hometown dialect. This disciplinary practice was relatively common until the 1950s, though it remained in use until the 1970s in some parts of the country.

The centralized government's universally standardized educational policies like those discussed above had both merits and demerits. With the standardized language and a specific knowledge set shared broadly throughout the country, people could now travel and move around more and ascend the social ladder with academic credentials. Indeed, social mobility increased to a degree unimaginable in the Tokugawa period. Additionally, standardization and increased access to obtaining

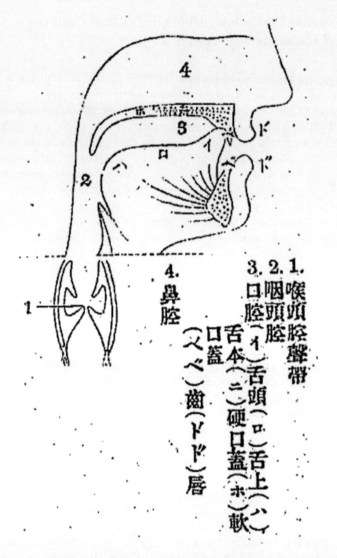

Fig. 9.3 Prior to the advent of record player, teachers taught correct enunciation with illustrations like the one here, which shows the location of the tongue in the palate. (Reproduced from Isawa 1909)

school credentials meant that the upper-class culture was no longer distinctive or exclusive to a small group of aristocracy and elite with old money. Nonetheless, standardization also had its downsides: it did not just obliterate the uniqueness of the regional community, but also rendered insignificant the act of remaining in a small local community and serving the well-being of the place and its people.

In the 1930s, the trend of standardization of education faced significant push-back. Some educators voiced the idea that kids should learn more about histories and legends unique to the communities they live in. This occurred against the backdrop of the Great Depression in the 1920s. The economic crisis that ravaged many small communities turned a lot of people toward rediscovering and reevaluating communal values, which also had an impact on school education. Here, the central government took a cautious attitude. In general the government was encouraging, but did try to channel popular interest in communal identities toward patriotism, so that the same popular interest would not later become grounds for critique against the state. The government explained that as love for a community was but a subset of nationalism, the two remained completely compatible. The official interpretation worked effectively, at least in school: most educators now discussed and evoked communal values in the classroom in order to strengthen the pupils' loyalty to the nation. This strategic link between communal and national allegiance persisted even after the Second World War and was still common in postwar education.

9.5   US Occupation and Educational Reforms

When speaking of the history of education in Japan, a series of educational reforms under the US occupation forces is also worthy of note. First of all, it is important to know that most classes had to be conducted in the open air as wartime US air raids had reduced much of Japan to charred ruins. The lack of proper classrooms and the government's depleted financial reserves caused locals to take initiative in rebuilding schools. Villagers in Chiyogawa, Ibaraki Prefecture, for instance, made a tough decision on felling and selling the local shrine's seven ancient trees in order to make money for school reconstruction. A plaque at the shrine says:

> There were once seven ancient trees here, piercing through the azure sky like dragons. Our ancestors worshiped them as the trees of god and we cherished them as the symbol of our shared community. But we had to cut down those very trees. The burden to build a school anew was too insufferable for our village to shoulder. At the same time, our children needed classrooms where they could study, protected from the elements. We thus felled the trees our ancestors treasured for generations and sold them to a merchant to cover the cost of the school's construction. It was difficult to make the decision and to hold back the tears. This occurred in November 1948, one quiet day of the village festival. (Nakauchi et al. 1987, p. 9)

This was not an exceptional case. Between 1947 and 1950, the total area of schools built covered 10.45 km^2, of which 6.1 km^2 were constructed with government subsidies, while 4.35 km^2 of these were paid for by the locals (Nakauchi et al. 1987, p. 9). Schoolteachers were also underpaid due to the economic instability and confusion in the immediate postwar period. One person recalls seeing local villagers sending vegetables to teachers. During that period, locals often provided financial succor in return for school education.

The impact of new policies during early years of the US Occupation cannot be underestimated either. The Supreme Commander for Allied Powers, or SCAP, represented the occupation forces in Japan, and one of the orders the SCAP issued to the central government was to devolve administrative power and authority to the schools' regional communities. SCAP specified that teachers had to confer with locals regarding teaching materials and curricula.

Many teachers at elementary and junior high schools responded quickly to this order. They went around in an attempt to discover what locals wanted from school education and then incorporated what they learned into their original curricula. This practice was common between the late 1940s and the early 1950s. For example, Uozaki Elementary School in Kobe, Hyogo Prefecture, set three principles for designing curricula:

1. The right to design curricula resides in the hands of the teaching staff and the people in our community.
2. Our teaching plans are to be in accord with the improvement of the lives [of the people in the community].
3. In principle, pupils' parents are welcome to participate in our classes.

In 1947, Uozaki teachers and locals founded the School Administration Committee and began fashioning curricula. Roughly 12,000 people in about 3,000 households lived in the town of Uozaki, where the school is located. The US air raids during the war had severely affected the lives of most people there—locals, kids, and teachers alike—and they still had found no way of escaping their misery. The first thing committee members agreed upon under the circumstances was to address the reality of the affliction from which most people suffered. The committee examined the living conditions of the town and its inhabitants, looking for effective ways to better the lives of the people. As a result, the 10 committee members completed a booklet that listed teaching objectives for the coming 6 years and a voluminous workbook of 550 pages for pupils to work on. The school principal at the time prefaced the booklet as follows:

> We believe that our life will be blessed with happiness. If we do not let the hardships of today be the cause of despair or lethargy, our society shall be infused with dreams. Let the hope for the realization of these dreams guide us through our miseries today, and our life shall improve and our society shall progress. Let us now commence the grand enterprise of reconstructing our educational system so that it ceases to serve itself and instead serves to better the society for our common good.

They groped for the best way to raise their children in the face of the immense task of reviving the town from the war-scorched earth. Such a proactive stance on the part of regional communities was quite common and was even encouraged by the central government. Government support of such dynamic approaches is evidenced by the fact that the Ministry of Education, between 1947 and 1957, designated its *General Policies Regarding Curriculum Formulation* (*gakushu shido yoryo*) as a "draft plan" (*shian*), or a sort of reference work for local schools to consult when designing their respective communities' own unique curricula. At the behest of the SCAP pushing for decentralization of educational administrative power, the government also set up a Board of Education office in every municipality. Each local government conducted public elections to appoint Board members, strengthening the link between communal educational needs and local school administration.

This combined effort did not last long, however. When the Korean War erupted in 1950, the SCAP changed its occupation policies, causing Japan to serve as a bulwark against Communist expansion. The *General Policies Regarding Curriculum Formulation* could no longer exist as a "draft plan" and were instead made mandatory in 1958 in order to ensure that local schools taught according to the new policies. The Ministry also required schools to notify the Board of Education in advance of the use of any teaching materials other than official textbooks. The public election of members of the Board of Education, which had helped translate local will into school education, was also abolished and now heads of the municipal governments appointed Board members. With this series of new educational policies, local schools became loyal agents of the central government, unrepresentative of local communities.

9.6   Regional Reorganization and Education in the Period of High Economic Growth

Japan went through a period called "high economic growth" or "economic miracle" between 1955 and 1973. In these years, the Japanese national economy changed drastically, with an annual 10% rise in GNP, as did those of the communal villages and towns throughout the country. In an attempt to facilitate high economic growth, the government initiated a number of regional development policies such as the "Comprehensive National Development Plan" and the "New Industrial City Development Plan." As a result, industrial cities with petrochemical complexes emerged all along the Pacific coast. The booming industry was in need of capable workers, which it recruited systematically from junior high and high school graduates. Many teenagers were encouraged to leave their home villages to work in factories in urban areas (Fig. 9.4).

In this period, junior high and high schools in the archipelago were newly defined as "labor production devices" for the newly constructed industrial areas. In other words, schools now played a new role in sending children away from their birthplaces. Tests and exams assessing academic progress became a routine in the everyday lives of junior high and high school students. Grades at school based on these tests were crucial in paving the road for each child's future because they determined what kind of jobs students could get after graduation and where they would be sent. During this period a string of teenage suicide cases occurred among young people from the countryside who were shamed by people ridiculing their regional dialects when they started to work in factories in cities. Feeling sympathy for the unfortunate children, many teachers were even more motivated to teach children how to speak standard Japanese. Standardized Japanese education robbed children of the languages and cultures unique to their birthplace and inevitably annihilated regional dialects and cultures which had once given rise to regional distinctiveness.

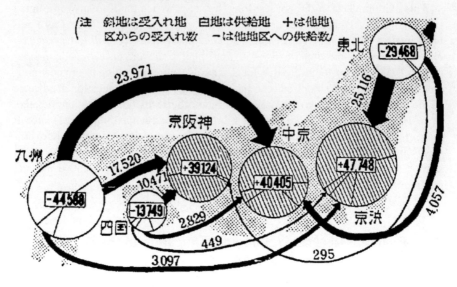

Fig. 9.4 A large number of junior high graduates migrated to major cities such as Tokyo, Nagoya, and Osaka for work during the 1960s. The image here shows that the number was more than 120,000 graduates in 1963 alone. ("The Asahi Shinbun", March 28, 1963)

9.7 Resistance Movements to Economically Oriented Regional Reorganization

In the face of these policies that favored industrial development, there were many cases in which locals and schoolteachers cooperated to stage resistance movements. Participants in these campaigns challenged the conventional ways in which local schools were conceived vis-à-vis local communities. Let us examine the exact nature of the resistance through the following two case studies: (a) the role schools and teachers played in antipollution campaigns and (b) the struggle against the merger or elimination of junior high and high schools in remote areas.

(a) The role played by schools and teachers in the antipollution campaigns

The rapid government-led industrialization brought on pollution issues in many parts of the country. Some such negative aspects of the excessive industrialization surfaced already in the 1960s. Some people endured air pollution in petrochemical complexes, others suffered from grave illnesses after eating inshore fish polluted with factory effluent that contained mercury, and still others became victims of occasional photochemical smog caused by automobile exhaust in urban areas.

People took action in the face of these rising problems. Some collectively opposed plant construction. In battling against a plan for a petrochemical complex, for instance, members of one community in Shizuoka Prefecture met and held study sessions more than a few hundred times and also staged an anti-factory rally in 1964 that a third of the constituents in the area joined. They successfully put an end to the plan for plant construction.

Local schoolteachers and high school students in this community helped the locals with scientific investigations and study sessions. The teaching faculty from the technical high school, in particular, made use of their expertise in sciences like meteorology, industrial chemistry, and geology. They conducted a series of scientific experiments that discredited the many scientific arguments the corporation in question had tendered in order to support their claims that the construction of the factory was safe. All along, the science teachers maintained close contact with the locals and kept them well informed of the scientific aspects of the debate. High school students, too, showed commitment to the cause and foresaw the potential danger of a community relying too much on petrochemical industry. The students sensed that such a community would last no more than 40 years, after which it would atrophy in the same way as many towns that relied primarily on the coal mining industry. The students actively conducted research and fieldwork to understand what was really happening in their community. The activities turned out to be highly educational, perhaps more so than the official textbooks, and the products of the research and fieldwork were enlightening not just to the students, but also to the people in the community.

Through these events, schools played a new role. They now offered a space where both students and people of the community could consider what nature of knowledge they wished to pursue and believe in and what happiness meant for the members of the corresponding community. This was an important juncture for the history of school education, as it was the first time communities became keenly and critically aware of some of the negative aspects of modernization that had been forced upon them subliminally through school education (Makabe 1971).

(b) The campaigns against the merger or elimination of junior high and high schools in remote areas

Between 1950 and 1979, the number of schools shrank from 25,800 to 24,800 for elementary schools and from 14,000 to 11,000 for junior high schools. Three factors can explain this decline. First, motivated by economic growth, the central government promoted municipal mergers that could minimize administrative inefficiency. Additionally, the central government instructed regional governments to merge small schools so that they would be "appropriate in size" and run cost-effectively. Finally, an increasing number of young men and women flooded into economically booming urban areas. As young adults of marriageable age moved away, this caused the number of children born in remote areas to diminish, and thus, inevitably, the number of school-aged children also decreased dramatically.

The 1970s were marked by various local political and social campaigns. Communities took issue with the central government's policy on school mergers and elimination. One instance happened when a town council in Gunma Prefecture passed a resolution to close a small school under its jurisdiction of only some 70 students named Yuzurihara Elementary School. As this decision paid no heed to the voices of most denizens of the town, they felt infuriated. Most people disagreed with the authoritarian resolution out of a strong attachment to the school as "their own local school," and so they continued to send their kids to the school even after its official closing. Without any government subsidies, the locals hired teachers and successfully managed the school on their own. It is surprising that the school was maintained smoothly for the brief yet significant duration of 2 years after the government shut it down.

In modern Japan, schools functioned primarily as an important place of "national education" that, through standardized and universalized curricula and textbooks, nurtured homogenized and loyal members of a modern nation state. The local opposition movements against the school merger policy posed a challenge to the dominant role schools played. People also started to ponder over the function of schools tied to communities and how they could be beneficial to the spiritual well-being of those living there. Most locals were now aware that schools could be emotional symbols of their communities but stopped short of challenging the nationally standardized curricula that completely disregarded local distinctiveness or needs.

9.8   New Policies: A Turn Toward the "Community School"

The nature of school education shifted in the 1980s, both regionally and nationally. School violence was a matter of grave concern for most educators. Some students attacked their teachers. Others bullied their fellow students, leaving them traumatized and pushing them to play truant in order to avoid torment. Schools often hastened to cover up such incidents, frequently without success. The media then criticized their attempts to hide these events and denounced the closed, secretive nature of many schools. The educational policies that emerged in response hence put forward the slogan of "open schools" based on healthy communication and cooperation with local families and communities. The Ad Hoc Council on Education (*Rinji kyoiku shingi kai*) set up in 1984 at the behest of the prime minister at the time reported 3 years later as follows:

> Schools should be considered community property, and thus, oriented towards forming a harmonious and cooperative relationship with the communities and families living there. This does not mean simply that school facilities should be open and available to the public. It also signifies that schools should be receptive to constructive criticism of school management from students' parents and communities, that schools and local communities should unite in adapting to the rapidly computerizing society, that pupils should spend more time doing outdoor activities as part of school curricula, and that schools should develop in a more globally-oriented direction. Those involved in school education ought to pursue new methods of school administration and management that can fulfill the new goals mentioned above. (Rinji kyoiku shingi kai 1987, p. 25)

In reality, though, other than school facilities becoming more available to the general public, few of these "goals" were achieved in the 1980s and 1990s. Schools redefined themselves as a place which provided the opportunity for people at various stages of life to learn. They therefore opened their swimming pools during the summer and their gymnasiums at night or on weekends for the locals. But schools did not go much further than that.

Many schools engaged in their respective regional communities in more meaningful ways from the late 1990s to the 2000s. Local people and students' parents were now more directly involved in school administration and management. The 1998 report from the Central Council for Education, the executive council at the Ministry of Education, Culture, Sports, Science and Technology ("MEXT"; formerly, Ministry of Education), defines the role of the school in a community:

> Schools must be accessible to the public and the administrators there must be held accountable for school management. This way, schools will contribute to creating an atmosphere where people can trust the schools in their communities and parents and schools can work together for better education [...].
>
> For schools to be increasingly accessible to their local communities in the near future, schools must be sensitive to and incorporate the voices of the locals and parents, and thus garner their support in school management. From this perspective, we suggest that a law should be passed that allows headmasters to be able to set up school councils where they can obtain advice and feedback on school management from well-informed locals outside of schools. Moreover, such school councils can also serve as a liaison between schools and local communities.

The lawmakers responded to the above suggestions and passed a law in 2000 that institutionalized the School Council Member System (*gakko hyogiin seido*) and placed school council members in public schools all over the country. The system, however, did not achieve the desired result of well representing the voices of parents and local people in school management. The root of the problem was that council members were appointed by the school principal, rather than through regional election. Furthermore, schools were not legally bound by the suggestions that council members made. Many councils hence ended up validating the authority of the headmaster's decisions regarding school management instead of constructively modifying such decisions. Somehow, it was in these very years that staff organizations—assemblies in which teachers made important decisions on school management—were legally demoted from the executive decision-making body in each school to an ancillary organ of the school. We could probably argue here that the central government showed more interest in the voices of regional people and parents in order to covertly weaken the teachers' former influence over school administration.

The basic framework of school education has not changed much even after the introduction of the Community School System. The Central Council for Education made the proposal for the system in 2007 in an attempt to take the School Council Member System a step further in the direction of "even greater local and parental participation in school management." The government set the target of converting about 10% of the public elementary and junior high schools into community schools by March 2017.

Community schools will surely bring about many benefits for school-aged children. With parental and communal involvement, schools can provide children with more fine-grained, flexible education than they did before, both academically and spiritually. Furthermore, children will profit from interactions with adults of different backgrounds from whom they can choose role models to emulate.

Nevertheless, the community school as it is currently conceived in Japan also has its limitations. First of all, it operates within the framework of the centralized bureaucracy. That is, the community school is still legally bound by the central government-designed curricula, and any textbook a community school wishes to use must first receive the central government's approval. Not much is left to the discretion of the school itself. Furthermore, community schools have little say in recruitment and personnel management, which are controlled by the regional Boards of Education. Regulations preventing a teacher from homerooming or serving as headmaster for the same cohort of students for more than 3–5 years also restrict teachers' long-term involvement in their pupils' education. Budgetary discretion still goes to the Boards of Education, which is yet another limiting factor for community schools. What is more, the school principal appoints the members of the School Management Board (*gakko un'ei kyogikai*), just as with the members in the Board's predecessor, the School Council. The Board selected hence has only an advisory function in school management. The original motivation behind the community school of constructive collaboration between parents, locals, and teachers is still hindered by multiple parties unwilling to renounce the power accorded them. Namely, the MEXT exercises curricular discretion, the regional governments (the 47 prefectures in total) have recruitment/personnel discretion, and the Board of Education has control over school principals.

The prospect that local schools will be teaching children their distinctive histories and cultures more systematically and meaningfully is even dimmer than before. It is true that, in recent years, a growing number of schools started "hometown education" to do just that. A closer look at what is actually taught in such classes shows, however, that the primary objective is often set to evoke the type of local identities that coincide with and can be effectively translated into love for the Japanese culture and loyalty to the nation. Hometown education as it is practiced now essentially rehashes the 1930s educational movement concerning teaching local distinctiveness. Just like in the 1930s, this form of pedagogy is emerging within the context of a rapidly widening economic gap between the haves and the have-nots. It is disturbing to think that hometown education might end up simply diverting economically disadvantaged people's attention away from their frustration with their situation and focus it instead on the idea of a collective nationalistic identity.

9.9   Conclusion

This essay has shown that throughout the history of modern Japan, school education in Japan has failed in instituting effective ways to teach children communal values and cultures unique to their respective hometowns. It has, however, succeeded in generating the grounds for equal access to educational opportunities and high social mobility propelled by school credentials. The "national education" that has dictated schools in modern Japan has forced on children an image of Japan as an ethically homogenized entity and has relegated a rich variety of regional languages to mere "dialects" that must be replaced by the supposedly standardized Japanese. This is a sheer denial of linguistic rights as defined by UNESCO.

There has been a new impetus for change in recent years. Japan is transitioning toward becoming a nation of immigrants. As of now, the number of non-Japanese in Japan amounts to over two million and accounts for approximately 2% of the whole population. Though this is still a small number, it does vary regionally: in some parts of the country, the number goes up to far more than 10%. The number skyrockets to above 30% in the Okubo area just outside central Tokyo. There, more than two thirds of pupils are of non- or half-Japanese descent. Communication between the schools and the parents in the area is made in seven different languages.

The Japanese policymakers are interested in bringing in more immigrants, who could help sustain the Japanese labor market as the young Japanese labor population shrinks and the retired population increases. Multi-nationalization is on its way. This can be a catalyst for change in school education in Japan that until now has done little to pass communal values and distinctiveness on to students. Are schools going to remain producers of a homogenized Japanese identity and culture as they have for more than a century? Or are they willing to transform themselves into intercultural and international hubs, where people from diverse backgrounds come together to create unique communal cultures that they can pass on to their children? School education in Japan will soon stand at a historic crossroads.

References

Chiba, M. (1962). *Gakkuseido no kenkyu: kokka kenryoku to sonraku kyodotai* [A study on the school district system: The state power and the village communities]. Tokyo: Keiso shobo.

Emori, I. (1990). *"Benkyo" jidai no makuake* [An opening of the era of *"Benkyo* (study)"]. Tokyo: Heibonsha.

Isawa, S. (1909). *Shiwa oyo tohoku hatsuon kyoseiho* [Visible speech: Correcting the dialect of Tohoku Region]. Tokyo: Rakusekisha.

Kyoto Municipal Museum of School History & Kyoto Municipal Board of Education. (2006). *Kyoto gakko monogatari* [Stories of schools in Kyoto]. Kyoto: Information Design Associates Kyoto.

Makabe, J. (1971). *Chiikiron, chiikiundo to kyoiku* [Regional theory: Local movement in communities and education]. In T. Morita (Ed.), *Kyoiku jissen to chiiki kyoto* [Educational practices and community collaboration and resistance] (pp. 9–32). Tokyo: Meiji Tosho.

Naka, A. (1962). *Meijishoki no kyoikuseisaku to chiho eno teichaku* [Education policy in the early Meiji era and its local acceptance]. Tokyo: Kodansha.

Nakauchi, T., et al. (1987). *Nihon kyoiku no sengoshi* [The postwar history of Japanese education]. Tokyo: Sanseido.

Nishimura, S. (1876). *Gakkujunshi kotei* [The inspection tour of the school districts]. *Nihon teikoku monbusho nenpo* [Bulletin of Ministry of Education of the Empire of Japan], *4*, 44–46.

Ogawa, T. (1963). *Seinenki ni okeru sabetsu no mondai* [Issues of discrimination during the adolescence]. *Kyoiku* [Education], *13*(5), 12–22.

Rinji kyoiku shingi kai. (1987). *Rinkyoshin dayori* [Newsletter of the Ad Hoc Council on Education], 39 (August special issue).

Tamaki, H. (1954). *Nihon kyoiku hattatsushi* [History of educational development in Japan]. Kyoto: Sanichi Shobo.

Tsuchiya, T. (1953). *Shugakutokusoku to kyohi no jidai* [The era of promoting school enrolment and the resistance against such efforts]. *The Japanese Journal of Educational Research, 20*(1), 74–86.

Chapter 10
Background of "Individualized Meritocracy" Among Japanese Youth: Social Circulation Model of Postwar Japan and Its Collapse

Yuki Honda

10.1 What Happened in Japan on 3.11?

Everybody is aware of what happened in the northeast of Japan on March 11, 2011. A huge earthquake that shook the ocean floor near the east coast of Japan caused gigantic tidal waves to roll inland, destroying a large number of towns on the coast and resulting in a huge loss of human life—around 19,000 people are dead, and about 2500 people are still missing to date. Waves also assaulted the Fukushima Daiichi nuclear power plant, inflicting severe damage on key areas of the plant that stored critical equipment. Since then, radioactive contamination has become a threat not only to the people living close to the damaged plant but also to the wider population living in Fukushima and neighboring prefectures. What made things worse was the electric power shortage caused by the destruction of the Fukushima Daiichi plant and the suspension of operations at other nuclear facilities on safety concerns. Thus, almost every industry located in the eastern half of Japan has been adversely impacted, leading to the unemployment of a large number of people; some estimate that unemployment and layoff figures caused by the 3.11 disaster could be well over 2,200,000 (Genda 2014, p. 104).

These incidents raise the following questions: do we know what really happened? What does this disaster really mean to the Japanese people, especially the young people on whose shoulders the destiny of Japan rests? Is this just an unlucky, natural calamity, the damage from which will be overcome sooner or later? Or does this imply a grave turning point for the entire Japanese society?

Y. Honda (✉)
Graduate School of Education, The University of Tokyo, Tokyo, Japan
e-mail: yuki@p.u-tokyo.ac.jp

© Springer Nature Singapore Pte Ltd. 2019
Y. Kitamura et al. (eds.), *Education in Japan*, Education in the Asia-Pacific Region: Issues, Concerns and Prospects 47,
https://doi.org/10.1007/978-981-13-2632-5_10

10.2 "They Were Victims of Disaster Prior to 3.11"

In order to understand what the 3.11 disaster implies to the people of Japan, we must reflect on the social situation before this catastrophe.

In a paper written just before the 3.11 disaster, Japanese sociologist Nozomu Shibuya (2011) describes the condition of Japanese youth after the bursting of the bubble economy at the beginning of the 1990s, referencing the concepts "disaster capitalism" and "shock doctrine" proposed by Naomi Klein (2007). According to Shibuya, the sense of discontent and despair produced by some kind of psychological shock is a condition of the self-actualizing "entrepreneurial self" that is indispensable for the sustenance of neoliberalism. Like natural disasters and hostile military operations, the marked deterioration of the labor market since the mid-1990s has infused shock or panic among Japanese youth. They have lost their sense of stability, and their only hope has been to behave as "entrepreneurs," who seek to actualize their objects by themselves despite the various risks and hardships.

Shibuya's argument is quite impressive because it suggests that Japan's younger generation had already suffered a sort of socioeconomic "disaster" prior to 3.11. We can detect various social phenomena in the late 1990s and first decade of the 2000s that support Shibuya's view. The Japanese youth labor market has undergone a marked change since the beginning of the 1990s. With a significant rise in the number of young workers uncertain about their job prospects and an increasing number of unemployed youth, the risks of poverty, social isolation, and despair have grown among the youth of Japan. Although some new youth policies have been enforced as countermeasures against these situations, their effects have been questionable because of their limited scope and the inadequacy of their contents.

Under these circumstances, the subjectivity of Japanese youth assumed some characteristic features. Our analysis of the social attitudes of Japanese adolescents (Honda et al. 2010), using data from a questionnaire survey conducted in 2009, indicates that the younger generations of the Japanese have high praise for meritocracy, though they are dissatisfied with the government and the labor market and harbor feeble hopes for any improvement in their situation (Figs. 10.1 and 10.2).[1]

[1] The data is from the first to third sweep of the Youth Cohort Study of Japan. Our original samples were randomly collected from 20-year-old young people from all over the country in 2007. The number of responses are 1357 for the first sweep (autumn 2007), 1097 for the second sweep (autumn 2008), and 966 for the third sweep (autumn 2009). Variables used in the analyses and their components are shown in the table below.

Components of the variables

	Variable	Questions used	Choices	α
Competencies	Activeness	I am always an active participant.	Strongly agree/agree/ disagree/strongly disagree	0.759
		I have an ability to contribute to society.	Strongly agree/agree/ disagree/strongly disagree	
		I have some advantages over other people.	Strongly agree/agree/ disagree/strongly disagree	
	Communication skills	Expressing my opinion	Completely able/able/ unable/completely unable	0.752
		Conversing naturally with people who you don't know	Completely able/able/ unable/completely unable	
		Directing a group of people with your leadership	Completely able/able/ unable/completely unable	
	Information skills	Making documents using Personal computers or word processer	Completely able/able/ unable/completely unable	0.808
		Collecting information from internet	Completely able/able/ unable/completely unable	
Social Attitudes	Meritocracy	Jobs should be provided for those who have appropriate abilities to fulfil their responsibilities.	Strongly agree/agree/ disagree/strongly disagree	0.655
		It is a good thing for those who have achieved better result than others to be compensated with high salaries and status for their own abilities.	Strongly agree/agree/ disagree/strongly disagree	
		It is a good thing for those who have achieved better result than others to be evaluated as a better human being than the others.	Strongly agree/agree/ disagree/strongly disagree	
	Hope	Japan provides opportunities for youth.	Strongly agree/agree/ disagree/strongly disagree	0.575
		Social problems can be solved by people.	Strongly agree/agree/ disagree/strongly disagree	
		It is the fault of the young who cannot get stable jobs, because they are not giving enough efforts.	Strongly agree/agree/ disagree/strongly disagree	
	Dissatisfaction	I am not happy with the government.	Strongly agree/agree/ disagree/strongly disagree	0.693
		I am not happy with the companies' attitudes towards employment.	Strongly agree/agree/ disagree/strongly disagree	

We allotted scores 1–4 to the answer to the questions and calculated the average score for each variables

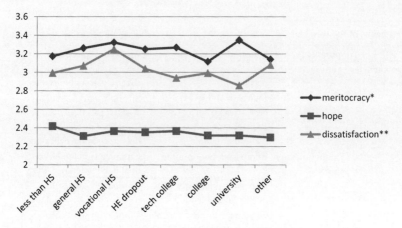

Fig. 10.1 Social attitudes of young people by educational background

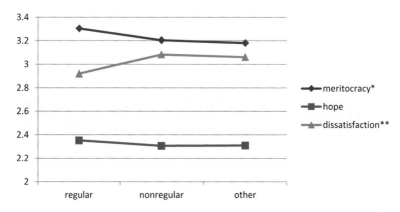

Fig. 10.2 Social attitudes of young people by job status

The results of multiple regression analyses of these three social attitudes (Table 10.1) indicate complex relations between one's background and social attitudes. The intensity of dissatisfaction is influenced by unfavorable conditions such as an economically disadvantaged family background, an educational background lower than a university diploma, and a non-regular job. The strength of the sense of hope correlates positively with the self-evaluation of one's activeness and communication skill. At the same time, the level of information skill has a positive effect on the approval of meritocracy.

Moreover, the interrelation between these three social attitudes is also worthy of note. There is a strong positive correlation between the approval of meritocracy and the feeling of hope. The approval of meritocracy also correlates positively with dissatisfaction, though weakly. On the other hand, a strong negative correlation is observed between hope and dissatisfaction.

Table 10.1 Multiple regression analysis of social attitudes (β)

		Meritocracy	Hope	Dissatisfaction
Gender	Female	−0.052	−0.040	−0.008
SES	Family affluence (age 18)	0.064	0.061	−0.081*
Education	University graduation	0.059	−0.103*	−0.122**
Work	Regular worker	0.044	0.001	−0.091*
	Income	0.012	0.019	0.022
	Work hour	0.047	−0.005	−0.009
Skills	Activeness	−0.003	0.231***	0.051
	Communication	−0.029	0.101*	0.008
	Information	0.186***	−.090*	−0.006
Social attitudes	Meritocracy		0.155***	0.068+
	Hope	0.168***		−0.202***
	Dissatisfaction	0.067+	−0.184***	
	Adjusted R2	0.066	0.139	0.055
	F	5.108	10.336	4.389
	Significance level	0.000	0.000	0.000

*:p<0.05, **:p<0.01, ***:p<0.001

How can we interpret these interrelations between social attitudes? Why does the approval of meritocracy show positive correlations both with dissatisfaction and with hope, while the latter two contradict each other? A possible explanation is that since the dissatisfaction with the status quo is based on a feeling that society does not treat these young people fairly, it tends to generate an expectation of meritocracy as an ideal social structure in which one could revive oneself. On the other hand, young people who have a stronger sense of hope are satisfied with the actual state of a society that properly appreciates their own competencies. In both cases, meritocracy is the dominant framework by which young Japanese people interpret their own positions in society.

It is also important to note that dissatisfaction with the government and the labor market is not accompanied by a feeling that one can make a change and improve the actual state—namely, a sense of hope—because those who are dissatisfied tend to lack confidence in their own competencies, abilities, or power. On the other hand, those who have hope do not think it necessary to change the actual state of society. Thus, the movement among young people to redress the deficits of Japanese society is very weak.

When we return to Shibuya's argument with these findings from our data analyses, we note that among Japanese youth, the notion of meritocracy spells the functional equivalence to the "entrepreneurial self," a concept originally stated by Michel Foucault. For Japanese youth, "merit" signifies competencies which individuals possess adventitiously and is actualized through the constant behaviors of individuals, rather than acquired systematically through some institutional education and training. Therefore, meritocracy in Japan seems to be quite individualized in two senses: the responsibility for the difference of "merit" both in quantity and

Table 10.2 Scoreboard for youth aged 15–24, Japan and OECD, 2007

	Japan	OECD
Employment rate (% of the age group)	41.5	43.6
Unemployment rate – UR (% of the labour force)	7.7	13.4
Relative UR youth/adult (25-54)	2.1	2.9
Ratio unemployed to population (% of the age group)	3.5	6.1
Incidence of long-term unemployment (% of unemployment)	21.3	19.6
Incidence of part-time work (% of employment)	25.5	24.2
NEET rate (% of the age group)	8.8	12.0
School drop–outs (% of the age group)	4.5	13.6

Source: OECD (2009, Table1.4)

quality between individuals is attributed to the individuals themselves, and the status of individuals is recognized as the outcome of their own "merit."

Japanese young people have lived through the economic disaster preceding 3.11 with this type of "individualized meritocracy" in mind. "Survive by yourself, or resign" was the message from the society which constantly surrounded them, permeated their minds, and incited their actions.

This argument, however, might provoke several questions, including the following: why has the situation of the youth labor market inflicted a "disastrous" impact on Japanese youth, despite the fact that the rate of unemployment and part-time jobs in recent times has not been noticeably high compared to other developed societies (Table 10.2)? Why has meritocracy in Japan become so individualized, despite the fact that Japanese society seems to have highly institutionalized systems of ability formation?

10.3 Postwar Japan's Unique Social Circulation

In order to answer these questions, we need to trace through Japanese history, identify the distinctive features of the Japanese social structure, and interpret the implications of change after the 1990s in light of the sociohistorical trajectory that Japanese society has followed over the years.

It is well known that postwar Japanese society, following the period of confusion and rehabilitation from the ravages of war, achieved a high level of economic growth, more than 10% against the average, every year, in the 1960s. Although this period of high growth ended because of the oil shock in the early 1970s, the Japanese economy maintained stable economic growth until around 1990. During these two periods, namely, the high economic growth period and the stable economic growth period, a social circulation model peculiar to Japan formed, developed, and matured.

The distinctive features of this social circulation model of postwar Japan are as follows (Fig. 10.3): (1) a strong one-way flow of resources between the three

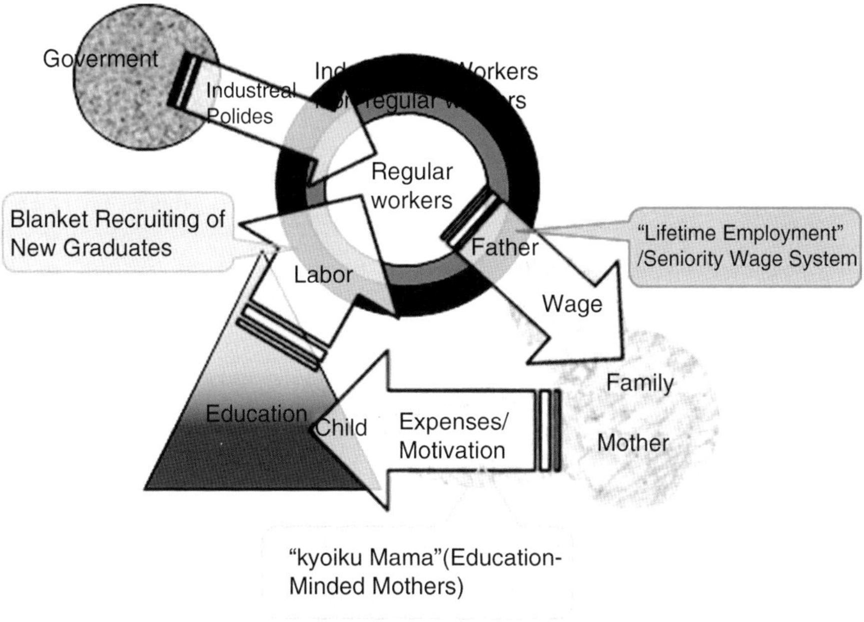

Fig. 10.3 Social circulation model of postwar Japan

social systems of education, work, and family, through which the output of one system is poured directly into another system as the input; (2) the limited role of the government outside this triangular circulation of resources to industrial policies, such as giving orders for public engineering works; and (3) a definite "division of labor" among people according to their age and gender into these three social systems, namely, the younger age bracket taking charge of school education, male adults taking charge of work, and female adults taking charge of family, the consequence of which is strong ageism and gender discrimination.

What is important is that the flow between systems assumed quite peculiar forms. First, the flow of manpower from education to work was characterized by the "blanket recruiting of new graduates." This meant that students searched for and found jobs while still in schools and universities, often with the intensive help of school-teachers or university professors, who often played the role of sorting applicants into job openings, and the students began regular work immediately after graduating. This unique process of transition from school to work, which had been prompted by a steady labor demand for new graduates whose labor costs were low and were deemed to be rich in trainability, apparently seemed to be quite efficient. Actually, this process contributed toward maintaining a very low youth unemployment rate in Japan compared to that of other developed societies during the 1970s and 1980s. This process, however, had a defect: within the school education system, the formation of vocational skills of youth and the matching of an individual's aptitude, ability, and willingness to work in a particular job had not been given much thought.

The most important issue that drove this process for students and teachers was the choice of which company to join as a member, rather than the choice of the job one might engage in.

Second, the flow of livelihood from work to family was characterized by the long-term employment and seniority-based wage system. Thus, once a person, generally a male, got a regular job at a company, a stable and better future was almost ensured. On the basis of this reliable prospect, they formed their own family, enriched it through consumption, and reproduced the next generation. Although the decline in the economic growth rate brought by the oil shock in the 1970s imperiled the expectation of stable employment, the government and employers chose to retain as many employees as possible to avoid an increase in the unemployment rate. This choice resulted in an intensification of the so-called Japanese employment system, whose distinctive features are frequent and flexible job rotations within a company, long-term competition for promotion among employees, and strong pressure to display loyalty and devotion to the company to which one belongs. Thus, in order to secure employment and earn an income to support their families, Japanese employees had no choice other than to submit themselves to the company's will.

Third, the flow of expenditure and motivation from family to education, the main actors of which had been mothers, also took a peculiar form. The word "education mothers," in Japanese *kyoiku mama*, which caricatured mothers who were quite zealous to have their child achieve good marks at school, appeared repeatedly in the mass media during the 1960s and 1970s. Not only typical "education mothers" but even ordinary mothers in Japan spared little effort to encourage their children to do well at school, enter prestigious schools and universities, and get jobs in big companies. They also spent as much money as they could on the education of their children, including fees for cram schools (after school) and activities such as sports, music, and arts. Japanese sociologist Toshiki Sato (2006) points out that Japanese parents sought to achieve their personal aspirations of attaining higher educational qualifications and better jobs through their children. The eagerness of parents, especially of mothers, in their expectations of their children's educational and vocational success, however, often caused severe conflicts and estrangements between parents and their children. The main motif of novels, TV dramas, and movies which depicted different facets of Japanese families during the 1970s and 1980s was the emptiness of family relations, the lack of affective sympathies, and the attempts to merely keep up appearances and statuses; this reflected the social reality of that time.

To sum up, these flows between education, work, and family, all of which were one-way, excessively tight, and instrumental in nature, dominated Japanese society until the 1980s. Children studied just to get a good job, fathers were devoted to their companies just to maintain their families, and mothers concentrated their energies on increasing their children's educational achievements. This circulation model was so predominant and normative in Japanese society that people could hardly realize an alternative way of life.

This social circulation, which accelerated throughout the 1980s, reached its peak during the bubble economy around 1990 and then abruptly began to crack.

10.4 The Partial Collapse and Ruined Remains

The change that occurred in this social circulation after 1990 was that the flow of resources from education to work, work to family, and family to education begun to split twofold: one was as stable as before, and the other was far more unstable than ever (Fig. 10.4). The latter fragile flows, making their appearance in the early 1990s and markedly expanding their scope since then, constitute the substance of the first "disaster" that primarily hit the young generation.

The initial change happened in the social domain of work. What has been observed since the beginning of the 1990s was a rapid shrinkage of labor demand for new regular workers, especially new graduates from schools and universities, on the one hand, and an equally rapid growing demand for non-regular workers on the other. This meant that quite a few young people were unable to find stable employment and, consequently, have had difficulty in stabilizing their own family life. Since, to date, the "male breadwinner norm" is still strong in Japan, a young man who does not earn as much as is expected to be sufficient to support a wife, let alone a child, is hardly regarded as a marriageable person. Hence, the share of unmarried persons among the young generation has continued to increase; it was 72.7% for men aged 25–29 years and 47.1% for men aged 30–34 years in 2015, thus accelerating the pace of aging of Japanese society.

Even if one could have a family, the increasing inequalities of various resources among families have had a direct impact on their children's educational attainment.

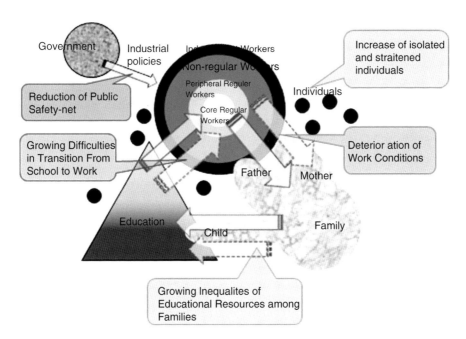

Fig. 10.4 Collapse of social circulation model

Affluent parents, aiming to reduce the risks of their children's future as much as possible, have come to utilize all their different kinds of resources, that is, "capital," into their children. In addition to the economic, cultural, and social capital theorized by Pierre Bourdieu (1984), a type of communication capital and experience capital, which are also passed on by parents to their children through daily interactions, seems to have become more important than ever. Thus, Phillip Brown's concept of "parentocracy" (1995) and "personal capital" (Brown and Hesketh 2004) has increasingly become a recent reality in Japan.

In brief, the social circulation model that dominated Japanese people's life courses and thoughts until around 1990 partially collapsed while retaining certain facets of the model. This split reality has been the source of "disaster" for Japanese youth, implying that although the opportunity to realize a "normal" life course is decreasing, objectively, the subjective normality of the "normal" life course remains the same or is even increasing in scarcity value more than ever.

10.5   Where Were the Seismic Centers?

Let us now discuss the seismic centers of this first "disaster" that preceded 3.11. The crucial turning point that occurred in the beginning of the 1990s cannot be attributed only to the bursting of the bubble economy. We can detect roughly two epicenters of the transfiguration of social circulation, especially the change in the Japanese youth labor market.

First is the "unfortunate coincidence" between economic fluctuation and the uneven age composition of the Japanese population. There are two huge age cohorts within the Japanese population: one is the first generation of baby boomers born in the late 1940s, and the other is the second generation of baby boomers born in the early 1970s. During the bubble economy that occurred in the latter half of the 1980s and reached its peak around 1990, Japanese companies recruited a large number of second-generation baby boomers as regular workers. After the bubble burst, they became a heavy burden on Japanese companies, as judicial precedents had made it very difficult for employers to dismiss regular workers. Moreover, during the 1990s, the first-generation baby boomers were reaching their 50s, and their labor costs were peaking under a wage system based on seniority. This double burden on Japanese companies, caused by incidental synchronicity between the economic wave and population wave, drove Japanese companies to refrain from recruiting new young regular workers and instead increased the utilization of non-regular workers. Although the large-scale retirement of the first generation of baby boomers is reducing the burden of personnel costs on employers, there is little noticeable improvement in employment opportunities and working conditions for the so-called lost generation—those who were hit directly by the shrinkage of the labor market for new graduates during the 1990s and the early 2000s.

The second epicenter of the change in the youth labor market is more fatal in its nature than incidental. It refers to the "diastrophism" both of industrial structures

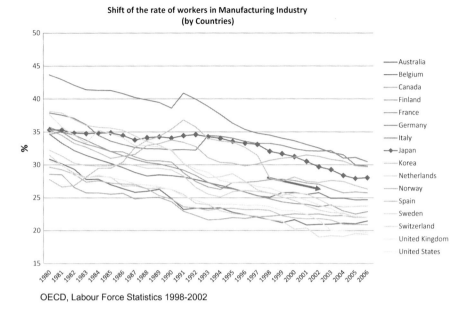

Fig. 10.5 Shift of the rate of workers in manufacturing industry (by countries). (Source: OECD, Labor Force Statistics 1980–2006)

and of the quantity and quality of labor demands in Japan, caused by the irreversible change in the global economic configuration. In every developed country, the industrial core has been shifting from manufacturing to services, partly because of the economic catching-up activities of newly developing countries in which manual labor costs are far lower than in developed countries (Fig. 10.5).

The manufacturing industry in developed countries including Japan has not only been shrinking in scale but also transforming its quality from mass production to small-lot multiple production, which is increasingly based on technological innovations. As Robert Reich (1991) states, under the so-called new economy within which the presence of the service industry is expanding, labor polarizes into highly intellectual and innovative on the one hand and low-tech face-to-face service work on the other. These global industrial trends stimulate the growing demands for non-regular workers in developed economies, which can be mobilized flexibly "just in time" both for factory production and labor-intensive services at reduced labor costs. Such a kind of industrial transformation had become prominent in Japan since around 1990, thus inflicting serious damage on the job opportunities for the younger generations ever since.

What is especially significant for Japan is that the shock waves that broke out from these two seismic centers have been exacerbated by the persistence of institutions and customs formed during the former social circulation. A typical example is the strong "dualism" within the Japanese labor market, in other words, the great gap in labor conditions between regular and non-regular workers (OECD 2009). Keiichiro Hamaguchi (2009) argues that this gap between regular and non-regular employment is derived from the difference in the principles of each type of employment. According to Hamaguchi, regular employment in Japan is characterized by the principle of "membership without job," while non-regular employment is characterized by the principle of "job without membership." The former implies that regular workers in Japan are not employed for a specific job but are conferred total membership by a company. The latter implies that non-regular workers in Japan are expected to perform a single job or task with almost no secure membership of a company. Within this stark dualism of employment, both regular and non-regular young workers suffer from an imbalance between membership and job.

One grave consequence of this dualism is the barrier to the transition from non-regular employment to regular employment, as employers tend to regard a person who has worked as a non-regular worker not worthy of full membership. Therefore, non-regular workers, who have increased significantly in number since the beginning of the 1990s, have found great difficulty in landing a more stable job. Moreover, there is a paradoxical relationship between regular and non-regular workers; non-regular workers function as buffers that help to maintain the employment security of regular workers, while at the same time, the low wages and employment insecurity of the non-regular workers contribute to the deterioration of the working conditions of regular workers. Thus, the strong dualism within the Japanese labor market fuels a vicious circle.

Another example of the persistence of the former social circulation model is the peculiar relationship between education and work in Japan that has also worsened the situation for young workers. The lack of vocational relevance in school education deprives youth of both market value and the power to bargain with employers. Owing to the custom of periodic blanket recruitment of new graduates, young people who do not acquire regular jobs upon graduation find it nearly impossible to enter a favorable labor market later.

These negative legacies of the former period have aggravated the situation for the young generation during the "lost decade" after the bursting of the economic bubble. However, this is not the only tragedy. Yet another problem to besiege Japanese youth is negative opinions about them.

10.6   Negative Opinions of the Young

We must not overlook the particularity of opinion of young people around the turn of the twenty-first century. One of the keywords quite often used to describe younger generation trends has been "freeter," coined by the editor of a job advertising magazine and referring to freelance, part-time workers. When the term first emerged in the late 1980s, it originally connoted "a vigorous and free young person." By the late 1990s, however, it had come to mean "a lazy and dependent young person," and in the early 2000s, the meaning changed again to imply "young people who pathologically lack vigor and volition." This drastic change in the connotation of "freeter" clearly indicates the social atmosphere in which the decline of employment opportunities for young people is being attributed to and explained by the mental shortcomings of the young people themselves.

Similarly, "NEET," an acronym for young people who are "Not in Education, Employment, or Training," has spread rapidly via the mass media throughout Japan since 2004 (Honda et al. 2006). The Japanese usage of the word NEET is different from that in Britain, where the term originated. In Japan, the official definition of NEET excludes unemployed youth who are seeking jobs. This definition provoked an image of a NEET as a "young person without the motivation to work." Such a stereotype of a NEET was reinforced by a widely held opinion that most NEETs had affluent middle-class parents. Moreover, the definition of a NEET in Japan included a broad age group from 15 to 34 years, resulting in a NEET population estimated at more than 800,000. This compounded the gloomy view of Japanese youth and their employment status.

The mass media played an important role in the diffusion of a negative image of a NEET in Japan. Several characteristics can be identified in representations of NEETs by the Japanese mass media. First, the term NEET was suggestive of young people with psychological problems. Second, commonality between NEET and *hikikomori*—a term referring to socially isolated young people who mostly stay at home, without going to school or work—is emphasized. Third, parents were often blamed for permitting their children to live as NEETs. Fourth, NEETs were stigmatized as losers, the term often being used derogatorily. Finally, various causes and solutions for the increase in the number of NEETs were asserted which were not based on scientific evidence.

In contrast to the negative meaning of the word NEET, the term *ningenryoku* or "human power" has been used to express whatever positive expectation and requirement the Japanese government and employers have regarding young people. Since the late 1990s, this term has frequently appeared in the mass media and policy papers. "Human power" signifies every desirable personal and emotional trait that a person should possess, such as communication skills and problem-solving competencies. The tacit premise of this word is that most of the problems of young people, including the problem of NEETs, can be resolved by nurturing their "human power."

Some empirical data on NEETs, however, denies the rough image of the NEET in its most simplistic form as a young person lacking the will to work. Most NEETs are either willing to work or have no need to work immediately, engaging in various activities with or without their families. Although some NEETs are inactive, this cannot be attributed solely to their mental state. Rather, social factors, such as the experience of bullying in school and the workplace, dropping out of school, and loss of a parent, have plunged them into the NEET situation. Therefore, what has been the most harmful is the fact that the word NEET has spread mistaken beliefs about young people, diverted social attention from implementing concrete measures for the improvement of objective conditions and opportunities for young people by blaming or scorning them, and has thus increased their hardship.

10.7 Desolation Resulting from the Individualized Meritocracy

Following the examination of the past processes of Japanese society, we are now ready to answer the earlier questions of why the situation of society since the 1990s inflicted a "disastrous" impact on Japanese youth and why has meritocracy among Japanese youth been so individualized. The answers are the uniqueness of the social circulation model established in postwar Japan, the coexistence of its legacies and its collapse, and a social climate that attributes structural problems to individual deficits. Confronted with these conditions, the Japanese, especially the younger generation, had few choices other than to act as "entrepreneurs," placing the responsibility for their situation on their own "merit" or lack of it, without accusing or reforming the deficiencies and dysfunctions of the social structure.

What is important is that this situation has created chaos in the formation, evaluation, and compensation of the "merit" of individuals in Japan. Essentially, "merit" is constructed and formed through social institutions, environments, and interactions, with certain established rules and public consensus about its sound treatment. However, in Japan in recent years, these social frameworks linked to "merit" have become increasingly obscure. Critical issues such as what is "merit," how to foster and identify it, and what is the appropriate price for a specific "merit" have been largely dodged or evaded, while arbitrary and illusive requirements and expectations for super "merit" such as "human power" have been propagated within political and economic discourse. The actual formation of and compensation for "merit" have become increasingly accidental or slipshod because the educational system has become obsolete and dysfunctional, with the curricula lacking relevance to the realities of society and the economy, and because the employment system, which has been split into "membership without job" and "job without membership," has lost sound criteria and wage standards for judging the "merit" of both types of workers. Therefore, peoples' "merit" has been trampled on, wasted, and exploited.

What can be derived from this situation is that those who are fortunate enough to enjoy the advantages of various kinds of resources at the beginning of their life course tend to gain and accumulate more "merit" than others and eventually acquire advantageous positions. In other words, the social reproduction of inequalities has been reinforced. Disadvantaged people are left with little social support and few opportunities to build a better life.

Thus, Japanese society, being inundated with an individualized meritocracy, has gradually but steadily taken steps into a miserable state of confusion and inequality over the last two decades.

10.8   After the Real Disaster

It was at this historic stage that the 3.11 disaster occurred. This real catastrophe convulsed a society that had already been ruined by the previous metaphorical disaster. What does this absolute disaster mean to Japanese society?

As mentioned earlier, there is no doubt that it inflicted serious damage on the Japanese economy and society. Despite the damage, several positive symptoms can be observed. For example, a large amount of relief material and donations were quickly gathered from across the country and sent to the devastated areas, mostly by citizen's groups. Sufferers themselves showed incredible perseverance and cooperation, voluntarily helping each other. It was as if the Japanese people had forgotten individualized meritocracy in the face of this tremendous threat from nature. Does this imply that a catastrophe following a disastrous situation brings about solidarity and cooperation, in the same way that a minus multiplied by a minus is a plus? Is this a utopia brought about by a disaster, as Rebecca Solnit (2009) argued in her book *A Paradise Built in Hell*?

Certainly, the obvious tragedy and crisis brought about by the catastrophe seemed to erode the differences in "merit" and social position between individuals, at least tentatively. The structural deficiencies of Japanese society, however, remain unchanged or rather are deteriorating, because of the effects of the disaster on industry, the economy, and employment. Economist Fumio Ohtake (2011) points out that the increase in the number of people who attach importance to cooperation after 3.11 is not a sign of growing unselfishness but is based on the pragmatic view that mutual help within a community is the most efficient way in a crisis. Although we cannot currently foresee the exact outcome of this disaster, what is certain is that the future of Japanese society depends on whether we make determined steps to overcome the remnants of the old social circulation, especially the chaos and growing inequality caused by the individualized meritocracy.

10.9   Steps Necessary for Japan to Recover from the Disasters

What then is needed to break through the existing tortured structure of Japanese society? An important step is to implement measures to change the concept of meritocracy from one that is individualized to one that is social. While an individualized meritocracy attributes the responsibility for developing "merit" to individuals themselves, a social meritocracy assumes that society is responsible for developing, appraising, and rewarding people's "merit." Therefore, governmental policies to actualize a social meritocracy will be indispensable in tackling the problems of chaotic anxiety, despair, and inequality among young people in Japan.

Possible measures to achieve this are as follows: first, the education system must be improved so that it functions better in empowering people, especially the younger generation. In particular, the vocational relevance of educational content taught in

Fig. 10.6 Model of
"Flexpeciality"

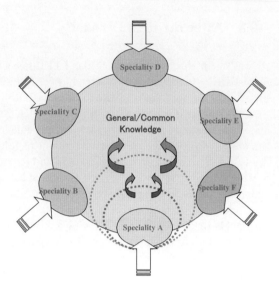

schools and universities should be strengthened. For example, technical and professional high schools, the number of which is too small in Japan, must be increased to serve a far wider set of people who wish to acquire stable jobs. In order to cope with the rapid change of technology and the global economic environment, the curricula of vocational education should be designed to allow for ample flexibility, while maintaining the outline of each specialized field. The term "flexpeciality" might be useful to depict the image of the formation of knowledge and skills which are expected to be achieved through education (Fig. 10.6).

Second, the convention of periodically blanket recruiting new graduates should be reformed in order to open employment opportunities to job seekers and non-regular workers. The chance to get a stable job should not be limited to particular social groups but must be opened to anyone who has the appropriate competence, experience, and volition. The current situation, in which a person who fails to get a regular job upon graduation from school and university tends to be trapped in pre-carious conditions for life, needs to be resolved.

Third, the wide gap in working patterns between regular and non-regular workers needs to be reduced. The wage level of non-regular workers should be improved on the basis of the principle of "equal pay for equal work," so that they can attain an acceptable standard of living. In order to reduce the polarity between "membership without job" of regular workers and "job without membership" of non-regular workers, it will be beneficial to increase intermediate types of work options which include, for instance, regular employment with shorter working hours and clear profiles of jobs or non-regular employment with more stable working conditions and an upward career path.

Fourth, greater opportunities for public vocational training should be created. Its necessity derives, at least in part, from the fact that companies' budgets for in-house training have been shrinking. Even regular workers are no longer guaranteed

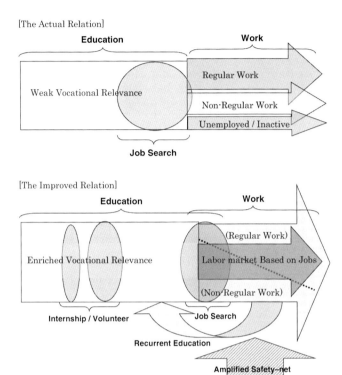

Fig. 10.7 The direction of the improvement of the relation between education and work

opportunities to improve their skill levels within their workplace, while non-regular workers have far fewer chances to develop their vocational skills. Therefore, inexpensive or free public training opportunities, which are very limited in Japan at present, should be amplified. The fact that new training courses in which unemployed trainees are provided with their living expenses were introduced recently for the first time in Japan as "the second safety net" is a sign of progress.

These propositions are integrated in Fig. 10.7. This is an envisaged model of the renewed relationship between education and work in Japan. In order to tackle the problems of an individualized meritocracy, it is imperative that the social framework for the formation, verification, and compensation of an individual's "merit" is reconstructed. Needless to say, such a social reform is no easy task, but the fact itself adds urgency to resolute social and political efforts. To leave the situation unattended will inflict major damage both on the well-being of individuals and the sustainability of Japanese society.

Was the 3.11 disaster a trigger for reforming the structure of Japanese society, which was already distorted by the first disaster that occurred in the 1990s? Or was it a grave gateway to further decay in this society? We do not know the answer yet. We need to determine what the answer will be through our actions.

References

Bourdieu, P. (1984). *Distinction: A social critique of the judgement of taste*. London: Routledge.
Brown, P. (1995). Cultural capital and social exclusion: Some observations on recent trends in education, employment, and the labour market. *Work, Employment and Society, 9*, 29–51.
Brown, P., & Hesketh, A. (2004). *The mismanagement of talent: Employability and jobs in the knowledge economy*. Oxford: Oxford University Press.
Genda, Y. (2014). Higashinihondaishinsai ga shigoto ni ataeta eikyou ni tsuite [Influence of 311 disaster on labor]. *Nihon Roudou Kenkyu Zasshi, 653*, 100–120.
Hamaguchi, K. (2009). *Atarashii roudou shakai* [New Society of Labor]. Iwanami Shoten.
Honda, Y., Naito, A., & Goto, K. (2006). *"Neet" tte iuna* [Don't say "Neet"]. Kobunsha.
Honda, Y., et al. (2010). *The differentiation of trajectories from school to work in present-day Japan*. A presentation at the XVII ISA World Congress of Sociology.
Klein, N. (2007). *The shock doctrine: The rise of disaster capitalism*. Metropolitan.
OECD. (2009). *Jobs for youth: Japan*. Paris: OECD Publishing.
Ohtake, F. (2011). *Tasukeai no seishin wo dokomade hirogerareruka* [How wide can we make the spirit of cooperation?]. Chuo Koron 2011.8.
Reich, R. (1991). *The work of nations*. New York: Alfred A. Knopf Inc.
Sato, T. (2006). Bakuhatsusuru fubyoudou-kan [Burst of the feeling of inequality]. In S. Sirahase (Ed.), *Henkasuru shakai no fubyoudou* [Inequality in the changing society]. Tokyo: Tokyo Daigaku Shuppankai.
Shibya, N. (2011) Antorepurenaa to Hisaisha: Neoriberalizumu no Kenryoku to Shinrigakuteki Shutai [Entrepreneur and disaster survivor: Neoliberal production of psychological subject]. *Japanese Sociological Review, 61*(4).
Solnit, R. (2009). *A paradise built in hell: The extraordinary communities that arise in disaster*. San Francisco: Viking Adult.

Chapter 11
Discussing the "Multicultural" in Japanese Society

Ryoko Tsuneyoshi

11.1 Introduction

As societies around the world face the forces of globalization, even societies like Japan's, which were often considered to be relatively "homogeneous," are facing diversity within. With the inflow of foreigners over the last several decades, there has arisen in Japan a discourse on what is "multicultural" in Japanese society, especially among the localities that are at the forefront of its diversifying society.

The challenge of meeting the needs of a diversifying population was met first by local governments with a concentration of foreigners and then by the national government. This is not surprising, since the localities cannot ignore the needs of foreign residents in their communities. At the national level, there is a sea of difference between a Japanese national and a non-Japanese, while in the localities, both Japanese and non-Japanese are residents of the same locality.

Now, it is conventional in Japanese academia to divide foreigners in Japan into two categories. First, there are the Koreans and Chinese in Japan who have resided in Japan since the prewar period; they are the ethnic minorities who have come as a result of Japan's colonial policies—the "oldcomers."

On the other hand, there are foreigners who have entered Japan in the postwar period as foreign labor, spouses of Japanese nationals, etc. who have been labeled the "newcomers." The local governments of the areas in which the "newcomers" clustered have seen their localities transform with the inflow of foreigners (Tsuneyoshi et al. 2011). For many of these alien-concentrated localities, the revisions to the immigration law in 1990 which allowed later-generation South Americans of Japanese descent to enter legally as unskilled labor signaled the beginning of a new phase of diversification. These South Americans of Japanese

R. Tsuneyoshi (✉)
Graduate School of Education, The University of Tokyo, Tokyo, Japan
e-mail: tsuney@p.u-tokyo.ac.jp

© Springer Nature Singapore Pte Ltd. 2019   177
Y. Kitamura et al. (eds.), *Education in Japan*, Education in the Asia-Pacific
Region: Issues, Concerns and Prospects 47,
https://doi.org/10.1007/978-981-13-2632-5_11

descent (Nikkeijin) often came with their families and stayed in Japan for extended periods. Though the collapse of the Lehman Brothers in 2008 is said to have hit this population very hard, since they were irregular employees and easy to lay off, the ones that have remained are said to be more rooted in the Japanese community.

"Multicultural" is the term localities with a concentration of foreigners have used to capture this diversification of their locality. In this sense, "multicultural" symbolizes the grassroots diversification of Japanese society. What is the reasoning behind this "multicultural," a term symbolizing the inner transformation of Japanese communities? What are the implications? This chapter addresses these questions by analyzing how representative localities voice the "multicultural."

11.2 The Background to "Multicultural" Understanding in Japan

Before we look at how individual localities portray the "multicultural" to the public, it is necessary to say a word about the context in which this is happening.

Terms such as international, multicultural, and global are used simultaneously in Japanese society today, albeit in different contexts. In the 1980s, there was a lot of media exposure of the term internationalization (*kokusaika*). This was an umbrella term that was used for anything from governmental policies to school practices.

From around the 1970s, as more Japanese businesspersons moved out of Japan and returned with their families as a result of Japan's postwar economic recovery, the plight of their children started to become sensationalized in the media. These children, the Japanese returnees, initially suffered from a lack of assistance in Japanese schools; they were sometimes placed in grades lower than their age and faced enormous adjustment problems (Sato 1997; Minoura 2003).

Eventually, from the 1980s, and especially after 1990, when the Immigration Control and Refugee Recognition Act was revised to allow later-generation South Americans of Japanese descent to work in Japan as unskilled labor, the numbers of this population soared in some regions. Other new types of foreigners came as well. As mentioned previously, these foreigners were called "newcomers" in comparison to the Koreans and Chinese in Japan, the "oldcomers." The "newcomers" were foreign laborers, spouses of Japanese nationals, Indochinese refugees and their descendants, returnees from China, etc. who came to Japan for different reasons than the "oldcomers." The existence of the "oldcomers" is related to Japan's colonial history, while the inflow of "newcomers" is related to Japan's bubble economy, work opportunities, etc.

Famous "oldcomer" regions include cities in western Japan such as Osaka and Kyoto, with effective "oldcomer" movements. On the other hand, "newcomer" enclaves emerged in the 1990s, especially Nikkei (South Americans of Japanese descent) enclaves. First used around the time of the 1995 Hanshin earthquake, it is said that NGOs and local governments with a diversifying resident population started to use the term "multicultural coexistence" (*tabunka kyosei*) as a goal of a diversifying society (Kim 2012). This eventually spread to the government.

For example, in an influential document, the Ministry of Internal Affairs and Communications (Somucho 2006, p. 2) notes that from the end of the 1980s, local governments have internationalized the local community using the two concepts of "international exchange" and "international cooperation" but that today, a third axis, "multicultural coexistence" is required. The Research Group concerning the Promotion of Multicultural Coexistence was thus erected in 2005 under the ministry. The ministry's report to "build alien-friendly communities" also frequently used the term "multicultural" (Somucho 2006). The framework is clearly for "Japanese residents and foreign residents to coexist" (p. 9) and what the localities, NGOs, etc. can do to facilitate this. For example, educators were asked to bring in a "multicultural" outlook when conducting international understanding education (p. 7), and human rights are mentioned as enabling "people who have different nationalities and ethnicities, etc., to recognize each other's cultural differences, and to build an equal (*taito*) relationship" (p. 3). More recently, "globalization" has become the buzzword in the media and the government. The latter is used more in the context of global competition.

Now, as mentioned, the term "multicultural" emerged as a result of the growing awareness of the diversification of Japanese society. One example will suffice to illustrate this.

For example, in Gunma Prefecture, an ethnic enclave for the South Americans of Japanese descent, international/multicultural measures in the 1980–1990s were still given the title of "international." In 1990, the International Exchange Association (*Kokusai Koryu Kyokai*) was established, and the prefecture issued its internationalization promotion plan.

However, after the immigration law was revised in 1990, the foreign population began to increase, and especially as the Nikkei population came as legal unskilled labor with their families, there emerged an awareness of the diversity within. In 2004, the prefecture set up a "project to construct a town to coexist with foreigners," and the next year in 2005, the "multicultural coexistence support room" was put in place. The 2006 Gunma Prefectural Comprehensive Plan (*13th Gunma ken sogo keikaku*) focused on "promoting coexistence with diverse people," and in October of 2007 the Gunma Prefecture Multicultural Coexistence Promotion Guidelines (*Gumaken tabunka kyosei suishin shishin*) were issued and revised in 2012 (Gunma 2012, pp. 3–4). The revised guidelines asserted that "multicultural" coexistence is certainly not just a matter for areas with a concentration of foreigners, like Gunma. As Japanese society globalizes, even in areas in which there are not that many foreigners, cultural exposure occurs daily (Gunma 2012, p. 4). It is this rising awareness of the diversity within that is spurring the use of the term "multicultural."

This paper focuses on how localities with a concentration of foreigners, at the forefront of multicultural Japan, present the emerging concept of "multicultural" to the public. What are the characteristics of the rhetoric on "multicultural" in Japan's representative ethnic enclaves? What are the implications for how "multicultural" is understood in Japan?

R. Tsuneyoshi

11.3   Method

Regions differ according to whether or not "multicultural" is relevant to them and who they think the term "multicultural" applies to. Of those regions that think that "multicultural" concerns them, those most likely to be aware of the growing "multicultural" sphere are the ones that have experienced diversification or have an active minority movement in the area which heightens the awareness of diversity.

In Japan, there are regions which are known in this regard, and the public understanding of these districts is associated with the foreign population they serve. Thus, some areas are known for their concentration of the Koreans in Japan, the "oldcomers," and others are known for an inflow of a certain type of "newcomers" such as the Nikkei. The enclave can be broken down even further at times. Some public housing projects have become popular for their foreign population, such as the Homi public housing project in Toyota City in Aichi Prefecture (Nikkei, etc.) and the Icho public housing in Yamato/Yokohama City, Kanagawa Prefecture, near the former settlement assistance center for refugees (Shimizu 2009, 2011).

This paper focuses on the rhetoric of representative "oldcomer" and "newcomer" enclaves, analyzing the definition of "multicultural" in the locality's guidelines for multicultural coexistence in these areas. Several examples of non-enclaves were added for comparative purposes.

Today, as the awareness of the diversification of Japanese society heightens, it comes as no surprise that many localities have tried to voice their position regarding what they see as "multicultural." The following sections will analyze both the contents and the implications of local efforts to define the diversification within.

11.4   "Multicultural" Targets and Their Justification

11.4.1   "Newcomer" Enclaves

Today, one has only to input the Japanese term for "multicultural" (*tabunka*) in a search engine on the Internet, and lines of names, from NGOs to government documents, appear on the screen in Japanese. However, the interesting point about the term "multicultural" in Japan is that it is almost always accompanied by the topic of "foreigners." Coexistence (*kyosei*) itself can be anything from coexistence of men and women to nature and human beings. But when the term "multicultural" (*tabunka*) is added in front of coexistence (*kyosei*), the headings on the screen start to contain the word "foreigner." What is happening? What are the implications? In this section, the meaning of "multicultural" in Japan will be analyzed through focusing on the rhetoric of "newcomer" districts. The next section will focus on the "oldcomers."

Now, as I have argued before, there are various districts in Japan which are emerging as enclaves for foreign populations, and the first of those types are areas in which new types of foreigners, the "newcomers," are concentrated.

There are reasons why a certain "newcomer" population is concentrated in a certain area. For example, initially, Nikkei foreign laborers were recruited into areas in which there was a labor shortage (e.g., subcontractors of automobile companies). In the larger Tokyo area, one of the reasons many Indochinese refugees initially located themselves in Kanagawa Prefecture was because there was a settlement center for refugees there in the 1980s–1990s and NGOs sprouted to render assistance (Shimizu 2009, 2011).

Since there are today enough areas in which there is a concentration of these "newcomers" and many other areas are witnessing diversification, there is now a joint conference for representatives of "the areas with a high concentration of foreigners" (*gaikokujin shujyu toshi*) called the "Association of Cities with a Concentration of Foreigners" (Gaikokujin Shujyu Toshi Kaigi). This conference is made up of "policy-makers, local associations of international exchange, etc. of cities in which foreign residents, the core of which are South Americans of Japanese descent, called 'newcomers', are concentrated."[1] The aim is to share information, and the first meeting was held in 2001 in the "newcomer" enclave of Hamamatsu.

Members of this group are prefectures/localities from Japan's largest "newcomer" enclaves and the regions that are known for their pioneering efforts in regard to foreigners. For this reason, members of this committee will be chosen for examination here.

11.4.1.1   The Largest "Newcomer" Enclave: Shizuoka

As prefectures, Shizuoka, Gunma, Aichi, Mie, Gifu, and Shiga, all members of the above-stated network, are known for their concentrations of "newcomers," especially the Nikkei from Brazil.

However, foreigners are not scattered throughout the prefectures but are clustered in certain cities, public housing, etc. which attract that population for a reason, such as the availability of jobs or low cost of living.

As can be seen in Fig. 11.1, Shizuoka Prefecture, with famous ethnic enclaves such as Hamamatsu City, has the most number of enclaves of the prefectural members as of 2015. Thus, it might be expected that Shizuoka Prefecture would issue a message on multicultural coexistence that is quite progressive. The explanation of the prefecture's Multicultural Affairs Division (*Tabunka Kyoseika*) is as below. As of December 2014, some of its cities consist of 4.0–5.0% foreign nationals, and the largest nationality groups were Brazilians, comprising 33.8% of the total in December 2014, followed by nationals from the Philippines.

---

[1] http://www.shujutoshi.jp/member/index.htm, retrieved July 2015.

Gunma Prefecture (Isesaki, Ota, Oizumi)

Nagano Prefecture (Ueda, Iida)

Gifu Prefecture (Minokamo)

Shizuoka Prefecture (Hamamatsu, Fuji, Iwata, Kakegawa, Fukuroi, Kosai, Kikukawa)

Aichi Prefecture (Toyohashi, Toyota, Komaki)

Mie Prefecture (Tsu, Yokkaichi, Suzuka, Kameyama, Iga)

Shiga Prefecture (Nagahama, Koka)

Okayama Prefecture (Soja)

Observer: Tokyo (Shinjyuku, Ota)

Source: The homepage of the member cities, http://www.shujutoshi.jp/member/index.htm, retrieved April, 2015.

Fig. 11.1 Member cities of the conference as of April 1, 2015

> Put simply, the **Multicultural** Affairs Division exists to look after **the non-Japanese popu-lation** of Shizuoka Prefecture, and to help put plans and procedures in place to allow non-Japanese people to assimilate into Japanese society. In addition to in-house native English checking and translations, the Multicultural Affairs Division sends Brazilian and American staff to various schools within the prefecture, where they give presentations in Japanese about their home countries **to try and raise global awareness among the youth of Japan**.
> Notes: Bold, mine
> Source: https://www.pref.shizuoka.jp/kikaku/ki140/multiculturalisminshizuokaprefecture.html#content_atcir, retrieved July 2015.

"Multicultural" is identified with foreigners, non-Japanese nationals, and the framework is mutual understanding. As we will see, this is a pattern repeated in other localities.

If we now turn our eyes to individual cities, we see a very similar picture. Multicultural means "foreigners," and mutual understanding and coexistence between foreigners and Japanese are emphasized. Nationality and culture are the main indicators of diversity. Examples are given below.

Iwata City

According to Iwata City, there are presently approximately 5,885 foreigners (March 1, 2014), which constitute about 3.4% of the entire population. The locality cites cases in which coexistence between Japanese and foreigners faces difficulties "due to differences in culture, the language barrier, and lack of communication, etc." However, foreign citizens are seen as a great asset for the community, and are "important actors in constructing a city built from many cultures." "It is important that everyone recognizes each other as **residents** of the community, regardless of **nationality**, culture, custom, gender and age, and to coexist (*tomoni ikite*) while building an equal relationship" (bold, mine).[2]

------

[2] http://www.city.iwata.shizuoka.jp/shisei/tabunka/torikumi.php, July 2015.

Kikugawa City

Kikugawa has the largest percentage of foreigners, mostly Brazilians, in Shizuoka Prefecture. On its homepage, it adopts the Ministry of Internal Affairs and Communication's definition of a multicultural society (see above). In its second Kikugawa City Multicultural Coexistence Promotion Action Guidelines 2013–2016 (*Dai niji Kikugawa shi tabunka kyosei suishin kodo shishin*), Kikugawa upholds, as its basic goal, a community in which "multicultural coexistence is attained by respecting the mutual differences of culture and customs" and to strive for a community in which "all citizens can reside happily and satisfied" (Kikugawa 2013, p. 12). Mutual understanding between Japanese and foreigners, assistance in daily life, and educational assistance are the three pillars of action, according to the guidelines above.

The basic framework for "multicultural" is the same. It is about the coexistence of Japanese with foreigners as residents, despite differences in nationality and other cultural differences. Mutual understanding is emphasized. Below is an example of prefectures with fewer enclaves than Shizuoka.

11.4.1.2 Gunma Prefecture

Unlike Shizuoka Prefecture, Gunma Prefecture is to the north of Tokyo. Again, with the revisions to the immigration law in 1990, the inflow of South Americans of Japanese descent, especially Brazilians, transformed some of the cities into ethnic enclaves.

As of 2016, there were 48,521 registered foreigners in Gunma Prefecture, forming 2.4% of the population. Of the prefecture's cities, Isesaki, Ota, Oizumi, Maebashi, and Takahashi City together contain 77.5% of the alien population.[3] Such figures attest again to how foreign populations are clustered in certain areas of a prefecture, not scattered throughout. Again, Brazilians are the most numerous, followed by Chinese, Filipinos, Peruvians, and Koreans, though in recent years, the number of Nikkei is decreasing and the numbers of Chinese and Vietnamese are growing (Gunma 2012, pp. 2–3).

According to the revised Gunma Prefecture Multicultural Coexistence Promotion Guideline, which was first issued in 2007, and revised in July 2012, "multicultural coexistence in the community" (*chiiki ni okeru tabunka kyosei*) means that "people who differ in **nationality**, **ethnicity**, etc., will respect **each other's** cultural differences, and while trying to form an equitable relationship, will contribute in their own way and in the manner they are capable of doing, in order to live together as **members of the community**" (bold, mine, Gunma 2012, p. 6). Here again, foreigners and Japanese, as residents of the community, are encouraged to respect each other and to coexist as members of the same community.

---

[3] http://www.pref.gunma.jp/04/c2200234.html, retrieved August 2017, the official homepage of Gunma Prefecture.

Gunma Prefecture includes districts like Oizumi, one of the largest Brazilian enclaves in the nation, where over 17.0% of the population were foreign in 2016.[4] Oizumi City erected a Multicultural Coexistence Communication Center (*Tabunka Kyosei Communication Center*) which issues a newsletter (GARAPA) in Portuguese and initiates various activities concerning the alien population. Ota has also responded to diversifying needs and now has institutionalized bilingual teachers at its schools.[5]

Gifu, Minokamo

In Minokamo City in Gifu Prefecture, its multicultural guideline, the Minokamo City Multicultural Coexistence Promotion Guideline, describes the process of building a multicultural coexistence society as the state in which Japanese and **foreigners**, as equal Minokamo **citizens**, live **together** comfortably and in safety. Both foreign and Japanese citizens are, according to the local law, **residents, equal** in standing. **Communication** between **foreigners** and Japanese, and **mutual understanding**, and establishing a relationship in which both assist one another are important (bold, mine, Minokamo 2014).

According to Minokamo City (2014), as of April 2013, the status of the residence of foreigners is 53.9% permanent residents (*eijyusha*), 28.8% long-term residents (*teijyu*), and 5.8% spouses of Japanese; in other words, most of the "foreigners" are likely to stay for a long time. Nationalities can be broken down to 51.4% Brazilian and 35.3% Filipino; the former are Nikkeijin, and the latter are one of the highest nationalities in the category of spouse of Japanese (p. 5). Thus, according to the City, "as (foreigners) stay permanently (*eijyuka*)," "there is an increase in the number of foreigners who acquire Japanese nationality," and in addition, "among children of mixed marriages, there are foreign children who were born in Japan and have never been to their homeland." This brings about new needs of "not just acquiring Japanese culture and language, but acquiring the culture and language of one's homeland (*bokoku*)," as well as the need to address "the identity issues of each citizen" (p. 5).

Tokyo, Shinjuku Ward

Shinjuku Ward in Tokyo is an Asian enclave. It is listed as one of the districts that has the highest percentage of Korean nationals (33.3%), alongside traditionally "oldcomer" districts such as Osaka and Kyoto. Its most numerous population is Chinese (37.3%).[6]

What is multicultural coexistence? On its homepage, Shinjuku Ward defines multicultural coexistence according to the previously stated ministry definition. It promises to build a multicultural coexistence community, in which people with

---

[4] http://www.town.oizumi.gunma.jp/01soshiki/02kikaku/03kokusai/ 1288067347-3.html, retrieved July 2015, homepage of Oizumi City.

[5] http://www.pref.gunma.jp/contents/100009676.pdf, retrieved August 2017, Gunma Prefecture, the number of alien residents by municipality.

[6] http://www.city.shinjuku.lg.jp/content/000142625.pdf, statistics, retrieved July 2015.

"different nationalities and ethnicities, etc. recognize each other's' differences in culture, and understand each other, and live together."[7]

Mie Prefecture

I end with Mie, since it exemplifies that these enclaves are not static. Unlike the clearly "oldcomer" or "newcomer" enclaves, Mie first started off in the late 1980s as a locality in which the numbers of Koreans in Japan and Brazilians were about the same. After the revisions to the immigration law in 1990, the number of Brazilians soared, and Mie became a "newcomer" enclave, a member of the above-stated association. At about the same time, the Chinese population overtook the number of Koreans in Japan. In recent years, the Filipino population has also over-taken the number of Koreans.

However, as a whole, in 2013, the numbers of foreign residents had been going down for 5 consecutive years (2.21% of the prefectural population in 2013). The prefectural breakdown by nationality in 2013 was 29.1% Brazilian, 21.9% Chinese, 13.7% Filipino, and 12.6% Korean.[8]

Mie has a strong human rights perspective and refers to the Koreans in Japan, part of its former "oldcomer" district legacy, but also shares the basic message with the other "newcomer" districts. When the word "multicultural" is used, as in the Mie Prefecture Internationalization Promotion Guideline (Mie 2011), the contents are similar to other "newcomer" enclaves in some respects and are similar to Kawasaki, an "oldcomer" enclave, in others. The document starts with the recognition that the first "foreigners" in Mie were the Koreans in Japan who had lived in Mie from before WWII. Today, the foreign population has diversified and expanded, with the inflow of "newcomers" now constituting "about 2.6 % of the prefectural population" (Mie 2011, p. 1). In this context, Mie asserts that there is a need for people of different nationalities and ethnicities to respect each other's differences, and as equal partners and members of the community, to construct a multicultural coexistence society where they can both live together in safety (p. 1). This is a district which combines features of "oldcomers" and "newcomers." Mie justifies its message as being in line with international human rights conventions protecting the **rights** of foreigners (Mie 2011, p. 4).

11.5   Out of the Concentrated Areas

What about the areas which are not identified as those with a concentration of foreigners? Though it used to be the case that "multicultural" was popular among those prefectures with ethnic enclaves, today, with the increase in the number of foreigners, many more localities have started to use this term.

---

[7] https://www.city.shinjuku.lg.jp/tabunka/bunka01_000101.html, retrieved, July 2015.
[8] http://www.pref.mie.lg.jp/TABUNKA/HP/data/gaitou/index.htm, from the Mie Prefectural Government, Multicultural Affairs Division, retrieved, June 2015.

As was seen, the above-stated ministry issued a notice to localities to adopt some kind of guideline for constructing a multicultural society, and it is easy to identify the influence of the government definition of multicultural, in the statements of the localities.

I will simply cite two non-enclave examples, Hachioji City and Saitama Prefecture, to illustrate.

Now, according to the Hachioji Multicultural Policy (Hachioji 2013), issued by Hachioji, a locality in Metropolitan Tokyo, this policy, effective from fiscal year 2013 to 2022, has the purpose of promoting the goal below:

> The time has come to embrace cultural breadth and diversity in daily life through the recent globalization that has led people to discover their new life in Japan. Local authorities are taking advantage of this great trend to develop a vigorous and unique community by supporting cross-cultural experiences for a better understanding and cultivation of international perspectives. In light of these circumstances, we are committed to consolidating systems to accept people from diverse ethnic backgrounds and to encouraging the sharing of cultural differences. We do this by providing various local programs to realize an inclusive community where everyone feels a sense of belonging. This policy is dedicated to our fundamental strategy of multicultural community development, starting from 2013, that leads our residents, corporations, universities, administration, and related entities themselves to take cooperative actions towards a cohesive and harmonious society.
>
> Note: Bold, mine
>
> Source: Hachioji 2013. http://www.city.hachioji.tokyo.jp/dbps_data/_material_/localhost/soshiki/gakuentoshibunkaka/kokusaikoryu/plangaiyoeng.pdf, retrieved July 2015.

Or take another example from Saitama Prefecture which now has a number of foreign populations. Saitama Prefecture Multicultural Coexistence Promotion Plan reads, "the new Saitama Prefecture Multicultural Coexistence Promotion Plan was issued in July 2012, so that both **Japanese and foreigners** can jointly support the local community, and to build a prefecture in which b**oth move forward with each other**...." Three barriers to understanding are mentioned. The barrier of language, the barrier of the system, and the barrier of the heart (bold, mine, Saitama 2012).

In all of these cases, there are a growing number of foreign residents, which are cited as evidence in all of the statements. The emphasis lies in incorporating the existing alien residents into the largely Japanese community. Here, diversification is given, rather than a goal. Given the diversity, the goal is to help foreigners coexist as residents with Japanese. The concept of "residents" of a locality cuts across nationality lines. The basic message is the same as the "newcomer" enclaves.

11.6 "Oldcomer" Enclaves

There is another older and more established type of ethnic/minority enclave in Japan. These are the enclaves of the long-standing minorities. The latter are Japan's representative involuntary ethnic minority (Ogbu and Simons 1998).

These groups are different from the "newcomers," which are composed of, for example, voluntary laborers, spouses of Japanese, and refugees. These "oldcomer" areas have a history of minority movement, and a human rights perspective is already in place. Here, the "newcomers" are thus, truly newcomers, in that there are former minority residents who have roots in that area.

Representative "oldcomer" districts include many areas in Osaka, Kyoto, areas in Kobe in Hyogo Prefecture, and some parts around Tokyo and Kawasaki.

Osaka City

Osaka City has the largest foreign resident population among the government-designated cities (*seirei shitei toshi*), and almost half of the foreigners there are Korean, followed by Chinese.[9] Areas in the city, such as Ikuno Ward, are known as Japan's "oldcomer" enclaves.

As a city with concentrations of "oldcomers," Osaka City has a strong human rights focus. Its homepage groups headings into three sections: "human rights, equal participation by gender, and multicultural coexistence." Multicultural coexistence is but one in the list of three.

The section under "multicultural coexistence" indeed refers to the foreign population, like the other Japanese localities mentioned previously. However, there is a strong emphasis on human rights, and human rights is the umbrella term which captures all the vulnerable groups, including foreign nationals. The topics that are listed under human rights are varied, including women, children, the aged, those with disabilities, the *dowa* issues, foreign nationals, those recovered from Hansen's disease, victims of crime, human rights violations due to the Internet, the victims of abduction by the North Korean authorities, homeless, gay/lesbian, the protection of individual information, other human rights issues, and hate speech.[10]

According to Osaka Prefecture, human rights are "a basic freedom and right which human beings have from birth (*umarenagaranishite*), and which is indispensable for people to have to live a happy life, and a right which should be assured, not just for the present, but for the entire future."[11] Osaka notes that human rights are protected by the Japanese constitution.

Osaka has a separate guideline for foreigners. The Basic Guidelines for Osaka Foreign Residents' Policy (*Osaka-shi Gaikokusekijyumin Sesaku Kihonshishin*) revised in 2004 includes a section on the realization of a multicultural coexistence society with a special emphasis on the education of Koreans in Japan (Osaka 2004). The Koreans in Japan are the ethnic minority population which has been traditionally linked to human rights issues. Osaka also notes that it includes "not only those whose nationality is presently foreign, but also those who have roots abroad"; those with "roots abroad" means "those whose parents or grandparents or either one of them have a foreign nationality."[12]

---

[9] http://www.pref.osaka.lg.jp/attach/4167/00000000/28_kokuseki_betsu.pdf, retrieved August 2017, from the homepage of Osaka Prefecture.

[10] http://www.city.osaka.lg.jp/shimin/category/1435-2-1-0-0.html, retrieved, June 2015.

[11] http://www.city.osaka.lg.jp/shimin/page/0000021513.html, July 2015.

[12] http://www.city.oosaka.lg.jp/shimin/page/0000275071.html, July 2015.

Next, the Osaka City **Multicultural** Policy Liaison Committee Establishment
Guideline (bold, mine, *Osaka-shi Tabunka kyosei Sesaku Renraku kaigi Secchi
Yoryo*) defines its purpose of establishment as follows:

First clause:
  From the viewpoint that those foreigners who reside in this city are **"foreign residents"**
  constituting the local community (*chiiki shakai*), in order to promote multicultural poli-
  cies comprehensively and effectively, toward the realization of a **"coexistence society"**
  (***kyosei shakai***) in which people (*minzoku*) who differ in nation and culture, etc. mutually
  understand and respect each other's difference and coexist, we have founded the Osaka City
  Multicultural Policy Liaison Committee Establishment (called the *Tabunka Kyosei Renraku
  Kaigi* below).
  Note: Bold, mine
  Source: Osaka 2005.

In some sections, we can identify similar rhetoric as in the "newcomer" enclaves.
Foreign residents are "residents" like the Japanese, and both should mutually try to
understand and respect differences and jointly contribute to the local community of
which both are a part. However, even in this statement narrowly focused on "multicultural," we see that Osaka adopts the term "coexistence society" rather than *multicultural* coexistence, emphasizing human rights.

Discussions of multicultural education in the United States and Canada, for
example, bring different cultural groups, including ethnic minorities, women, etc.
into the larger framework of the "multicultural." A human rights perspective is built
into the definition of what is multicultural because of its history rooted in the movement of minorities.

In the Osaka case, since "multicultural" in Japan is linked to being a foreigner, in
order to bring in a larger set of minority cultures, "human rights" serves as the
umbrella concept, and "multicultural" (foreigners) becomes a part of this. The
emphasis in Osaka is ethnicity. In the above-stated basic guidelines for city policies
on foreigners, the section under "the realization of a multicultural coexistence society" and "international understanding education," there is a description that states
that understanding "different ethnicity, culture, customs" is important. Here, ethnicity is used instead of the term nationality as in the other localities; however, the
emphasis on understanding "mutual interdependence" is the same (Osaka 2004,
Introduction).

In other words, the Japanese concept of "multicultural," as it is reflected in the
official homepages of pioneering localities, identifies it with issues of foreigners of
that locality and emphasizes mutual understanding with Japanese.

The term "resident," which includes both Japanese nationals and non-Japanese
nationals, is more inclusive than separating people in regard to their nationality. It is
no secret that localities with a concentration of foreigners have been on the cutting
edge of pioneering policies toward foreigners, ahead of the national government.
However, although the term "resident" makes it possible to be more inclusive to
foreigners, it also limits the target population to "residents" of that locality.

This same emphasis on residents also brings about deviations from the international trend. For example, in the basic policy of Osaka City above, "assistance to

foreign students" is listed under the realization of a multicultural coexistence society, alongside Koreans in Japan, although the first is about a temporary population in higher education, and relatively elitist, and the latter are Japan's largest involuntary minority (Osaka 2004, Table of Contents).

Kawasaki

Kawasaki is an area that has a strong Korean movement, and until the 1980s, most foreigners in the region were the Koreans in Japan. Because of this, the tone of the Kawasaki Multicultural Society Promotion Guidelines (*Kawasakishi Tabunka Kyosei Shakai Suishin Shishin*) has a strong human rights emphasis like in Osaka. The goal of the multicultural coexistence society is "to celebrate the differences in nationality, ethnicity and culture, and for all to respect one another, for **human rights** to be upheld, so that each can live together as an independent citizen" (bold, mine, Kawasaki 2008). The three key concepts of this society are (1) respect for human rights, (2) promotion of social participation, and (3) assisting independence.

What is characteristic of Kawasaki, as is the case with Osaka, is that the "oldcomer"/*dowa* human rights issues procede the inflow of "newcomers," setting a discourse focusing on human rights.

Analyzing the Dilemmas

In sum, after analyzing the multicultural rhetoric in "newcomer," "oldcomer," and other categories, there are common tendencies. First of all, the Japanese "multicultural" is basically about foreigners. If we follow this line of thought, this means that differences in culture as a part of "multicultural" are basically understood as differences in the national culture of the foreigners. The language, therefore, focuses on the need for coexistence between Japanese and foreigners, understanding each other's culture and coexisting as equal residents. I would argue, however, that such understandings of the "multicultural" present localities with dilemmas and that the dilemmas reveal underlining thoughts about the "multicultural."

Dilemma 1: The Human Rights and Multicultural Divide

Having analyzed how progressive localities voice the "multicultural," it seems that because "multicultural" is so strongly associated with foreigners in Japan, localities that have a strong human rights perspective (e.g., speaking out for the rights of various vulnerable populations in general), such as Osaka, have trouble linking their existing human rights perspective with the rising usage of the "multicultural" (referring to foreigners). The former refers to various vulnerable Japanese populations, such as the aged, the physically challenged, and those with chronic diseases, and the latter to "foreigners" which may include vulnerable populations such as foreign workers but may also encompass not so vulnerable populations such as foreign students.

As seen above, the image of the multicultural coexistence society (*tabunka kyosei shakai*) is evoked by all of the localities in question. This image associates "multicultural" with foreigners. These foreigners and the Japanese are seen as mutually understanding and respecting each other's cultures, living "together" (*tomoni* is a favorite term), and contributing to the community together as "residents" in the multicultural coexistence society. The image is basically harmonious.

However, in reality, the status of foreigners and Japanese is far from equal, and the reality is filled with exploitation. As an example, foreign laborers tend to be clustered in jobs at the bottom of the social ladder and can be exploited more easily than Japanese nationals, especially if they are not working legally. Seen from this light, "multicultural coexistence" is actually a human rights issue.

The interesting thing, however, is that the Japanese localities adhere to a harmonious image of "multicultural" and seem to have trouble reconciling this image with human rights language, since the latter is intertwined with conflict, issues of discrimination, and inequality. Because of this, the theme of the Koreans in Japan, who are not only "foreigners" but also clearly human rights subjects, tends to serve as the bridge used to link the "multicultural" and "human rights" language in localities that have a strong human rights perspective preceding the inflow of "newcomers," as can be seen in the case of Osaka and Kawasaki. The "newcomer" enclaves trying to emphasize a human rights perspective also seem to follow this example.

"Oldcomer" enclaves tend to emphasize the special meaning of the Koreans in Japan in understanding "multicultural" human rights. For example, Kawasaki City's Multicultural Coexistence Society Promotion Guidelines (2008) does just that. It starts with the discrimination that Koreans in Japan have faced and moves on to mention the "newcomers," thus, effectively linking "foreigners" with human rights language.

Even some of the "newcomer" enclaves feel compelled to mention that they are not ignoring Japan's representative involuntary ethnic group—the Koreans in Japan. For example, Gunma mentions that the "number of Koreans in Japan may be decreasing," but "in order to promote multicultural coexistence, it is not sufficient to focus on only the South Americans of Japanese descent, etc., but to embark on comprehensive initiatives that take into consideration the historical process by which Koreans in Japan have advanced in Japanese society" (Gunma 2012, p. 2).

Another tactic of localities facing the multicultural vs. human rights dilemma seems to be to just acknowledge the split between multicultural and human rights. Such localities not only have multicultural guidelines but also have created a separate human rights guideline as well. In these human rights guidelines, we see the names of groups that are commonly regarded as discriminated against minority groups by the international community, such as people with disabilities and the aged.

For example, the Mie Prefecture Human Rights Policy Basic Guidelines (*Mie ken jinken sesaku kihon hoshin, daiichijikaite*) starts with a definition of human rights, referring to the various UN conventions on human rights, and goes on to list *dowa* issues, children, women, people with disabilities, foreigners, victims of diseases such as HIV, family victims of crime, Internet abuse, and other human rights violations such as those against the Ainu, former criminals, sexual minorities, the homeless, etc. (Table of Contents, Mie ken 2006). It even talks about the "need to respect various cultures and diversity" but connects that to "the realization of a coexistence society (*kosei shakai*) in which individuals are respected" (p. 3). The term "multicultural" is dropped perhaps because most of those mentioned are vulnerable Japanese nationals. The guidelines call on citizens, corporations, resident groups, NPOs, and civil society in the localities to come together; the actors called upon are basically similar to those asked to realize a multicultural society (p. 3). On the other hand, in its Mei Prefecture **Internationalization** Promotion Guidelines (bold, mine, *Mie ken kokusaika suishin shishin, daiijichi kaite*), in its comments on "multicultural" coexistence, human rights protection for **foreign** residents tops the list; Mie notes that the promotion of multicultural coexistence policies will "lead to respecting the human rights of **foreigners**" as is upheld in the international conventions (bold, mine, Mie 2011, p. 4).

Kawasaki, a representative "oldcomer" district in the Kanto (larger Tokyo) area, adopts a strategy which combines both approaches above. First, the Koreans in Japan are seen as the core of the "foreign" residents, and human rights issues are seen as central to the realization of a multicultural coexistence society.[13] As a representative "oldcomer" enclave, the "oldcomer" human rights movement far preceded the entry of "newcomers" in Kawasaki. The city had already issued the Kawasaki City **Foreigners** in Japan Education Basic Guidelines with the subtitle, "Mainly the Education of **Koreans** in Japan," in 1986 (italics, mine). This title reflects the effectiveness of the Korean movement in the area. In 1998, the subtitle of the above document was renamed as "Towards a **Multicultural** Coexistence Society" (bold, mine).

Kawasaki also uses the second tactic of dividing the multicultural and human rights language. The Kawasaki City **Human Rights** Policy Promotion Guideline was issued in 2000 and then the city's **Multicultural Coexistence Society** Promotion Guidelines of 2005 (revised in 2008) (bold, mine). The multicultural guideline (Kawasaki 2008) lists "respecting human rights" as one of the central ideals which constitute multicultural coexistence. Under multicultural coexistence education, it lists "respect for minority cultures," in those words. Like Mie, Kawasaki (2008) also calls for the formation of a "coexistence society" (without the multicultural) in which "all citizens respect each other's differences and contribute in building a society in which they can live together" (p. 4) and distinguishes this from "the promotion of **multicultural** coexistence education" (bold, mine, p. 3), which refers to foreigners or ethnic Japanese.

Osaka, another representative "oldcomer" enclave, pioneered the nation in its Korean movement to abolish the nationality clause in public housing, childcare allowance, etc. As we saw, Osaka, with its long history of minority human rights movements, solved the multicultural and human rights split in its own way; it used "human rights" as an umbrella term and inserted "multicultural" into this. Since human rights are a wider concept in Japan than multicultural (foreigners), this actually makes sense if one is trying to combine the two.

In the usual usage of "multicultural" in an international context, there would be no problem in including discriminated against cultural groups in the definition of a multicultural society, so this association of "multicultural" with foreigners (bicul-

---

[13] http://www.city.kawasaki.jp/250/page/0000041067.html, retrieved July 2015, the homepage of Kawasaki City.

tural) is a Japanese characteristic. Localities which try to deal with the human rights of vulnerable populations seem to be the ones struggling most with the (perhaps unconsciously) narrow definition of the term multicultural in the Japanese content.

Dilemma 2: The Japanese versus Foreigners Divide
Another issue linked with the above-stated "dilemma 1" is that the foreigner versus the Japanese divide is so strong in Japan that ethnic minorities, even those that have Japanese nationality, are basically conceived of as foreigners.

While the vast majority of those labeled "foreigners" in the community indeed held foreign nationalities, this dichotomous category may not have presented a major problem. However, today, in the ethnic enclaves, localities are discovering that there are an increasing number of individuals who do not fall into this dichotomous pattern, such as those whose parent(s) or ancestor(s) were from another culture but who themselves have Japanese nationality. From the mid-1980s, children can acquire Japanese nationality from their mother as well as their father. Most Koreans in Japan marry Japanese nationals, so their children acquire Japanese nationality.

Localities reviewed in this chapter are those with a concentration of foreigners or ethnic minorities and thus are at the forefront of the cultural diversification of Japanese society. It is thus not surprising that some have started to challenge the simplistic category of foreigners versus Japanese and to try to voice that in various ways.

For example, in Gifu, Minokamo City notes that "we should not forget the existence" of those that do not fall into the dichotomous categories of Japanese and foreigners, such as "Japanese" who have a Japanese nationality but were born abroad and do not speak Japanese or "foreigners" who were born in Japan and who have never been to their "homeland" (*bokoku*) (Minokamo 2014, p. 1).

Kawasaki also notes that Kawasaki City "includes not only residents with foreign nationality, but Japanese nationals who have a foreign cultural background" and lists them comprehensively under an intentionally different term—foreign "citizens" (Kawasaki 2008, p. 1). Similarly, Mie, an "oldcomer" turned "newcomer" district, notes in their internationalization guidebook, those Japanese nationals "who have a cultural background or roots in a foreign country." Mie also includes transient foreign populations (Mie 2011, p. 2).

Dilemma 3: Quantity to Quality
Another point of issue is that in almost every locality, the rhetoric of "multicultural coexistence" is linked to the *increase* in the number of foreigners in the locality and the recognition that there is a *rising* need for Japanese to coexist with the "foreigners." Since the need for multicultural coexistence is justified in this manner, there is a potential problem when the number of foreigners starts to decrease.

The collapse of the Lehman Brothers in 2008 resulted in a decrease in the number of foreigners and the layoff of foreign laborers. The Great East Japan Earthquake in March 2011 also led to a decrease in new foreigners and a heightened awareness of the need to provide support to foreigners during disasters, which is mentioned by some localities (e.g., Gunma 2012, p. 1).

One manner in which localities seem to try to get around the fact that the number of foreigners, at least a certain group of them, is decreasing is to note that though the numbers may be decreasing, the foreigners who remain are staying longer and are increasingly more important as members of the community, in other words, maintaining that these foreigners are becoming a permanent part of the landscape of multicultural Japan (Onai 2009; Onai and Sakai 2001; Ikegami 2001; Kajita et al. 2005).

Take the case of Gunma. It notes that "Brazilians are dramatically decreasing" (Gunma 2012, p. 3) but they are increasingly rooted in the Japanese community. Mie also noted that with the Lehman collapse, the number of foreigners has decreased, but those who are permanent residents and those who are school-aged have rather increased, highlighting the need for a multicultural coexistence society (Mie 2011, pp. 1–2).

11.7 Conclusion

This chapter discussed how localities with a concentration of foreigners have defined what is "multicultural" in the Japanese context. The regions were divided into three categories, "oldcomer" and "newcomer" enclaves, as well as those in-between, or not part of either.

Defining both foreigners and Japanese as "residents" enabled localities to move away from the exclusion of foreigners and to envision a community in which Japanese and foreigners were equal. The emphasis on communication, coexistence, and togetherness resulted in a harmonious image of a multicultural coexistence community. Residents were encouraged to overcome differences in their nationality and culture.

However, the identification of "multicultural" with foreigners, a dichotomous definition of the "multicultural," and a harmonious understanding of the multicultural coexistence society presented problems for localities which felt a need to link the "multicultural" with a human rights perspective. An analysis of the dilemmas revealed how localities built on their different minority/ethnic traditions in recognizing and breaking the narrowness of the conventional "multicultural" framework which was increasingly becoming obsolete in the light of a changing Japanese society.

References

Gunma ken. (2012). *Gunma-ken tabunka kyosei suishin shishin* [Gunma prefecture multicultural community advancement guidelines] (revised version of 2007 guidelines), issued by Gunma Prefecture. Retrieved July 2015, https://www.pref.gunma.jp/04/c1500176.html

Hachioji. (2013). *Tabunka kyosei suishin puran* (this is the Hachioji multicultural policy statement). http://www.city.hachioji.tokyo.jp/kurashi/shimin/004/002/tabunkakyouseisuisinpuran/p023108_d/fil/plan.pdf. Retrieved July 2015.

Ikegami, S. (Ed.). (2001). *Burajirujin to kokusaika suru chiiki shakai* [Brazilians and the globalization of local communities in Japan]. Tokyo: Akashi Shoten.

Kajita, T., Tanno, K., & Higuchi, N. (2005). *Kao no mienai Teijuka—Nikkei burajirujin to kokka/shijyo/imin nettowaku* [Invisible residents: Japanese Brazilians vis-à-vis the state, the market and the immigrant network]. Nagoya: Nagoya Daigaku Shuppankai.

Kawasaki (2008). *Kawasakishi tabunka kyosei shakai suishin shishin—tomoni ikiru chiiki shakai o mezashite* [Kawasaki's promotion guideline for a multicultural, harmonious society: Aiming to be a harmonious community] (abbreviated edition), 2008, March. Revised from the 2005 version.

Kikugawa (2013). *Dai niji Kikugawa shi tabunka kyosei suishin kodo shishin* [Kikugawa City's 2nd guidelines for promotion of multicultural coexistence] (2013–2016). Retrieved July, 2015, http://www.city.kikugawa.shizuoka.jp/chiikishien/documents/dainijisisinn.pdf

Kim, C. (2012). Hanshin/Awaji Daishinsai kara Higashi Nihon Daishinsai e tabunka kyosei no keiken o tsunagu—chiiki niokeru tagengo hoso ga tabunka kyosei shakai kochiku ni hataseru kanosei [Passing on the lessons of multicultural coexistence to Great East Japan earthquake from the Great Hanshin-Awaji earthquake: The potency of multi-lingual broadcasting in a local community]. *GMEC Journal, 7*, 36–37.

Mie ken. (2006). *Mieken jinken sesaku kihon hoshin (dai ichiji kaitei)* (Mie Prefecture basic policy for human rights measures [lit.], first revised edition). Mie ken, 2006, March. Retrieved July, 2015, http://www.pref.mie.lg.jp/JINKEN/HP/hoshin/hoshin.pdf

Mie ken. (2011). *Mieken kokusaika suishin shishin (daiichiji kaitei)-tabunka o tomoni ikiru Mie o mezashite* [Mie Prefecture Guidelines for Promoting Internationalization: Toward a Harmonious Multicultural Society, first revised edition]. March 2011. Mie Prefecture. Retrieved June, 2015, http://www.pref.mie.lg.jp/TABUNKA/HP/shishin/up/sisinnhonbun1.pdf

Minokamo City. (2014). *Dai 2 ji Minokamoshi tabunka kyosei suishin puran* [2nd Minokamo City multicultural coexistence promotion plan] Issued by Minokamo City, Gifu. July, 2014.

Minoura, Y. (2003). *Kodomo no ibunka taiken—Jinkaku keisei katei no shinri jinruiguku teki kenkyu* [Inter-cultural experiences for children: Psychological anthropology on the process of forming the identity of children]. Tokyo: Shin Shisaku Sha.

Ogbu, J., & Simons, H. (1998). Voluntary and involuntary minorities: A cultural-ecological theory of school performance with some implications for education. *Anthropology & Education Quarterly, 29*(2), 155–188.

Onai, T. (Ed.). (2009). *Zainichi Burajirujin no kyoiku to hoiku no henyo* [Transformation of education and childcare among Brazilians in Japan]. Tokyo: Ochanomizu Shobo.

Onai, T., & Sakai, E. (2001). *Nikkei Burajirujin no teijyuka to chiiki shakai—Gunmaken Ota/Oizumi chiku o jirei toshite* [Settlement of Japanese Brazilians and local communities: A case study on the Ota and Oizumi areas in Gunma Prefecture]. Tokyo: Ochanomizu Shobo.

Osaka. (2004). *Osakashi Gaikokuseki Jyumin Sesaku Kihonshishin* [Osaka city basic guidelines on measures for residents with foreign nationality]. March, 2004, by Osaka City.

Saitama ken. (2012). *Saitama ken tabunka kyosei suishin puran (Heisei 24 nendo-28 nendo)—kenmin daremoga kokuseki/bunka no chigai o koete tomoni tsukuru katsuryoku no aru Saitama no jitsugen o meashite* [Saitama Multicultural Society Promotion Plan [2017–2021]: Aiming to Further Invigorate Saitama Together, Overcoming Differences in Nationality/Culture], 2012, July. Retrieved, July, 2015, https://www.pref.saitama.lg.jp/a0306/keikakutoukei/tabunkaplan.html

Sato, G. (1997). *Kaigai/kikokushijyo kyoiku no saikochiku—Ibunkakan kyoiku no shiten kara* [Reconstructing the education of Japanese children abroad or recently retuning home: From the perspective of cross-cultural education studies]. Tokyo: Tamagawadaigaku Shuppanbu.

Shimizu, M. & 'Stand by Me'. (2009). *Ichodanchi hatsu! Gaikokujin no kodomotachi nochosen* [Challenges tackled by children with foreign background living in the Icho housing complex], Tokyo: Iwanamishoten.

Shimizu, M. (2011). Schools, communities, and newcomer children: A case study of a public housing complex. In *Minorities and education in multicultural Japan: An interactive perspective* (pp. 173–190). New York: Routledge.

Somucho. (2006). *Chiki ni okeru tabunka kyosei suishin puran ni tsuite* [On Prefectual/Municipal plans for the promotion of multicultural coexistence]. Issued March, 27. Retrieved June, 2015, http://www.soumu.go.jp/kokusai/pdf/sonota_b6.pdf

Somucho (Ministry of Internal Affairs and Communications). (2006). *Tabunka kyosei no suishin ni kansuru kenyukai hokokusho: Chiiki niokeru tabunka kyosei no suishin ni mukete* [Report by the council for the promotion of multicultural coexistence: Toward promotion of multicultural coexistence in prefectures/municipalities] (March). Retrieved June, 2015, http://www.soumu.go.jp/kokusai/pdf/sonota_b5.pdf

Tsuneyoshi, R., Okano, K., & Boocock, S. (Eds.). (2011). *Minorities and education in multicultural Japan: An interactive perspective*. New York: Routledge.

Chapter 12
Higher Education Reform: Focusing on National University Reform

Akiko Morozumi

12.1 Easing Government Regulations to Promote Results Orientation

At one time, there was a trend toward strong governmental control in higher education in Japan, even from an international perspective (Clark 1983). This approach attempted to ensure the best educational quality by limiting the number of universities, establishing minimum standards of adherence, and strictly applying "prior regulations." However, although this governmental regulation ensured consistent quality, the policy was criticized as it was perceived to discourage individuality and the diversification of universities. Thus, in the 1990s, the government adopted a different approach by easing regulations to allow greater university autonomy. For example, in the 1991 Deregulation of University Act, universities were granted a greater degree of freedom in terms of educational content and curricula. Based on the Koizumi administration's strong move toward structural reform of market principles and free competition, the policy of controlling new extensions to universities and departments was essentially annulled in 2003; instead, a policy was established that changed prior regulations to post-checks, and a third-party evaluation system was introduced.

At the same time, from society there is a strong requirement for universities to achieve visible results. However, the relevance of private universities is also being severely questioned. For instance, 46% of private universities do not meet their quotas. Moreover, despite the fact that approximately half of all university students take out student loans to attend a university, they are not always assured of employment in their field of specialization. Such social opinions are closely associated with the distribution of finances during a time of financial restraint by the government.

A. Morozumi (✉)
Graduate School of Education, The University of Tokyo, Tokyo, Japan
e-mail: morozumi@p.u-tokyo.ac.jp

© Springer Nature Singapore Pte Ltd. 2019
Y. Kitamura et al. (eds.), *Education in Japan*, Education in the Asia-Pacific
Region: Issues, Concerns and Prospects 47,
https://doi.org/10.1007/978-981-13-2632-5_12

There has also been a surge in competitive funding distribution schemes for specific programs in the last decade. In addition, as noted later in this chapter, few criticisms state that the inability of universities to produce results is due to poor-quality structures. Addressing this issue from the perspective of university governance is significant. Although results and accountability have been consistently emphasized in recent times, there has also been a policy shift in terms of increasingly strong governmental controls on university activities and structure. This chapter discusses national university reforms as a typical example of such policy changes.

12.2 Aims and Design of Incorporation

The governance of national universities in Japan is undergoing reform as is the case in many foreign countries. From this aspect, the symbolic point of diversion was the incorporation of national universities in 2004. Prior to that, Japanese national universities were part of an administrative agency that had little decision-making authority as an agency and lacked autonomy (OECD 2003). The incorporation of national universities was intended to provide autonomy as an agency and to stimulate momentum for university reform.

The fundamental design of the National University Corporation (NUC), which is detailed in CNUFM (2008), can be summarized in the following five points. The first states that strong state participation in the management of the NUC impedes university reform. Awarding the universities' corporate status makes them more independent, while being the management head of the organization strengthens the president's authority. The second point is increased discretion, which is achieved by easing various national regulations such as budgets and by means of a non-bureaucratic-type personnel system. The third is legitimization for external parties to participate in the director and management council committees and president selection committees to promote a diversity of perspectives for better management of the corporation. The fourth point is that the management of universities occurs on the basis of a 6-year plan with specific midterm targets, the results of which are evaluated and reflected in the government's operating grant assessments. Based on the midterm plan and targets, which are mutually approved by the state and the NUC, a contractual agreement is then established whereby the state adopts the necessary financial measures and the university works toward achieving its devised targets. The fifth point states that, in contrast to the former system of financial support where the budget allocated specific amounts for each expenditure, universities have been granted more autonomy in the form of block grants, which are not restrictive in terms of how the money is used. Such schemes have increased the discretion of universities in various ways.

In the NUC, the president serves as the head of both the corporation and the university and is entrusted with the final decision-making authority. This system does not exist in any other country, wherein the president of a university is personally entrusted with such authority (Kaneko 2009). This administrative system of endowing greater authority to the presidents was devised to negate the problems encountered by the pre-incorporation national university presidents. As agency heads, they possessed no authority, whereas the power rested primarily with the Ministry of Education, Culture, Sports, Science and Technology (MEXT) and the academic units (faculty, department, etc.), and this was perceived as a significant problem. The discretion of the university has been increased by changing the system design, which is expected to engender autonomous management and promote reforms, based on the increasing influence of the president.

12.3   Effects and Issues After a Decade

What has changed in the decade since incorporation? After 6 years of incorporation, which was the first period for the midterm targets, MEXT investigated and compiled the latest effects and issues (MEXT 2010). This research was conducted by gathering opinions and evaluations not only from university officials but also from students and community members. Some of the effects have been explored by Honda (2013) and Oba (2014), but the effects and issues are summarized below.

12.3.1   The Effects of Incorporation

The objectives and the reform philosophy of the NUC system were positively evaluated by society in general, and positive results have consistently been manifested in the management and education/research/social contributions since the beginning of incorporation. Furthermore, there have been many positive comments about the initiatives for enriching educational content and improving the quality of educational activities. There has been a drastic rise in the amount of collaborative research and competitive funding, as well as Grants-in-Aid for Scientific Research. The ratio of total income from competitive funding (competitive subsidies, funded research, donations, etc.) has increased from 8% to 14%. With the acquisition of external funding to ensure sufficient university hospital income, the total income has surged by nearly 120% (Fig. 12.1) in the decade since incorporation. Social contribution activities have also witnessed notable progress.

We have also observed examples of management reorganization. Historically, Japanese universities have been characterized by a closed structure supported by a chair system and research-oriented academics (Clark 1983; Oba 2014), and this feature has prevented educational reform. For example, Kanazawa University separated faculty organization and student organization and divided student organization into bigger groups. Akita University changed from a three-faculty system to a four-faculty system, and the structure of human resources was reviewed. However, it is important to note that even before incorporation, Kyushu University had conducted reorganization, and those initiatives have not necessarily been enabled as a

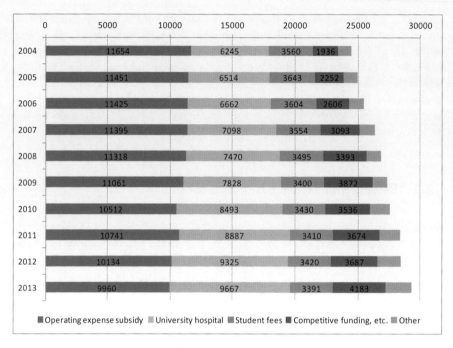

Fig. 12.1 The transition in ordinary revenue (income) in the NUC over the last decade

consequence of incorporation. Thus, undoubtedly, opportunities for reform have increased in the NUC as a result of incorporation.

12.3.2 Challenges Since Incorporation

However, many challenges have been identified simultaneously. The first challenge is the reduction in operating grants. In the decade since incorporation, the total income has increased, but operating grants for fundamental expenses have decreased from 48% in 2004 to 34% in 2013. The first midterm planning and target period introduced a uniform 1% efficiency coefficient, and budget for the NUCs was subsequently reduced by 1% each year. During the second period, a "university reforms promotion coefficient" was introduced with the purpose of reviewing existing organizations and businesses. However, if such reorganization was not carried out, basic operating grants were decreased, including a decrease of 1% for universities without a hospital. These changes in the financial structure exerted a significant influence on educational and research activities. For example, for some universities, there was a decrease in personnel expenses for full-time academic staffs, leading to a decrease in the number of academic staffs. In turn, this led to an increased workload for instructors and professors. The research area faced serious challenges: the number of published research papers since incorporation has decreased. In addition, due to the longer time required to acquire external funding, the academic staffs have less time to commit to research. Qualitative differences among universities have also increased. While there is a group of universities for which external funding has increased considerably, such as the former imperial universities, the challenges for teacher-training colleges have been maximized because they are unable to secure as much external funding and are greatly affected by the reduction in operating grants.

The university presidents often argued that the reduction in operating grants was in violation of the agreement because the government guaranteed autonomy to university management for a period of 6 years. Moreover, the contract between the government and the NUCs was rather based on the midterm planning and target period. National universities do not have an endowment fund of their own. After incorporation, considerable effort was made to acquire donations. Some universities increased their income from donations, but there were still some systematic restrictions, such as private donations to NUCs not being tax deductible and income deductions being restricted to employment income only. Although there were numerous other routes to private funding and competitive funding, there is no assurance of funding each year; and this makes it difficult for management to take a long-term perspective. Moreover, universities are not entirely free to borrow money. These constraints were significantly impacted by the gradual reduction in operating grants.

The second challenge is related to the midterm plan and targets. While the cycle of plans and target, implementation, and evaluation was found to be functional, the troubles associated with it are believed to have increased. Moreover, in the original design of the incorporation, midterm targets are established by the university, and the 6-year period evaluation results would be linked to future financial support; however, in practice, these mechanisms are not functioning effectively (Kaneko 2012). It is apparent that the challenge in evaluating university activities lies in the lack of nearly any indicators to measure the achievement level; the target level for each university is not standardized, and it is difficult to establish differences when evaluating the results of educational activities. However, in order to reflect accurate evaluation results for operating grant assessments, a weighted comprehensive score is calculated that combines achievement, level evaluations, and quality improvement evaluations. These scores are publicly announced in the media, similar to a university ranking system, which some universities have opposed. Defects in such evaluation criteria would also lead to a decrease in evaluation reflections. For example, despite being fifth in terms of comprehensive evaluation points, Ochanomizu University only received a small increase in operating grants in the range of hundreds of thousands of yen. Although universities are asked to expend great efforts, they are not rewarded for their hard work, which leads to dissatisfaction. Having completed the first midterm planning and target period, it has become apparent that the design of the incorporation is not yet completely functional.

12.4   Increasingly Strong Government Influence

After reflecting on the first midterm planning and target period, the NUC reforms continue into their second stage. Instead of the NUC carrying out autonomous reforms, as was the original intention of the NUC Act, the direction has shifted so that the government has an increasing influence.

12.4.1   NUC Reforms Plan and Redefinition of the Mission

The basic objectives of the new policy are summarized in the NUC Reforms Plan,[1] which was announced by MEXT in November 2013. The NUC Reforms Plan was designed by the current Liberal Democratic Party, but in general it has followed the same direction as the former Democratic Party's "University Reform Action Plan." The current policy that embodies the University Reform Action Plan is the "NUC's redefinition of the mission." The reforms suggest an exchange of ideas between the NUC and MEXT, both of which organize each university's strengths, characteristics, and role in society (mission). This is designed based on objective data, such as the level of research, educational results, and industry-academic cooperation. In other words, the reforms can be regarded as a functional enhancement policy, wherein each university can expand their strengths and characteristics, thus fulfilling their role in society. The results of redefining the mission for every field are published for each university on the MEXT website.[2] The redefinition of the mission is derived from individual exchanges of ideas between each department in each NUC and MEXT. However, the process itself has not been clarified, although results clearly indicate that the intentions of MEXT have been included.

12.4.2   Subsidies for Promoting Reform

The NUC Reforms Plan comprises a drastic revision to the distribution methods used for the operating grants, which includes annual evaluations of the progress of reforms, key distribution for universities that promote reforms in order to extend the redefinition of the mission, and subsidies under the "priority issue promotion framework" (Table 12.1).

For example, under the leadership of the president and in addition to dealing with governance reforms, A-1 NUC reforms strengthen the promotional subsidies, which provide a centralized and significant support for leading initiatives. Such initiatives

---

[1] http://www.mext.go.jp/english/topics/__icsFiles/afieldfile/2014/03/13/1345139_1.pdf
[2] http://www.mext.go.jp/a_menu/koutou/houjin/1341970.htm (in Japanese).

Table 12.1 Prioritized budget distribution

Schemes		Start	Budget amount
A. NUC reform strengthening promotional project	A-1. NUC reform strengthening promotional subsidies	2012	FY 2012 13.83 billion yen (14 selected universities) FY 2013 14 billion yen (7 selected universities) FY 2014 13.8 billion yen (11 selected university) budget request of 17 billion yen
	A-2. University reforms basically strengthening promotional expenses (key support, such as maintenance of basic equipment and advanced equipment)	2014	FY 2014 4.8 billion yen FY 2015 budget request of 6 billion yen
B. Key support for reform philosophy by means of operating grants, etc.		2014	FY 2014 7.7 billion yen (18 selected universities) FY 2015 budget request of 23.2 billion yen

include personnel renewal and initiatives toward the reorganization of education and research across university and departmental frameworks for the optimization of resource distribution within the universities on the basis of the redefinition of the mission. Furthermore, it provides significant support for leading initiatives such as increasing the employment of excellent young researchers. The selection process is based on applications from each NUC, but the details of the evaluation/selection process are ambiguous. There are conflicting opinions and criticisms from universities, such as "essentially, instead of accepting applications, MEXT draws up scenarios that are then proposed to universities."[3]

In 2014, "Key support for reform philosophy by means of operating grants, etc." was enforced. This is a pivotal distribution budget that promotes reform, including optimizing the distribution of resources (within the schools across departments/postgraduate courses, etc.) of each NUC (budget, personnel, facilities/spaces, etc.), cooperation across university frameworks, and functional enhancement by means of personnel training. Naturally, that amount is taken from the operating grant budget that is distributed to other universities. Operating grants are awarded for leading and bold initiatives for a university reform model that supports strategically positioned items, which are a part of the overall university midterm reform philosophy. As a replacement for budgetary distribution, such philosophies must promote a flexible HR payroll system (including a salary system). Until 2013, those initiatives that matched the educational and research needs of each university, centering on the

---

[3] Between information report: "What happened to 'homework' in FY 2012? Progress of NUC reforms as shown in the university reform action plan." April 24, 2013, Shinken-Ad Co., Ltd., Between Editorial Department http://shinken-ad.co.jp/between/report/pdf/201304_01.pdf

ideas of departmental and academic staffs, were supported. However, in 2014, this changed so that functional enhancement would be promoted in order to utilize each university's strengths and characteristics based on the direction of national policy and the ideas of the presidents. Moreover, by converging university numbers, the amount of support for each university increased (from approximately 70 million yen to approximately 290 million yen). The selection process for universities with regard to the distribution process was again ambiguous.

When compared to the amount of NUC-evaluation management subsidies, the key distribution budgets for each university are very large. While operating grants continue to decrease, universities are desperately trying to acquire the budgets necessary to implement the reforms proposed by MEXT. While governmental control over universities was initially planned to be indirect and to emphasize the autonomy of universities, it has rapidly transformed into being policy-oriented in recent years.

12.4.3   Demand for Further Governance Reforms

Since incorporation, we have witnessed relatively more reforms under the president's leadership. However, according to extensive evaluations from society and corporate fields, this is inadequate. In order to implement further reforms within universities, governance reforms were discussed by the Central Council for Education in June 2013, and a summary of the deliberations was published in February 2014.

Two specific challenges were identified. The first is that the faculty council (*Kyoju-kai*) has significantly more authority, and the president cannot completely demonstrate leadership. The School Education Act was therefore revised in April 2014 to restrict items for deliberation by the faculty council to education and research activities, and in order to strengthen the president support system, new regulations for vice-presidents were established. Corresponding to the revised act, MEXT provides guidance to all universities to review the internal school regulations.

The second challenge is that the budget, which is required for the president to demonstrate able leadership, is lacking. Operating grants have decreased as a basic expense; however, most university expenses are fixed expenses, such as personnel expenses, and there is no margin for the president to extract a management budget. The ratio of strategic expenses, such as the president's discretionary expenses, comprising the budget is extremely low, and the ratio is as low as between sub-1% and 5% at some universities (National Institute for Educational Research 2012). Therefore, with regard to expanding discretionary expenses (indirect costs, etc.) for effective distribution based on presidential leadership and budget support for education and research activities including university governance reforms, assisted projects, etc., support is being provided through the budget so that the president can demonstrate leadership for fixed governance reforms. This direction is also confirmed in the "NUC operating grant ideals for the third period of midterm targets" (midterm summary) announced in April 2015.

12.5   What Management Reforms Are Needed in the NUCs?

Contrary to the initial plan, the influence of MEXT is being strengthened. Such demands on the universities may appear to be MEXT policy, but it cannot be ignored that the background to this is the demand from the Ministry of Finance, the country, private businesses, etc. for the transparent presentation of apparent results at universities. The international trend is to emphasize increased accountability and results orientation. Despite the increased autonomy in the system and a greater amount of total income, it is only appropriate for critics to demand an explanation for its apparent lack of an effect on education and research results. Universities have to respond to this demand, and the fact is that more drastic changes are required.

The series of policies from MEXT have been designed effectively. However, they are not necessarily consistent, as the long-term perspective tends to crumble in terms of, for example, the feasible limits of the policy in budget negotiations with the Ministry of Finance. With an increasingly complex society, as long as MEXT can completely grasp the present conditions and the future of all NUCs, there may no longer be a need for incorporation. Today, the content of policy discussions is adopted from ideas from individual NUCs, not from MEXT, and negotiations must be held with external organizations, including MEXT. Management reforms are actually necessary at present in the NUCs, recognizing the challenges that have been underscored.

12.5.1   Management Personnel Training

In order to carry out a series of reforms, the authority of the president was strengthened during the discussions; however, the government's direct involvement in implementation does not necessarily provide solutions. What is currently lacking is not the systematic authority of the president but is actually the ability, knowledge, and symbol of the president as the manager of the university. Morozumi (2015), who analyzed the awareness and behavior of the academic staffs with regard to university business management, clearly stated that university academic staffs have become increasingly busy in recent years, and, despite the fact that research time has decreased, they are required to increasingly participate in university management. This demand for participation stems from a strong distrust of executives and presidents, while academic staffs who doubt the ability of the president as a manager strongly feel that "we cannot leave things up to the president." Thus, simply strengthening the authority of the president will only create opposition from such

	Managerial staffs with academic background (including experienced workers)	General academic staffs
Increasing academic results	56.8%	61.0%
Preparation to give good lessons and effort put into student guidance	62.5%	61.5%
Individual contact with students and dealing with their concerns	35.0%	25.8%
Contributing to social demands and problems	20.8%	19.1%
Contributing to everyday university management through managerial duties	15.0%	7.3%
Future planning and efforts towards reforms in committee activities, etc.	20.0%	9.3%

Ratio of "Very important" from Law 4

Fig. 12.2 Prioritization of duties for management academic staffs and general academic staffs. (Source: Calculated from an academic staff survey carried out in 2013 by CRUMP)

academic staffs, which will impede the process of achieving improved educational quality and research activities.

Rather than strengthening the authority, improving the management ability of presidents is the first challenge that needs to be addressed. In Japanese universities, there is an underdeveloped external labor market for managers, which originates from the academic staffs and management by so-called amateur presidents. Figure 12.2 demonstrates the different priorities of managerial academic staffs and general academic staffs. With regard to education and research activities, almost no difference can be observed between the priorities of the two groups. Operation and management activities are important to managerial academic staffs, but they are not as important as education and research activities. Many presidents have experience in general managerial positions, such as directors/councilors or as deans; however, they generally do not possess specialized training. For example, according to a survey of top-level university managers conducted by the Tokyo University Center for Research on University Management and Policy (CRUMP) in 2015, as much as 47% of university presidents had not received education or training in operations and management, and the education or training received by most of those who had was limited to short courses. This was particularly true of deans; nevertheless, there is a strong culture of rotation in university management. Even in a survey of university academic staffs conducted by CRUMP in 2013, 55% responded positively to the question "Would you take up a position as a manager in the future if asked?"

which suggests that there is a trend to perceive academic management as an extension of a teaching position.

In Japan, the job of managing a university is perceived to be easy; however, in a social environment with financial constraints, it is extremely challenging to control an organization that is pursuing several missions, including educational, research, and social goals. In private businesses in Japan, employees are motivated by the value of the next task, but it is difficult for top-level managers to lead the education and research activities of university academic staffs and to promote dedication and hard work among their employees with incentives. University management is a tough job, and a reformed level of awareness is needed to unearth personnel who can be good managers and to train, evaluate, and support them.

Of course, there are some excellent university managers, but it is the exception to observe them displaying effective business skills at another university. The tendency in today's culture is to select managers who are superior in terms of education and research and respected by their colleagues, which underscores the trend toward older presidents. Effective structures are necessary to select and train young, progressive individuals, and it is important to cultivate not only presidents but also deans and other leaders for every department within the institution. We also need to expand the range of university management personnel.

12.5.2 Establishing a Primary Actor Responsible for Long-Term Development

In order to find and train presidents as successful university managers, a primary actor responsible for the long-term development of the university is undoubtedly required by the current NUCs. In NUCs in Japan, the president is both the head of the corporation and the university, and the president selects the board of directors. Therefore, when there is a change in the president, there is often a complete change in the members of the board of directors, which is an issue regarding continuity for the board. The tenure of the president generally does not exceed 6 years, and thus it is essentially impossible for the board of directors to consider the future of the university from a long-term perspective. In comparison to other countries, while the structure of the NUC is inadequate in terms of the separation of management and education, its functions and role as a corporation must be strengthened. There are two remedies for this dilemma, namely, either create a monitoring agency such as an overarching board of directors or use a legislative organization that represents the whole university as the highest decision-making agency. Obviously, there is no such organizational structure in the current system, and this may be impacted significantly by the fact that the managerial ability of the president has not yet been cultivated. In NUCs in Japan, agencies have different ways of handling results when

Table 12.2 Method of selecting president/deans

	President			Deans		
	Essentially decided on the basis of election by staffs	There is an election, but the board of directors and election committee make the choice	The board of directors and election committee make the choice without an election	Essentially decided on the basis of election by staffs	There is an election, but the board of directors and election committee make the choice	The board of directors and election committee make the choice without an election
National	51%	47%	2%	96%	4%	
Public	39%	21%	40%	71%	16%	13%
Private	39%	17%	44%	55%	10%	35%

Source: Calculated from an academic staff survey carried out in 2013 by CRUMP

selecting a president, including selection by academic staffs (also known as the vote of intention)[4] (Table 12.2).

In the presidential selection process, it is extremely important to consider the opinions of the academic staffs, but internal members may not have enough information about who would be the ideal president, or they may not even want to take responsibility in case they choose an incapable president. It is thus risky to entrust the final decision to the result of an election directly.

The presidential selection committee can decide to overturn the election results to select a secondary candidate, which could lead to legal cases if the academic staffs do not consent. This can eventually become an impediment to university management. However, in the current governance of NUCs in Japan, the president is the final decision-making agent, and it is difficult to modify this mechanism. There are many private businesses that advocate eliminating the current presidential election by modifying the relevant policies. However, in this context, it is more important to provide direction from a long-term perspective, to establish a primary actor for decision-making, to consider such decision-making as a single choice, and to be able to implement such decisions. In order to carry out real, autonomous reforms, such changes to governance are necessary.

References

Clark, B. R. (1983). *The higher education system: Academic organization in cross-national perspective*. Berkeley and Los Angeles: University of California Press.
CNFUM (Center for National University Finance and Management). (2008). *Japanese national university reform in 2004*. Tokyo: CNFUM. http://www.zam.go.jp/n00/n000k001.htm

---

[4]Presidential selection by academic staffs is not required by the law. It is a decision left to the university. Some universities, such as Tohoku University, no longer have presidential elections.

Honda, S. (2013). Japan's higher education incorporation policy: A comparative analysis of three stages of national university governance. *Journal of Higher Education Policy and Management, 35*(5), 537–552.

Kaneko, M. (2009). Incorporation of national universities in Japan: Design, implementation and consequences. *Asia Pacific Education Review, 10*(1), 59–67.

Kaneko, M. (2012). Evaluating incorporation of National Universities in Japan. In CNFUM (Ed.), *Cycles of University Reform-2011*. Tokyo: CNFUM. http://www.zam.go.jp/n00/pdf/nk002004.pdf

MEXT (Ministry of Education, Culture, Sport and Technology). (2010). *Kokuritsudigaku hou-jinnkago no genjo to kadai nitsuite* [Current status and challenges post-national university cor-poration] (in Japanese).

Morozumi, A. (2015). Faculty participation in university decision making and Management in Japan. In J. C. Shin, G. A. Postiglione, & F. Huang (Eds.), *Mass higher education development in East Asia-strategy, quality, and challenges* (pp. 325–341). Dordrecht: Springer.

National Institute for Educational Research. (2012). *Daigaku no Zaimu-unei no arikata ni kansuru chousahoukokusho* [Investigative research report into the ideals for university financial man-agement]. Tokyo: National Institute for Educational Research (in Japanese). http://www.nier.go.jp/05_kenkyu_seika/pdf-report/h23/23-2-report.pdf

Oba, J. (2014). Reforming national universities in Japan. In M. Shattock (Ed.), *International trends in university governance-autonomy—Self-government and the distribution of authority* (pp. 107–124). New York: Routledge.

OECD (Organization for Economic Cooperation and Development). (2003). Changing patterns of governance in higher education. In OECD (Ed.), *Education Policy Analysis*. Paris: OECD Publishing.

Chapter 13
English Language Teaching and Learning in Japan: History and Prospect

Yoshifumi Saito

13.1 Introduction

The history of English language teaching (ELT) in Japan for the last hundred years is quite often depicted, deploringly as well as deplorably, as one of constant failure and confusion. This is largely because Japanese people on average tend to stay toward the lowest end of English proficiency on some international scales (including TOEFL and IELTS), most of them failing to reach a level they find satisfactory despite the time and energy they spend on learning the language. On the assumption that their time and energy have been misspent and that Japan has taken wrong approaches to ELT, a considerable number of progressive scholars and teachers proposed, at every turn of the abovementioned history, various innovations, most conspicuously, of teaching methodologies. The methodological innovations have mostly taken the form of introducing West-born methods and approaches, each of which, however, in turn has proved or is almost sure to prove not as effective as it first looked. The same assumption has also urged political or educational dignitaries to propose more administration-based "root-and-branch" innovations, only to aggravate the complications of classroom ELT situations all over Japan.

There are multifarious and multileveled reasons behind this seeming "failure" of ELT in Japan. Firstly, Japanese people are not highly motivated to study English, because they hardly feel any inconvenience in their daily lives without it. Another possible reason is that they are not very good at linguistic communication in the beginning, living in a relatively homogeneous society where they can understand each other nonverbally or without saying as much as they would possibly be expected to elsewhere. We may also need to consider the linguistic distance between Japanese and English, the former being more widely different from the latter—in

Y. Saito (✉)
Graduate School of Education, The University of Tokyo, Tokyo, Japan
e-mail: ysaito@p.u-tokyo.ac.jp

© Springer Nature Singapore Pte Ltd. 2019
Y. Kitamura et al. (eds.), *Education in Japan*, Education in the Asia-Pacific
Region: Issues, Concerns and Prospects 47,
https://doi.org/10.1007/978-981-13-2632-5_13

terms of phonetics, phonology, graphology (Japanese people use Chinese characters and the *hiragana* and *katakana* syllabaries instead of the alphabet), vocabulary, syntax, and pragmatics (e.g., they often use a phrase of apology in making a request, giving a denial, or expressing their gratitude)—than many other languages. For these and possibly many other reasons, Japanese people's proficiency in English on average has stayed rather low, which might have produced the wrong impression that ELT in Japan has been unsuccessful. If we are to make any improvements in ELT in Japan, therefore, it will be necessary to take a broad view of the complication of these reasons as well as its history, rather than just to denounce all the preceding language policies and teaching methodologies as outmoded and inefficient, and to sort out what *can* be improved. What this chapter purports to do is firstly to take a brief historical look at the teaching and learning of English in Japan, secondly to analyze the fallacy of reiterative methodological and administrative "innovations," and lastly to discuss some possible ways to improve ELT in Japan with special attention to some of the insights gained from its history and some case studies of successful Japanese learners of English.

13.2   A Brief History of English Language Teaching and Learning in Prewar Japan

In reviewing the history of English language teaching and learning in Japan, it is customary to refer to the "Phaeton Incident" of 1808—an incident involving the intrusion of a British frigate, the Phaeton, into Nagasaki Harbor—as its starting point, for the Tokugawa Shogunate, awakened for the first time to the military power of Britain, subsequently commanded Dutch-language interpreters in Nagasaki to start learning English (and Russian) the next year. The first incentive for English studies in Japan, it should be noted, was thus a pressing concern for national defense *against* an English-speaking nation. For the next 40 years, Dutch-language interpreters made slow but steady progress in their study of English until they were suddenly provided with an opportunity to be taught by an American named Ranald MacDonald, who had smuggled himself into Japan in an American whaling ship, firmly believing this Far Eastern island to be the home of his maternal ancestors. Before long he was arrested as an illegal immigrant but was treated rather generously as a precious native speaker of English and sent to Nagasaki, where he taught the language to Dutch-language interpreters through the grating of his confinement room. MacDonald's memoirs of his voyage to and stay in Japan include a description of how he was requested, as the word "duty" suggests, to take a grammar- and translation-based approach to language instruction which had proved most efficient in their professional experiences of Dutch learning through many generations of professional service to the Shogunate.

> Their habit was to read English to me: One at a time. My duty was to correct their pronunciation, and as best as I could in Japanese explain meaning, construction, etc. (…) They

were all well up in grammar, etc., especially Murayama [Moriyama Einosuke]; that is to say, they learned it readily from me. They were all very quick, and receptive. It was a pleasure to teach them.

The discussions as to signification and different applications of words were, at times, a little laborious, but, on the whole, satisfactory, by aid of the dictionaries, and my own natural aptitude in that way—of which I had no idea till developed by the effort.

(A passage from *Japan: Story of Adventure of Ranald MacDonald, First Teacher of English in Japan A.D. 1848-1849* as cited in Kawasumi, ed., 1998: 273)

Among those highly motivated language learners and professional interpreters, Moriyama made such outstanding progress in learning English as to be able, 5 years later when Commodore Perry came to Japan to establish trade and diplomatic relations between Japan and the United States, to speak "English well enough to render any other interpreter unnecessary" (a passage from *A Journal of the Perry Expedition to Japan* as cited in Kawasumi, ed., above: 263). However, during the process of contact between Japanese officials and the American envoy, English was still no more than a subsidiary medium of casual communication, Chinese and Dutch being two official languages for serious negotiations. No one at this point would have imagined the key role English was to play from the Meiji Restoration onward in Japan's modernization.

English studies in Japan made remarkable progress in the years following the opening of the ports at Shimoda, Hakodate, and Yokohama. Fukuzawa Yukichi (1835–1901: enlightenment thinker and educator; founder of Keio University) and Niijima Jo (1843–1890; Christian educator; founder of Doshisha University), who were then up-and-coming Dutch scholars, shifted their focus to English study, and many language teachers and official interpreters began publishing English dictionaries, grammar books, and textbooks. The first decade of the Meiji era witnessed the sudden emergence of English studies as a discipline primarily for obtaining Western knowledge and technology. The Meiji government employed many foreign teachers, mostly from Britain and the United States, as providers of higher education, and high proficiency in English consequently became a prerequisite for gaining access to advanced education. This government-driven Anglicization of education suddenly slowed down almost to a halt, however, when the Meiji government was confronted with serious financial difficulties caused by the Seinan War (1877) and had to drastically reduce the number of those high-salaried foreign teachers in its employ. Around the same time, the new domestic system of education had been well under way, and in 1885 the government at last put forth the policy for Japanizing the medium of instruction at all levels of education. Thus, as the result of "the well-ordered development of education in Japan" after its "humiliating" Anglicization, as the famous novelist put it (Natsume 1911; my translation), English was dethroned from its former dominant position in learning and education in Japan. In the latter half of the Meiji era when Japan grew quickly into a full-fledged modernized nation with due wealth and power, English studies, deprived of their practical functions, gradually shaped themselves into highly specialized disciplines of language and literary studies, and English was incorporated into school education as just one of the major subjects with its own routine functions of instruction and assessment. On the other hand, it is worth mentioning that there were many Japanese—including those masters of English such as Nitobe Inazo (1862–1933; agricultural economist, educator, and politician; author of *Bushido, the Soul of Japan*, 1900), Okakura (Tenshin) Kakuzo (1862–1913; art critic and administrator; author of *The Book of Tea*, 1906), Saito Hidesaburo (1866–1929; English grammarian and lexicographer), Suzuki Daisetsu (Daisetsu T. Suzuki; 1870–1966; Buddhist scholar and philosopher; author of *Zen and Japanese Culture*, 1970, which is the revised version of *Zen Buddhism and Its Influence on Japanese Culture* published in 1938, and many other books on Buddhism), and Iwasaki Tamihei (1892–1971; scholar of English)—who, born in the Edo or Meiji era, acquired a high command of English by means of grammar- and reading-based self-study (Saito 2000).

The ELT reform that took place in the 1920s in the Taisho era against the backdrop of the popularization of education deserves special notice in relation to the history of English language education in the world. For the first time in its history, the teaching of English as a foreign language (EFL) was highlighted in a state-driven educational reform. Howatt and Widdowson (2004: 264) give a biographical description of Harold E. Palmer, who played a central role in those projects, as follows:

> The second phase of [Palmer's] life was almost exclusively devoted to English as a foreign language. He became Linguistic Advisor to the Japanese Ministry of Education in 1922 and the following year he was appointed Director of a specialized institute set up by the Ministry called the Institute for Research in English Teaching (IRET). It eventually became the focus of world attention and attracted a large number of interested teachers, both native-speaking British and Americans, and Japanese. Among them was A.S. Hornby who arrived in Tokyo in the late 1920s and collaborated closely with Palmer on a number of projects.

Despite the enthusiastic acclaim his Oral Method achieved in many parts of Japan immediately after its implementation in language classrooms, however, it did not have any noticeable effect, as can be seen from the talk Ichikawa Sanki, Professor at the University of Tokyo and his IRET colleague, gave at the Conference of the Teachers of English in Tokyo in 1926, warning the conferees of the risk of putting scientific oral-based teaching methodologies too rigorously into classroom practice at the sacrifice of the development of students' reading skills (see Saito 2015). Thus, ironically enough, Palmer's Oral Method reform is historically significant not only as the first major EFL project in the world but as marking the point from which started in Japan the endless succession of rise and fall of ELT methodologies—the Direct Method, the Oral Method, the Audio-Lingual Method (especially C.C. Fries's Pattern Practice), Communicative Language Teaching (CLT), Task-Based Instruction, Focus on Form, Extensive Reading, Content-Based Instruction, Japanese Translation Handed Out First, Content and Language Integrated Learning (CLIL), etc.—as well as the confusion of ELT policies which we will see in the next section.

13.3 Never-Ending Quest for Practical and Communicative Skills in English

After suffering great hardship during the period of militarism leading up to the Pacific War (1941–45), in which English was designated as the language of the enemy and any pursuit even tangentially related to it was regarded as unpatriotic, English studies in Japan resumed their practices of research and education centered around universities, diversifying their respective disciplines and at the same time isolating themselves from the much proliferating ELT-related disciplines (see Saito 2007). The diversification and proliferation of English-related disciplines firstly brought about a structural division between the theory-based English-related academia and the practice-based ELT arena and, secondly, a dissociation of identity, especially among scholars of English literature and linguistics, most of whom were at the same time teachers of English and teacher-trainers by profession at universities but tended to prefer to define themselves in terms of specialization rather than profession (see also Nagatomo 2012). The power relationship thus established between specialized high-class English studies and low-class English education continued to dominate the English-related discourse and policy-making well into the middle of the Showa era (1926–89), when many newly established universities and colleges employed high-school teachers as ELT experts. Around the same time, budding theories of Western applied linguistics—one of which was audio-lingualism—were brought into Japan to help ELT emerge as a scientific discipline to be pursued academically.

Toward the end of the Showa era, as communicative foreign language ability drew more attention as one of the key abilities for surviving in the "globalized" world and CLT as reportedly the most efficient methodology for teaching English, the tables were turned, and ELT experts, many of whom in Japan were (and still are) SLA-based applied linguists, molded their discipline in such a way that it might meet the social and educational demands for communication-oriented ELT and at the same time kept out old literature-oriented disciplines, sometimes even as resentfully as Hatori (2002), thereby widening the professional gap between the traditional English studies camp and themselves. Today, as a result of further diversification of English studies as well as of ELT-related studies, there are an enormous number of subdisciplines in either camp, which are pursued by individuals or small in-groups with little connection or overlap with each other. The comment Mark Turner (1991: 6) made nearly 30 years ago on the profession of English is particularly true of what has happened and is still happening in Japan: "What is missing from the profession of English is *English*."

At the beginning of the Heisei era (1989–), the nationwide structural reform of higher education started, and faculties and departments of such "impractical" disciplines as liberal arts and literary studies (including English studies) began to close down. The same utilitarianism and rationalism that characterized this reform has also found its way into ELT in the form of national language policies. Urged on by the social demand for practice- and communication-oriented language education and based on the assumptions that ELT in Japan had focused "wrongly" on grammar-based reading and writing and that the skill of "practical" oral communication is a prerequisite for its people to survive in the twenty-first century and the age of "globalization," the Ministry of Education launched a large-scale reform of English education policies. In 1998 and 1999, the Course Guidelines for junior high schools and high schools were revised (and enforced, respectively, in 2002 and 2003) so that greater emphasis should be placed on oral communication. The Course Guidelines for elementary schools were also revised, and the subject of "Comprehensive Learning" was introduced to enable "English conversation" to be taught in the name of "foreign language education for cross-cultural understanding." In 2002 "the Strategic Design for Producing Competent Japanese Users of English," which strongly reflected the ELT-related proposal made in 2000 by the Japan Business Federation, was put out with specific action plans for introducing listening comprehension tests into examinations provided by the National Center for University Entrance Examinations, promoting the "Super English Language High School Project," increasing English-medium classroom activities, utilizing English-speaking assistant language teachers, establishing teacher-training courses, and incorporating other language activities for improving the English proficiency of the Japanese. In 2009 the Ministry of Education, Culture, Sports, Science and Technology (MEXT; the Ministry of Education reconstituted) revised the Course Guidelines for high schools (to be enforced in 2013), stipulating that English classes should be conducted primarily in English. In 2011, MEXT enforced the new Course Guidelines for elementary school, making compulsory the subject of "foreign language activities" in which the "foreign language" is virtually English.

The latest ELT-related MEXT policy can be seen in "English Education Reform Plan corresponding to Globalization" (December, 2013) with specific guidelines for:

(a) Successive ELT reforms in consideration of the 2020 Tokyo Olympic Games
(b) More English-specific compulsory class management in elementary schools
(c) English-medium instruction at the level of secondary education
(d) The introduction of a consistent assessment scale based on the CEFR (Common European Framework of Reference for Languages) and description of learning targets to all levels of primary and secondary education
(e) The extensive use of English proficiency tests organized by individual organizations (TOEFL, Eiken, etc.)
(f) Proactive trainer training at the levels of primary and secondary education

Except for the prospect of the Olympic Games and the use of the CEFR—or rather its misuse, for the CEFR is a plurilingualism-based guideline for describing and assessing language learners' achievements and not to be used as a learning target for any single language—nothing is quite new about the abovementioned MEXT plan; even ELT in elementary schools and many other types of early English learning have already been tested and practiced individually since the Meiji era, not surprisingly, without any long-term effects. The Olympic Games and the CEFR not being directly related to language learning, it is highly unlikely that the plan, for all its flamboyant statements of innovative prospects, will produce any dramatic effect on ELT in Japan at least before 2020.

13.4 The Failure Hypothesis Reexamined

As I suggested in the first and third sections, it is very often argued that ELT in Japan has long been unsuccessful because of wrong approaches to language learning, wrong methodologies, and wrong teaching materials. This failure hypothesis sometimes presents itself as a set of syllogisms, all of which always start with the primary proposition "ELT in Japan has been unsuccessful." Some of the examples are:

(1) ELT in Japan has been unsuccessful.
(2-a) English has been taught in liberal arts education in Japan.
(2-b) *Yakudoku* (literally "translational reading"; the method which is often confused with the Western grammar-translation method; see Saito 2012) has been the most popular method for teaching English in Japan.
(2-c) ELT in Japan has focused too much on grammar and reading.
(2-d) English classrooms in Japan have been mostly teacher-centered.
(2-e) The most popular material for teaching English in Japan has been literature.
(2-f) Most Japanese people start learning English in junior high school.
Therefore, what is responsible for the unsuccessful ELT in Japan is:
(3-a) The liberal arts approach to English education
(3-b) The *yakudoku* method
(3-c) Grammar- and reading-focused ways of ELT
(3-d) Teacher-centered class management
(3-e) The use of literary texts as ELT materials
(3-f) The lack of earlier ELT programs in public education

These questionable syllogisms are the basic assumptions underlying the promotion, respectively, of:

(a) The practice-oriented approach to English education
(b) English-medium CLT
(c) Speaking- and listening-focused ways of ELT
(d) Student-centered collaborative learning
(e) The use of nonliterary "authentic" materials
(f) Communicative activities in English in elementary schools in the large-scale ELT reforms that have taken place for the last 20 years

Despite these reforms, the English proficiency of Japanese people stays at the same low level or even seems to have gone down during those 20 years. Many university teachers of English testify to the decline of undergraduate students' reading skills (Namekata 2014), and the recent MEXT research into the English proficiency of Japanese high-school students (reported on March 17, 2015) suggests that the proficiency of Grade 3 high-school students (17–18 years old) is almost equal to the MEXT-stipulated target proficiency for junior-high-school graduates. Saida (2010) verified the gradual and constant decline of the English proficiency of high-school students in Ibaraki Prefecture over 14 years from 1995 to 2008. On the other hand, since the late Edo era, there always have been successful Japanese learners of English who acquired their respective target skills mostly through grammar- and reading-based self-study regardless of the school education they went through. These observations and pieces of evidence will enable us to make a modest proposal for questioning again the validity of the failure hypothesis and replacing it with an empirical theory based on a fuller acknowledgment of what has happened in the history of ELT in Japan. Some of the insights gained from the history are:

- That English (e.g., in comparison with Korean) is a difficult language for many Japanese people to master
- That school ELT in Japan as it is cannot fully meet the expectations of its people to equally acquire advanced skills in English
- That Japanese learners of English acquire reading and writing skills more easily and quickly than oral and aural skills
- That highly successful Japanese learners of English tend to have been self-motivated enough to take to intensive grammar- and reading-based self-study
- That, in the Japanese system of ELT, oral- and/or communication-oriented approaches do not work as efficiently as some CLT proponents suggest

These insights will serve as the basic assumptions on which the final section takes further steps to make some suggestions for the improvement of ELT in Japan.

13.5   Back to the Basics

We have seen how the ELT reforms in Japan based on the failure hypothesis—the hypothesis which attributes Japanese people's low proficiency in English to the failure of Japanese school education to take the right approach to ELT and provide students with proper skills in English—have had little or, in some cases, negative effects on the development of their target skills. This legitimately suggests that the hypothesis itself is questionable. In its place, I would propose to have as the basis for constructing proper ELT systems for Japanese people a theory that is capable of accommodating two different approaches, one teaching-centered and the other (self-)learning-centered, to English education. The teaching-centered approach focuses more on what school education can do and should do to provide students with basic skills, and the learning-centered approach more on what students can choose to do extensively in addition to the school education they go through. The assumption here is that school ELT in Japan has not been mistaken, but has been extremely limited in the range of things it can do for students.

One of the important facts that are not fully understood in ELT in Japan is that English is primarily an exercise-based subject, just like music, art, and physical education. As long as it is, it should start from the students' conscious learning of correct forms and subsequent acquisition of basic skills. ELT reformists for the last 30 years have tended to refer to the natural acquisition model and encourage Japanese learners to be exposed to and communicative in as much English discourse as possible, ignoring the fact that natural acquisition is only possible when learners are consistently exposed, from morning till night from early childhood, to *the correct system of native-speaker discourse*. To make matters worse, CLT reformers often blended their firm belief in oral communication with the idea of World Englishes to argue, without any understanding of how those varieties of English have been linguistically systematized, that Japanese people should be encouraged more to use Japanese English (which in fact is nothing more than broken English or classroom pidgin) to communicate in classroom situations. What they have done is, to use a metaphor from jazz improvisation, to encourage jazz-piano learners to try to play, before they have fully learned the system of jazz chords and available scales, some jazzy tunes on the keyboard. Their students will never acquire their target skills this way.

The importance of accuracy in language education is appropriately emphasized by Palmer (1964: 65–66), who argues:

> The method of trial and error, to which we have already alluded, is in direct opposition to the principles of accuracy; it is the method of sink-or-swim, of die-or-survive, of flounder-and-grope-until-you-hit-on-the-right-way. To replace this method by something less cruel is the function of such things as guides, teachers, and pedagogic devices. For let us remark that the environment of the young child who acquires language spontaneously (…) is such that error has little or no chance of surviving; the persons with whom he is in contact are providing him continually with accurate models of whatever the dialect may happen to be; he is given no chance of imitating wrong models, and he is not intelligent enough to create them himself in any appreciable degree. (…) One of the most important advances in the art of language-teaching will have been made when the principle of accuracy is understood, accepted, and adopted by all who are engaged in this work either as teachers or as trainers of teachers.

Although his Oral Method did not work as a whole in Japan, presumably because he focused too much on speaking and underestimated the roles of written grammar and reading texts in Japanese people's foreign language study, Palmer's principles of accuracy need to be revaluated and brought back into classroom practice together with those prescriptive grammar- and reading-based activities which Japanese students have proved to be good at. Considering the overall aim of school education, classroom ELT should focus primarily on providing students with rudimentary skills in English—pronunciation, lexical selection, reading, listening comprehension, writing, and speaking—which, though not necessarily applicable to real-world communication, constitute the very basis of their English proficiency on which they can build up the skills they need by means of self-study and optional learning.

This is where the learning-centered approach comes in; focusing on self-motivated individual learning, it complements the teaching-centered approach in my back-to-the-basics theory. In this approach, in order to make individual learning possible, we aim to establish as many public institutes and educational programs as possible to provide self-motivated advanced learners of English with various learning opportunities. Those institutes (language centers, conversation schools, research libraries, etc.) may be operated by local governments and programs (skill-oriented language courses, intensive lecture sessions, English seminars, reading groups, symposiums, etc.) by universities or other educational institutes, but the point is that the self-motivated demands for advanced learning opportunities are always met. The funds needed for establishing those institutes and programs will be much less than the national budgets which MEXT is (mis)spending on "Super-Global" projects and other short-sighted English language programs based on their failure hypothesis.

References

Hatori, H. (2002). *Ikinokoru-ka, eigo-kyoshi* [Will teachers of English survive?]. *The English Teachers' Magazine*, May special issue, Taishukan-shoten, p. 51.

Howatt, A. P. R., & Widdowson, H. G. (2004). *A history of English language teaching* (2nd ed.). Oxford: Oxford University Press.

Kawasumi, T. (ed.). (1998). *Shiryou Nihon eigakushi: 1-ge bunmeikaika to eigaku* [A documented history of English studies in Japan: Modernization of civilization and English studies]. Tokyo: Taishukan-shoten.

Natsume, S. (1911). *Gogaku youseihou* [Methods for developing foreign language proficiency]. *Gakusei* [Students' Magazine], the January issue.

Nagatomo, D. H. (2012). *Exploring Japanese university teachers' professional identity*. Bristol: Multilingual Matters.

Namekata, A. (2014). *Eikaiwa fuyouron* [No need for English conversation]. Tokyo: Bungei-shunju.

Palmer, H. E. (1964). *The principles of language-study*. London: Oxford University Press Originally published by George G. Harrap & Co. Ltd. In 1922.

Saida, C. (2010). *Koumoku-outou riron wo mochiita jigoteki-toukahou ni yoru eigo-gakuryoku no keinen-henka ni kansuru kenkyu* [A study on the secular change of English proficiency by means of test equating methods based on the item response theory]. Unpublished PhD thesis. Nagoya University.

Saito, Y. (2000) *Eigo tatsujin retsuden* [Stories of the Japanese Masters of English]. Tokyo: Chuou-koron Shinsha.

Saito, Y. (2007). English studies in Japan at the crossroads. In M. Araki et al. (Eds.), *English studies in Asia* (pp. 191–198). Kuala Lumpur: Silverfish Books.

Saito, Y. (2012). Translation in English language teaching in Japan. *Komaba Journal of English Education, 3*, 27–36.

Saito, Y. (2015). Ichikawa Sanki (1886-1970): Expert in English philology and literature. In H. Cortazzi (Ed.), *Britain & Japan: Biographical portraits* (Vol. IX, pp. 357–367). Folkestone: Renaissance Books.

Turner, M. (1991). *Reading minds: The study of English in the age of cognitive science*. Princeton: Princeton University Press.

Chapter 14
Safety Education from the Perspective of Education for Sustainable Development (ESD)

Yuto Kitamura

14.1 Introduction

Today, the environment surrounding children is changing dramatically. A review of children's situations from the perspectives of "safety" and "security" will reveal various kinds of risks, including traffic, crime, and disaster. Do children have sufficient capabilities to respond to such risks? If not, how can they acquire these capabilities? With these interests and based on a holistic understanding of safety, this chapter studies the shape of safety education, that is, education required for the development of a safe and secure society (i.e., a resilient and sustainable society), particularly in the context of Japan. In addition to that objective, this chapter aims to verify what kind of safety education should be provided through the new educational concept of "Education for Sustainable Development" (ESD).

The Great East Japan Earthquake of 2011 has heightened public interest in safety education in Japan. It is of course important to promote comprehensive safety education covering not only disaster prevention but also crime prevention and traffic safety. However, since safety education is a relatively new field, practices and academic verifications have been insufficient. Under these circumstances, employing the viewpoint of ESD, an international discussion of education, enables development of a comprehensive concept of safety education. Thus, this chapter examines the form of ESD-based safety education theoretically while presenting the results of research on how parents and teachers actually perceive such safety education.[1]

---

[1] This chapter is a modified version of Kitamura (2014).

Y. Kitamura (✉)
Graduate School of Education, The University of Tokyo, Tokyo, Japan
e-mail: yuto@p.u-tokyo.ac.jp

© Springer Nature Singapore Pte Ltd. 2019   221
Y. Kitamura et al. (eds.), *Education in Japan*, Education in the Asia-Pacific Region: Issues, Concerns and Prospects 47,
https://doi.org/10.1007/978-981-13-2632-5_14

14.2   What Is Safety Education?

Safety education is defined as education to facilitate the acquisition of capabilities to predict and avoid danger and qualities and capabilities to contribute to the safety of others or society.[2] Safety education deals with the areas of (1) safety in daily life (which means safety against crime that could happen in everyday life), (2) traffic safety, and (3) disaster safety. Although conventional safety education has handled each of these areas individually, the Central Council for Education under the Ministry of Education, Culture, Sports, Science and Technology (MEXT) pointed out the need to provide education across these areas for the purpose of considering the safety and security of children in their daily life in its 2008 report on the improvement of curriculum guidelines for kindergartens, elementary schools, junior high schools, high schools, and special schools.

The report emphasizes the need to enhance holistic safety education covering the safety of children's surroundings, traffic safety, and disaster safety, with the goal of enabling children to make the right judgment about safety information and transfer the judgment to acting safely. In order to achieve that goal, or to help children acquire the capabilities to predict and avoid danger to themselves and others, schools should work on safety education through overall education activities in light of the stage of development. By citing that reason, the report indicates the need to make children understand that, in order to ensure safety, they must pay attention to their own mental and physical condition as well as the way they behave.

The report also emphasizes the importance of deepening the connection between schools, homes, and local communities and improving the living environment throughout the entire country in providing such safety education. This reflects the idea that the connection between enhanced safety education and an improved living environment in the local community leads to the development of a sustainable society.

Enhancing safety education from that perspective, however, requires the development of interdisciplinary programs because the earlier-mentioned areas of safety range widely from daily life to traffic and disasters. It is also essential to think about safety education in a way that takes into consideration children's surroundings. School training on appropriate action may not enable children to protect themselves in a dangerous situation if it is provided without thinking about safety in light of their actual living environment. Therefore, in planning safety education, cooperation with the local community and the active involvement of parents and local residents must be encouraged. Furthermore, clearly positioning safety issues in the local community's "town development" efforts is also required.

---

[2]For the definition of safety education, this chapter referred to MEXT (2012), Plan on the Promotion of School Safety (http://www.mext.go.jp/a_menu/kenko/anzen/__icsFiles/afieldfile/2012/05/01/1320286_2.pdf [Web. 14 November 2013.]), and Tokyo Metropolitan Board of Education (2010), Safety Education Program (http://www.kyoiku.metro.tokyo.jp/press/22anzenkyoikupro.pdf [Web. 14 November 2013.]). These were also referred to in organizing concepts of safety education in this section.

Another issue to be noted is the need to plan safety education in accordance with the children's stage of development or process of growth. The content of safety education must vary depending on changes in the children's living environment and their mental and physical development and personal growth. To take the example of traffic safety education for elementary school children, Japanese children, in general, start to use bicycles more frequently when they become fourth graders, although conditions vary depending on the situation of the school or local community. This requires a shift in the focus of traffic safety education from pedestrian activity to bicycle activity for children up to the third grade. With such a change in children's behavior, necessary initiatives, such as protecting children from sexual violence in safety in daily life education, must also be discussed in ways that are appropriate for their mental and physical development.

Compared with elementary school students, junior high school students have a wider sphere of action as their school district is wider and their circle of friends becomes broader. This fact must be taken into account in safety education. It is also important to develop cooperative relationship beyond the level of schools, for example, cooperation between elementary schools and junior high schools, as well as cooperation between multiple schools in a school district (or multiple schools beyond a school district in some cases) when necessary.

Despite the importance of considering safety education from a multifaceted and holistic perspective, sufficient study results on school safety and safety education have not been accumulated, as pointed out in the previously mentioned report by the Central Council for Education (2008).[3] It is hard to say that multifaceted and holistic safety education has been developed based on objective evidence.

Meanwhile, as the importance of the previously mentioned "development of a sustainable society" was emphasized in the curriculum guidelines revised in 2008 and 2009, awareness that the development of a safe and secure society is essential to the development of a sustainable society gradually spreads. One of the triggers for the argument was the stabbing spree at Ikeda Elementary School affiliated with Osaka Kyoiku University.[4] The occurrence of other cases, accidents, and natural disasters in which children became victims—particularly, the Great East Japan Earthquake on March 11, 2011, and the accident at the Fukushima Daiichi Nuclear Power Station that had a major social impact and a series of tragic accidents in school zones in 2011 and 2012—highlighted the importance of children having a minimum level of knowledge and behavior.

With the increasing social interest in children's safety, MEXT formulated the Plan on the Promotion of School Safety in April 2012, which requires all schools to

---

[3] MEXT Central Council for Education report (2008). Regarding the revision of courses of study for kindergarten, elementary school, lower secondary school, upper secondary school, and schools for special needs education (http://www.mext.go.jp/component/a_menu/education/detail/__icsFiles/afieldfile/2010/11/29/20080117.pdf [Web. 14 November 2013]).

[4] A knife-wielding man stormed into an elementary school (which is affiliated with the university) on June 8, 2001, and fatally stabbed 8 children and wounded 15 others (13 children and 2 teachers) (*The Japan Times*, June 9, 2001). This tragic affair shocked Japanese society and raised public awareness and consciousness to strengthen school security.

develop a risk management manual. The MEXT plan also calls for the development of a plan to enhance safety education in teacher-training courses. It is mandated that the results of school-level plans must be reviewed periodically.

In light of cases in which children decided by themselves that the evacuation site was dangerous and took refuge in a safer place during the Great East Japan Earthquake, the MEXT plan points out that education that helps children develop an attitude to take proactive action must be covered in formulating a plan for promoting safety education. It suggests that, as health and physical education classes are not sufficient to nurture that attitude, time for other subjects, homeroom, and special activities may be used.[5]

Additionally, in line with the concept of safety promotion,[6] the MEXT plan stresses the significance of developing a mechanism to implement measures based on scientific evidence and conducting an assessment and argues that it is indispensable to properly collect information about cases, accidents, and disasters that happened at schools while giving due consideration to the burden on teachers, to analyze the information, and to take positive initiatives based on the analysis to reduce future cases, accidents, and disasters.

Although the importance of promoting holistic safety education at the school level is widely recognized, schools, in fact, have not taken sufficient initiatives. This reality prompted MEXT to formulate the Plan on the Promotion of School Safety, but many schools that have already spent many class hours on school events besides ordinary classes cannot afford to include safety education in their curricula. Taking into account this situation, MEXT calls for the flexible provision of safety education, but the outlook is unclear as to how much initiatives will be actually taken. It is necessary to continue to watch school initiatives and enhance administrative support for schools.

Preceding studies on safety education in the area of traffic safety include the following: Suzuki et al. (2000) studied practices of safety education through safety mapping; Ogawa et al. (2006) studied the development of a measure of safety education's effects; and Sekine et al. (2007) studied traffic safety education using a simulator. Nagayama et al. (1998) compared traffic safety education between Japan and Germany, the UK, Sweden, Finland, the USA, and Australia, which provides interesting implications. Widely known crime-prevention studies and practice include a study by Komiya et al. (2008) and Nobuo Komiya's practice of providing guidance in creating local safety maps. As an overview of previous studies on

---

[5] The importance of safety education that encourages children to take proactive actions is exemplified in the so-called miracle in Kamaishi, a case in which many children survived the Great East Japan Earthquake and subsequent tsunami. In Kamaishi City, 99.8% of elementary and junior high school students evacuated safely because of the disaster-prevention education that encourages children to think for themselves. For proactive safety education, refer to Shaw and Takeuchi (2012), Teramoto (2012), and Yamori (2012).

[6] Safety promotion means to prevent accidents and crimes with cross-occupation or cross-sector cooperation or with intervention that can be scientifically evaluated. Schools that are conducting activities linked to local-level safety promotion initiatives promoted by a collaborating center of the World Health Organization (WHO) are certified as international safety schools (ISS).

disaster-prevention education, Takahashi and Nunokawa (2010) pointed out the fact that studies on earthquake-related disaster-prevention education have been increasing following the Great Hanshin-Awaji Earthquake in 1995 and the Mid-Niigata Prefecture Earthquake in 2004. Among a wide variety of studies on safety education for other types of disasters, Yamori (2010) raised an interesting issue in the traditional view of disaster prevention; he suspected that the efforts made in disaster-prevention education to bridge the gap in awareness and information between citizens and experts might have actually widened the gap. Including these, there are numerous preceding studies on safety education, but many of them deal with daily life, traffic, and disasters, separately. Few studies have discussed safety education from a holistic perspective, as this chapter intends.

14.3 ESD Perspective for Safety Education

Education for Sustainable Development (ESD)[7] means "education to nurture citizens that have a global perspective who can recognize the finite nature of resources on the earth at an individual level and create new social orders based on their own thinking."[8] As a total of 15 strategic themes from 3 perspectives are set for ESD, organically connecting themes in wide-ranging areas is crucial in studying the shape of safety education (Sato 2009). In other words, challenges for a sustainable society (e.g., the environment, poverty, human rights, peace, development) are so complex that it is crucial to handle challenges in different areas, such as the environment, society, and economy, in a holistic manner (Hopkins and McKeown 2002).

The basis of this principle of ESD is the idea of achieving "development that meets the needs of the present without compromising the ability of future generations to meet their own needs" (World Commission on Environment and Development 1987). What is essential to that idea is the notion of taking the present affluence and passing down a higher quality of life to the next generation and beyond.

Sustainable development refers to activities to create a fair and affluent future by advocating human rights, building peace, promoting cross-cultural understanding, promoting health, maintaining natural resources, preventing disasters, reducing poverty, and promoting corporate responsibility, among others, while guaranteeing democratic social systems in which everyone can participate and social systems that consider environmental and social impacts and respect the uniqueness of individual

---

[7] The description of ESD in this chapter is based on the content on the MEXT website explaining "What is Education for Sustainable Development (ESD)?" (www.mext.go.jp/a_menu/kokusai/jizoku/kyouiku.htm [Web. 30 July 2013]).

[8] The concept of ESD was first advocated at the World Summit on Sustainable Development held in September 2002 in Johannesburg, the Republic of South Africa. In response to the discussions at the summit, the United Nations General Assembly adopted United Nations Decade of Education for Sustainable Development (UNDESD) [2005–2014] in December 2002.

cultures. These activities, which form the foundation of developing a safe and secure society, cannot be ignored in discussing safety education.[9]

Based on these ideas ESD aims to help children develop "the ability to make proactive responses" by connecting social issues to daily life to create new values and take new actions.[10] Learners must develop their abilities to review values and participate in the process of building a better society, rather than simply acquiring knowledge. They must be provided with participatory learning through local activities and education in which they face various issues about the sustainable society and solve problems. ESD should also be promoted not only by schools but also by individuals, organizations, and institutions from diverse positions in society, including businesses, government, NPOs/NGOs, and social and educational institutions.

This chapter advocates the importance of taking into account the ESD concept in understanding safety education from the holistic perspective because of the necessity of incorporating holistic and comprehensive approaches like ESD into safety education and developing problem-finding and problem-solving types of participatory programs.

In doing so, it is indispensable to design safe "town development" and provide education to deepen the understanding of it, as well as to use knowledge in such areas as traffic engineering, urban engineering, environmental studies, and economics. Providing education to improve risk communication and mental control abilities is also important to make a flexible response in the event of danger or an unexpected situation. These abilities cannot be nurtured without the use of knowledge of psychology, medicine, and business administration (risk management). Furthermore, in contemplating a safe and secure society, it is crucial to cover education to nurture a sense of citizenship or publicness and awareness of being a member of the local community, by referring to knowledge gained from philosophy, political science, and sociology. Studies related to safety education argued here include classic studies on town development by Lynch (1960) and Appleyard (1981), as well as recent study results by Appleyard (2013). Moreover, safety education based on the ESD concept should make best use of local knowledge, which exists in the local community (see the example in Yamori (2012)).

It must be noted that ESD was originally expected to function as an agent in town development. Accordingly, in the context of safety education, it is necessary to encourage children to think about what makes a safe and secure town and diverse stakeholders in the local community to think about how to develop a safe and secure environment for children. Therefore, safety education must be provided with the use of knowledge from different disciplines as mentioned earlier and with the participation of local people. In doing so, schools should be positioned as one of the centers of town development.

---

[9] For the concept of ESD, see the UNESCO website (http://www.unescobkk.org/education/esd/ [Web. 4 December 2013]).

[10] See the website of the NPO, the Japan Council on the UN Decade of Education for Sustainable Development (ESD-J) (http://www.esd-j.org/ [Web. 9 October 2013]).

When considering the ESD perspective, Yamori (2006) provides a good reference. In terms of disaster-prevention education, Yamori stresses the importance of positioning safety education in the process of reorganizing "community of practice" as a platform for social practice, rather than transferring knowledge and skills from educators to learners. Lave and Wenger (1991) and Wenger (1999) explained the concept of community of practice theoretically, expecting that people contribute to the maintenance of a community of practice as they play various roles and take actions in it. As they do so, the skills and knowledge of learners change, the relationship between them and their external environment changes, and their self-understanding (a kind of internal environment) changes. That has something in common to the earlier-mentioned ESD perspective that focuses on the relationship between the brain, body, mind, and town.

Safety education based on the ESD concept does not overlap with conventional safety education that has been introduced in schools. Rather, it will be developed as an educational program that is mutually complementary with conventional safety education. (Conventional safety education in this context includes safety education provided independently by schools, as well as traffic safety classes and disaster-prevention drills provided through cooperation between municipalities; public agencies, such as police and fire departments, traffic safety associations, or other organizations; and private companies, such as automobile manufacturers and security companies.)

The adoption of the ESD approach to safety education is expected to improve educational methods for the purpose of prompting children to take proactive actions, bringing about educational methods that focus on participatory learning through problem-solving education and local activities or leading to the development of educational programs that address daily life, traffic, and disaster issues in an interdisciplinary manner.

The importance of organizing concepts, as this chapter attempts to do, in developing such interdisciplinary safety education programs can be seen in the arguments on the development of safety education programs around the world. One example, which focuses on the area of traffic, is a report on a study conducted on traffic safety education in 25 EU countries in 2005 (Rose 25 2005). The report presents cases and issues in each country in an organized manner and specifically provides a definition of traffic safety education, which consists of goals, methods, knowledge, skills, and attitude. A report on risk management at schools published by the Royal Society for the Prevention of Accidents (RoSPA) provides a conceptual diagram as to how children learn safety-related risks (RoSPA 2012). Based on the comprehensive concept of risk, the report suggests various possible learning opportunities, including opportunities provided through cooperation with related organizations.

14.4 Parents' and Teachers' Awareness of Safety

This chapter has organized the conceptual framework of safety education from the perspective of ESD. How is safety education that covers a wide range of areas, including traffic safety, safety in daily life (crime prevention), and disaster safety (disaster prevention), actually provided at schools and homes (or is it provided at all)? To clarify answers to these questions, surveys were conducted with parents and teachers on the awareness of safety and safety education.

14.4.1 Survey Outline

The surveys were conducted with parents of elementary and junior high school students and educators (teachers) in December 2012. After a questionnaire was prepared, the questionnaire was distributed, and completed questionnaires were collected via the Internet. Parent respondents consisted of 250 parents of first to third graders, 250 parents of fourth to sixth graders, and 500 parents of junior high school students. Among them, 553 lived in urban areas while 447 lived in suburban areas. As for teachers, elementary school teachers totaled 474, junior high school teachers 379, and special school teachers 147; 407 lived in urban areas while 593 lived in suburban areas. (Urban areas refer to government-ordinance-designated cities, Tokyo and the top 100 central cities in terms of population. Suburban areas refer to all samples that do not fall under urban areas.)[11]

14.4.2 Survey Results

14.4.2.1 Parents' Awareness

Among the survey results, the first to introduce is parents' awareness.

The survey asked parents if they felt secure about their children's surroundings. Parents had high feelings of security regarding safety in daily life, including home life and school life. On the other hand, their feeling of security about safety from disaster, which includes fire and earthquake, was very low, at the 10% level, for most of the items. Notably, about 50% felt insecure about accidents at nuclear power plants. Parents' feelings of security about traffic safety were lower than that about safety in daily life, particularly in the following items: when riding bicycles, motorcycles, and cars and traffic accident prevention. Looking at parents' feelings of security by children's school age, parents of elementary school children felt less secure than parents of junior high school students. Parents of first to third graders

---

[11] Implementation and summarization of the survey were outsourced to a research company, Cross Marketing Inc. Respondents were the company's registered monitors.

felt least secure about local and social life, walking on and crossing roads, and when using transportation.

The survey next questioned parents about the recognized level of children's interest in safety. As a result, children's interest in safety reached 50% in such items as traveling to and from school, school life, and when riding bicycles. It implies that children are interested in items that are more familiar to their lives. Their interest in disaster safety was also high in all items, including 49% for earthquake disaster. Meanwhile, children's interest in local and social life, checking and maintaining bicycles, and motorcycles and cars, was at the 30% level, which was lower than for other items. It may be because these items are things they cannot do easily or things they don't use and are therefore not familiar to them. When parents were asked if they had known the level of their children's interest in safety, only around 40% answered yes; nearly 60% did not know about it until they talked with their children for the survey. By children's school age, parents of first to third graders had a slightly higher recognition than parents of older children, while parents of fourth to sixth graders had the lowest recognition at the 30% level. One possible reason for this is that parents pay more attention to their children's interest while they are in the lower grades and children become less likely to communicate closely with their parents as they get older.

After explaining that there were three areas (safety in daily life, traffic safety, and disaster safety) of safety education, the survey asked parents to what degree they knew about safety education. Slightly over 10% answered they knew all of the three areas. Over 50% answered they did not know fully about safety education. In terms of traffic safety, which was comparatively highly recognized among the three areas, less than 40% recognized the area in relation to safety education. These results reveal that safety education is not so familiar to parents.

Parents' recognition of safety education was comparatively higher on the following items: traveling to and from school, school life, walking on and crossing roads, when riding bicycles, and response to earthquakes. As these items are related to safety guidance, general traffic safety classes and disaster-prevention drills seem to have penetrated to some degree.

The survey also requested parents to reconsider safety education and describe the type of safety education that they would demand from schools. In response, parents answered that they wanted many items of disaster safety to be covered as part of school subjects. In particular, nearly 60% wanted schools to be more proactive in providing earthquake-related safety education. This may be because the Great East Japan Earthquake of 2011 was still fresh in their minds and many parents were recognizing earthquake as an immediate danger. Regarding safety education items to be covered as part of after-hours classes, 60–70% of parents demanded the safety education for motorcycles and cars, checking and maintaining bicycles, using transportation, and local and social life. When asked about the issue of covering safety education in school curricula, over 40% thought it was difficult, citing such reasons as lack of children's awareness and concern over the possibility of ending up as a temporary measure. In addition, 40% pointed out lack of teachers' knowledge. The older the children's school age, the more parents pointed it out.

When asked how much safety education was provided at home, over 50% answered they were providing children with some kind of guidance on safety in daily life, which is close to family life. On the other hand, less than 40% of households were giving guidance on similarly familiar issues of traffic safety, including checking and maintaining bicycles and response to motorcycles and cars, and of disaster safety, including fire and weather disasters. As reasons for not providing sufficient safety education at home, parents cited lack of knowledge by both children and parents and concern over the possibility of ending up as a temporary measure. ("Temporary" refers to the tendency for people to become passionate about safety education immediately after a disaster of significant social impact, such as the Great East Japan Earthquake, but to pay less attention to it over time.)

After these questions, the survey asked what parents thought were keys to safety education for children. Parents seemed to value awareness, including children's awareness and parents' awareness. They also cited knowledge of school teachers and parents, as well as knowledge of children who receive education, as key factors. Parents also recognized the importance of methodology, including educational content that was appropriate for their children's characteristics, participatory education method, and educational content that matched the social situation. As these are emphasized in ESD, the significance of incorporating the ESD perspective in safety education was confirmed.

Multiple regression analysis of the parent survey data regarding the provision of safety education in schools revealed the high contribution of traffic safety and disaster safety to safety education. The contribution of checking and maintaining bicycles to traffic safety, as well as the contribution of response to nuclear disasters to disaster safety, was particularly high (see Fig. 14.1). The results show that, among the three areas, traffic safety plays a key role in promoting safety education and that providing education on elements that directly relate to accidents, such as bicycle maintenance and motorcycles and cars, is crucial.

14.4.2.2 Teachers' Awareness

The teacher survey brought the following results.

The survey first asked teachers about the level of security they feel about their students' surroundings. Teachers' feelings of security were the highest about school life; only this item was cited by over 60% of teachers. The result was more or less expected because school life is within their sight. What supports that is the fact that only 23% of teachers felt secure about Internet use. Many educators seemed to worry about whether children were living a safe life when they were out of their teachers' sight.

While 30% to 40% felt secure about disaster safety, teachers did not feel secure enough about traffic safety as just over 10% answered they felt secure in each of the traffic safety items, including bicycles and motorcycles and cars. The same tendency is observed among parents. Parents and teachers share concern over their children's traffic safety as an immediate issue.

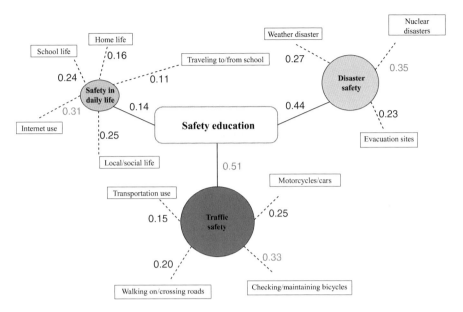

Fig. 14.1 Relationship between safety education and the three areas (parents' awareness)

As with the parent survey, the teacher survey next described the definition and three areas of safety education (safety in daily life, traffic safety, and disaster safety) and asked questions to find out the level of teachers' awareness. It was found that 65% recognized all of the three areas as the content of safety education. Nearly 90% recognized one of the three areas. These figures are significantly higher when compared with the results of the parent survey, implying a significant penetration of an understanding of safety education among school teachers.

Among the three areas, recognition of traffic safety was the highest at over 80%, while over 70% recognized safety in daily life and disaster safety. Recognition was particularly high among elementary school teachers; about 70% recognized all three. However, when comparing teachers by school type, recognition of each of the three areas was the lowest among special school teachers. Efforts should be made to raise recognition among teachers of that school type.

The survey also investigated the frequency of safety being talked about in schools. Nearly 80% of teachers answered they had talked about safety, particularly traffic safety, with students or colleagues. A comparison by school type revealed that elementary school teachers had been more proactive in talking about the topic with students or colleagues, while special school teachers had talked less about it. The percentage of teachers who pointed out such problems as lack of teachers' knowledge, lack of teachers' skills, and lack of teachers' awareness was higher among special school teachers than teachers at other types of schools.

That may be because situations in which teachers become conscious of safety and talk about the topic are less likely to arise at special schools due to conditions that may not be found in other types of schools. On the other hand, as living a safe life may be most difficult for students who need special support, there seems to be more need to discuss the topic more aggressively. Generalization may not be appropriate as situations vary between schools, but this issue may need further verification.

In response to a question asking teachers what they thought of including safety education into the school curricula, teachers shared a wide recognition that it is important to develop consistent curricula, which prevent safety education from ending up as a temporary measure, or curricula that matched the prevailing social situation. At the same time, however, they cited lack of teachers' knowledge and skills as a concern. Some teachers called into question to what extent children's awareness could be raised.

When asked how much safety education was provided in schools, over 80% of teachers answered they were providing safety education on the following items: traveling to and from school and school life in safety in daily life, walking on and crossing roads and traffic accident prevention in traffic safety, and response to fire and response to earthquakes in disaster safety. Meanwhile, only 30–40% answered that they had provided safety education on items that are difficult to teach only with their own knowledge and skills, such as checking and maintaining bicycles, motorcycles, and cars and nuclear disasters.

Junior high school teachers provided safety education on Internet use and special school teachers on the use of transportation, at a higher rate than teachers at other types of schools. These results suggest that teachers are picking up safety education themes that are more essential for their students. In other words, teachers are responding to junior high school students who use the Internet more actively and to special school students who must have more difficulties in using transportation when traveling.

Regarding a question asking teachers about content that they thought schools should focus on in providing safety education, the number of teachers who pointed to safety education on the use of the Internet was the highest by far at 63%. As for items to be covered as part of after-hours classes, over 70% pointed to motorcycles and cars and checking and maintaining bicycles. As mentioned earlier, these are content that many teachers cannot teach under the current situation but consider as necessary.

When asked about what teachers thought were key items in safety education for students, many teachers thought heightened awareness was important for teachers, as well as for parents and students. Teachers were more likely to consider that their knowledge and skills were important. Apparently, they placed a stronger emphasis on these than on the knowledge and skills of parents and students. Teachers seemed to recognize that they must acquire knowledge and skills to provide safety education. This seems to reflect teachers' sincere attitude toward safety education.

As with the data on parents' awareness, multiple regression analysis of teachers' awareness was conducted to show the relationship between safety education and the three areas. It revealed the high contribution of traffic safety and disaster safety to safety education. The contribution of checking and maintaining bicycles in traffic safety, as well as response to nuclear disasters in disaster safety, was particularly high (see Fig. 14.2).

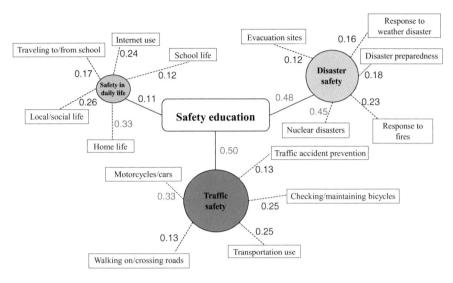

Fig. 14.2 Relationship between safety education and the three areas (teachers' awareness)

These results imply the necessity of promoting further safety education by providing education with a focus on the two items in the area of traffic safety that are directly related to accidents—motorcycles and cars—as shown by the results of the parent data analysis and nuclear disasters in disaster safety, public awareness of which has been growing after the Great East Japan Earthquake.

14.4.3 Comparison of Awareness Between Parents and Teachers

A comparison between parents' awareness and teachers' awareness based on the survey results revealed the following. It must be noted that any difference in awareness attributable to residential area, namely, urban area vs. suburban area, was not clarified either among parents or teachers.

14.4.3.1 Feelings of Security About the Surroundings

In a comparison of the feelings of security about children's (students') surroundings, parents felt more secure about safety in daily life than teachers did. This tendency is particularly evident in items such as home life and Internet use. As for traffic safety, parents' feelings of security were slightly higher than teachers' for

Table 14.1 Feelings of security about surroundings

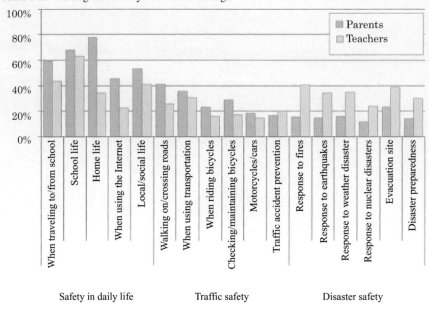

items such as walking on and crossing roads and checking and maintaining bicycles. Regarding overall traffic safety items, however, the feelings of security of both parents and teachers were low. On disaster safety, teachers felt more secure than parents in all items. The discrepancy between the two was greater for fires and earthquakes (Table 14.1).

14.4.3.2 Recognition of Safety Education

With regard to the recognition of safety education and its three constituent areas (safety in daily life, traffic safety, and disaster safety), teachers' recognition is overwhelmingly higher than parents. Notably, the percentage that recognizes all of the three areas was less than 20% for parents but exceeded 60% for teachers (Table 14.2).

14.4.3.3 Key to Safety Education for Children

Parents considered children's awareness and parents' knowledge as the keys, while teachers considered that their awareness, knowledge, and skills were crucial. What both parents and teachers considered as important were educational content that was appropriate for children's characteristics and a participatory education method. These results provide significant implications for incorporating the ESD perspective into safety education, on which this research project is working (Table 14.3).

Table 14.2   Recognition of safety education

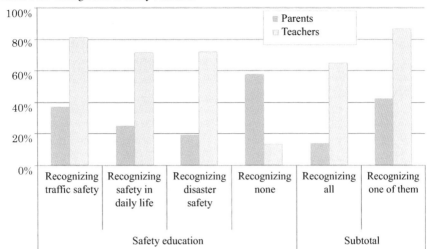

Table 14.3   Keys to safety education for children

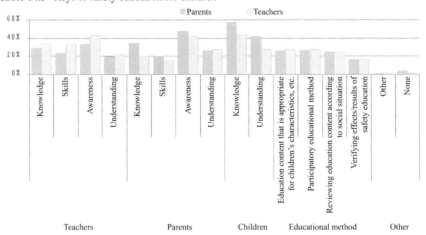

14.5   Conclusion

This chapter attempted to verify a new shape for safety education by holistically understanding safety from the areas of traffic, disaster, and daily life based on the ESD perspective. As this is a new approach, there are not many preceding studies in terms of organizing concepts or developing practical programs. Discussions in this chapter may not be satisfying but identified the following.

Firstly, this chapter identified the need to provide multiple software support for existing safety education. Many safety education programs have not sufficiently incorporated the perspective of understanding safety in a comprehensive manner but still focus on a particular area of traffic, disasters, or daily life. In light of this issue, this chapter recognized the importance of incorporating the perspective of problem-solving and participation-oriented ESD into a holistic understanding of safety education.

Secondly, the survey of the awareness of parents and teachers revealed their high interest in traffic safety among the safety education areas. It seems possible to start safety education from "traffic" and then broaden the scope to daily life and disasters. The survey also clarified that the parties involved considered raising children's awareness as the most important aspect in safety education.

As a future challenge, it is necessary to develop ESD-based curricula for holistic safety education through cooperation between schools and to verify their effects. This chapter examined the shape of safety education based on the ESD perspective only in the context of Japan. Further verification must be conducted with regard to possible safety education in different societies. Across the world, initiatives to understand safety education from the ESD perspective have just begun and are still groping for direction. It is imperative to continue our research efforts to present a new shape for safety education.

References

Appleyard, D. (1981). *Livable streets*. Berkeley: University of California Press.

Appleyard, B. (2013). Livable streets for schoolchildren. In D. Mohn (Ed.), *Safety, sustainability and future urban transport*. New Delhi: Eicher Goodearth Pvt. Ltd..

Hopkins, C., & McKeown, R. (2002). Education for sustainable development: An international perspective. In D. Tilbury, R. B. Stevenson, J. Fein, & D. Schreuder (Eds.), *Environmental education for sustainability: Responding to the global challenge*. Gland/Cambridge: IUCN Commission on Education and Communication.

Kitamura, Y. (2014). The possibility of holistic safety education in Japan: From the perspective of education for sustainable development (ESD). *IATSS Research, 38*(1), 40–47.

Komiya, N., Shiomi, T., Sato, H., Obinata, M., & Yamagata, F. (Eds.). (2008). *Anzen anshin no kankyo zukuri* [Creating safe and secured environments: Protecting by community, protecting by oneself]. Tokyo: Gyousei.

Lave, J., & Wenger, E. (1991). *Situated learning: Legitimate peripheral participation*. Cambridge, MA/New York: Cambridge University Press.

Lynch, K. (1960). *The image of the city*. Cambridge, MA: MIT Press.

MEXT (2012). Gakko kaizen no suishin ni kansuru keikaku [Plan on the Promotion of School Safety]. http://www.mext.go.jp/a_menu/kenko/anzen/__icsFiles/afieldfile/2012/05/01/1320286_2.pdf. [Web. 14 November 2013].

MEXT Central Council for Education report (2008). Yochien, shogakko, chugakko, kotogakko oyobi tokubetsushien gakko no gakushu shido youryo tou no kaizen ni tsuite [Regarding the revision of courses of study for kindergarten, elementary school, lower secondary school, upper secondary school, and schools for special needs education] http://www.mext.go.jp/component/a_menu/education/detail/__icsFiles/afieldfile/2010/11/29/20080117.pdf. [Web. 14 November 2013].

Nagayama, Y., Suzuki, H., Nagae, K., & Renge, K. (1998). *Shogaikoku ni okerukoutsu anzen kyoiku no jittai ni kansuru kenkyu* [Report on the study of traffic safety education in different countries]. Tokyo: The International Association of Traffic and Safety Sciences.

Ogawa, K., Ota, H., Renge, K., & Mukai, M. (2006). *Anzen kyoiku no koka wo sokutei surutameno monosashi zukuri* [Report on the development of the "measurement" for effectiveness of traffic safety education]. Tokyo: The International Association of Traffic and Safety Sciences.

Rose 25 (2005). *Inventory and compiling of a European good practice guide on road safety education targeted at young people* (Final Report). Rose 25 (Project funded by the European Commission).

RoSPA. (2012). *Managing safety in schools and colleges*. Birmingham: The Royal Society for the Prevention of Accidents.

Sato, M. (2009). *Jizoku kanouna kaihatsu no tameno kyoiku no kokusaiteki doukou* [Study on the international trends of education for sustainable development]. A report commissioned by City of Yokohama.

Sekine, T., Okano, M., Fukuda, A., Furukawa, O., & Miyamaru, Y. (2007). *Simulator wo katsuyo shita koutsu anzen kyoiku no kentou* [Report on the application of the simulator for traffic safety education]. Tokyo: The International Association of Traffic and Safety Sciences.

Shaw, R., & Takeuchi, Y. (2012). *East Japan earthquake and tsunami: Lessons for the education sector*. Bangkok: UNESCO Bangkok.

Suzuki, H., Oka, N., Takuma, S., Nakai, M., Matsumura, M., & Yokoyama, M. (2000). *Hiyari chizu zukuri no teian to sono unyo ni kannsuru kenkyu* [Report on the impacts of "safety mapping" and its implications]. Tokyo: The International Association of Traffic and Safety Sciences.

Takahashi, J., & Nunokawa, N. (2010). Bosai ryoku wo takameru tameno jishin bousai kyoiku ni kansuru kenkyu [Study on education of earthquake disaster prevention: Educational program of disaster prevention for junior high school in Tochigi Pref.]. *Bulletin of Oyama National College of Technology, 43*, 163–168.

Teramoto, K. (2012). Bousai kyoiku no jikouka to shakaika no hatasu yakuwari [Adaptation to school course of study of the protection against disasters and the part of the social studies]. *The Geographical Reports, 114*, 29–37.

Tokyo Metropolitan Board of Education (2010). Anzen kyoiku puroguramu [Safety Education Program]. http://www.kyoiku.metro.tokyo.jp/press/22anzenkyoikupro.pdf. [Web. 14 November 2013].

Wenger, E. (1999). *Community of practice: Learning, meaning and identity*. Cambridge/New York: Cambridge University Press.

World Commission on Environment and Development. (1987). *Report of the world commission on environment and development: Our common future*. New York: United Nations.

Yamori, K. (2006). Bosai kyoiku no tameno atarashii shiten [New perspective for education for disaster prevention: Recreating the community of practice]. *Journal of Japan Society for Natural Disaster Science, 24*(4), 344–350.

Yamori, K. (2010). Saigai jyohou to bosai kyoiku [Disaster information and education for disaster prevention]. *Disaster Information, 8*, 1–6.

Yamori, K. (2012). Tsunami tendenko no yottsu no imi [Revisiting the concept of '*tsunami tendenko*']. *Journal of Japan Society for Natural Disaster Science, 31*(1), 35–46.

Postscript: Toward Education that Truly Enhances People's Well-Being

Yuto Kitamura

Education sector is basically working with domestic interests. National governments pursue educational reform within their respective nation-state frameworks, reflecting their specificities in historical, political, economic, societal, cultural, and other aspects. In this process, challenges are identified, and policy measures are formulated to overcome them, within each country's domestic context. At the same time, however, in today's increasingly globalizing world, many countries, confronted with similar challenges in the area of education, are taking a somewhat uniform approach to educational reform. In particular, the influence of neoliberal ideology can be found in many such countries' educational reforms. That is to say, the principles of deregulation, decentralization, and market competition have been brought into the sphere of education, prompting autonomy and independence on the part of schools and teachers while causing such problems as widening educational disparities and intensifying races for educational credentials. Education-related problems are particularly clearly manifested in disparities.

Under such circumstances, in this book we have attempted to analyze, from diverse aspects, various issues relating to Japan's educational reforms mainly since the end of World War II. In doing so, we provide an overview of the evolution of Japan's educational reforms in the 30-year period starting in the 1980s, when neoliberal influence began to appear in the country's education policies. We examine prewar school teachers' narratives to discern how they perceived and practiced education. Moreover, we establish historical facts concerning how ordinary people supported local schools as the modern school education system developed and spread and how schools have contributed to local communities in turn. We also introduce the practice of Lesson Study, illustrating how Japanese school teachers engage in a highly creative educational endeavor. It is without doubt through the accumulation

Y. Kitamura (✉)
Graduate School of Education, The University of Tokyo, Tokyo, Japan
e-mail: yuto@p.u-tokyo.ac.jp

© Springer Nature Singapore Pte Ltd. 2019
Y. Kitamura et al. (eds.), *Education in Japan*, Education in the Asia-Pacific
Region: Issues, Concerns and Prospects 47,
https://doi.org/10.1007/978-981-13-2632-5

of such educational experiences that the quality of Japan's school education has greatly improved over the years.

Today, however, Japan's school education needs to be reexamined within the globalizing world context. Japanese schools have not necessarily responded adequately to the increased number of pupils of foreign origin, and not much effective reform has been carried out in English language education to realize a substantial improvement in students' English proficiency. Moreover, educational disparities are growing to such an extent that it is becoming morally irresponsible to leave them unrectified. We believe that, reading through the book, the readers have come to a good measure of understanding of these issues.

In modern Japan, educational policymaking has been based on the functionalist notion that the spread of school education should lead to society's development. Accordingly, the social roles of education have basically been viewed in a positive light. Policymakers have traditionally promoted national integration and institutional maintenance and reproduction through education. Japan's educational reforms conducted along the same vector have produced both positive and negative results. For example, modernization of the country's educational system under the banner of National Education has greatly contributed to making qualitatively homogeneous formal schooling available all over Japan. On the other hand, problems deriving from the compelling force of the National Curriculum (i.e., the Courses of Study) and imposition of uniform educational models have turned many schools into closed and stifling spaces, as illustrated by the practice of obligating teachers to hoist the national flag and sing the national anthem at graduation and other school ceremonies. In such a situation, neoliberalist trends in educational reform have, on the one hand, generated a range of refreshing ideas for educational practice while, on the other, widening disparities between regions and social strata. Furthermore, decentralization in the administration of educational affairs has led to the inability of certain social strata to actively participate in school administration to become undeniably visible, resulting in even wider disparities.

Meanwhile, the roles the national government is expected to play in Japan's educational reforms from now on are inevitably changing. Needless to say, this does not mean that the government must abandon its traditional role of setting norms and standards by presenting national goals in education or readjusting or establishing administrative and financial systems so that these goals can be attained. One increasingly strongly needed change is the government's attitude toward educational reform that clearly includes citizens' perspectives.

This is all the more so because the primary importance of school education as a vehicle for carrying over and developing democratic ideals is unlikely to change in the future. In *Democracy and Education*, John Dewey (1916/1944) emphasized the functions of school education as promoting social integration, correcting socioeconomic inequalities, and assisting individual character development. Behind this thesis were the ideals of liberal education that developed amid the social situations in Western countries in those days marked by accelerated industrialization and urbanization, democratic movements led by workers and citizens, raised awareness of social rights, women's social participation, and so forth.

Dewey's argument that was at the source of liberal education is still extremely suggestive in addressing educational reform in Japan today. This is because, in examining how the right to education that should be secured for all persons can be realized, it is essential to deeply contemplate on what constitutes education aimed at developing autonomous individuals who will lead democracy in the future, what "well-being" means to people, and what roles education can play in enhancing people's well-being.

In this regard, it is essential that further research be conducted from the perspective of education and people's well-being on themes not sufficiently explored in this book, such as special needs and disabilities, teacher education and training, gender in education, and analytical demographical changes in the future (partially discussed in some chapters). When these themes are also taken into consideration, we believe that further research should be pursued on Education for Sustainable Development (ESD), taken up in the final chapter, a new approach to education that Japan has been actively advocating and promoting in the international community.

As stated above, education is an extremely domestic enterprise. Yet, in today's rapidly globalizing world, the educational practices and reforms that Japan as a single country has experienced over the years have probably something significant to offer to those living in other societies as well. It is our hope that by reading this book, you have not only learned of unique and original aspects of Japanese education but also recognized certain commonalities with your respective societies in terms of challenges in education. It would be a great pleasure for us if the Japanese experiences presented in this book could serve as a reference for contemplating how education should be carried out in enhancing the well-being of people living in your respective societies and communities.

Reference

Dewey, J. (1916/1944). *Democracy and education*. New York: The Free Press (Macmillan).